Res Judicata

Res Judicata

A Handbook on Its Theory, Doctrine, and Practice

Robert C. Casad

John H. and John M. Kane Professor of Law Emeritus
University of Kansas

Kevin M. Clermont

Flanagan Professor of Law
Cornell University

Carolina Academic Press
Durham, North Carolina

Library of Congress Cataloging-in-Publication Data

Casad, Robert C.
Res judicata : a handbook on its theory, doctrine, and practice /
Robert C. Casad, Kevin M. Clermont.
p. cm.
Includes index.
ISBN 0-89089-705-0
1. Res judicata-United States. 1. Clermont, Kevin M. II. Title.

KF8992.C28 2001
347.73'77--dc2l

00-069771

Carolina Academic Press
700 Kent Street
Durham, North Carolina 27701
Telephone (919) 489-7486
Fax (919) 493-5668
E-mail: cap@cap-press.com
www.cap-press.com

Printed in the United States of America.

Summary of Content

Part I: Theory

Part II: Doctrine

Part III: Practice

Contents

Res Judicata

PART I

THEORY

"The defense of res judicata is universally respected, but actually not very well liked."

Riordan v. Ferguson,
147 F.2d 983, 988 (2d Cir. 1945)
(Clark, J., dissenting)

CHAPTER 1

INTRODUCTION TO RES JUDICATA

Liked or disliked, res judicata is certainly misunderstood. Most people view it as an arcane jumble of technical and arbitrary rules blocking access to court, rules that often sacrifice short-run justice to a dubious pursuit of long-run justice. Most people also think that res judicata applies only when a litigant has taken a misstep. Both of these positions are myths.

This book will set straight these and other misunderstandings. The place to start is specifying the focus of the book. The focus is the impact of a *previously rendered adjudication* in the course of *subsequent civil litigation.* Within this focus on former adjudication in civil procedure, the most important subject by far is res judicata. Accordingly, the book will treat the central doctrine of res judicata in detail. In Chapter 2 below, the book first will briefly give necessary attention to doctrines related to res judicata that appear just within the focus's periphery, as well as sketch other related doctrines that lie just beyond the focus. That next chapter will also survey res judicata's own extensions outside the focus, such as a judgment's effect in subsequent *criminal* litigation. These early detours will inform the book's later emphasis on the application of res judicata in civil litigation.

A. Significance

Res judicata is a major and critical topic from the basic law-school course in civil procedure. At a mundane level, res judicata specifies the effect that any adjudication has on all subsequent litigation. Although courts tend to discuss res judicata principally when a litigant somehow went wrong and so got mired in repetitive litigation, it has much wider application. Although res judicata appears to be a jumble of rules, it actually has the straightforward but profound mission of defining the scope of a prior adjudication. It is good to remember that *res judicata* literally means the thing, or matter, adjudged.

Let's get specific. A judgment is the concrete embodiment of what a court has decided. Res judicata performs the job of delineating the content of a judgment. Res judicata dictates whether decided matters are subject to reopening, as well as which actually undecided matters nevertheless fall within the bounds of a judgment and so receive treatment as if decided. It fixes the boundaries of the judgment, and thus is critical in interpreting the judgment. And it applies to every judgment ever rendered.

- Because a judgment, as delineated by res judicata law, is the primary objective of most adjudicative proceedings, a knowing eye trained on res judicata will greatly affect the litigant's implementation of *procedure*, both way before and way after judgment. From contemplating pleading in an initial lawsuit to settling or otherwise ending the case and then to attacking judgment by a second lawsuit, the litigant must bear res judicata in mind.
- At a more profound level, res judicata does much more. It is essential to *judicial operation*, to the orderly working of the judicial branch. If disputants could just reopen their adjudicated disputes, there would be no end to litigation, nor any beginning of authority. Finality is not just an efficient policy, it is a necessary condition for the existence of a judiciary.
- Res judicata is the law that specifies what a judgment decides and what it does not decide or, in other words, that shores up *separation of powers* by setting the boundaries on the output of the judicial branch of government. It is the law that restrains the applicability of judicial decisions to nonparties and the retroactivity of legal change to adjudicated matters. Because res judicata thus determines how a judgment differs from legislation and administration, the doctrine is of basic importance in understanding our governmental system.
- Moreover, res judicata implies at least some respect for prior adjudication, even across legal systems linked by *federalism*. Without such respect, the more powerful courts would inevitably extinguish their competitors. If disputants could reopen their disputes in the superior court, they would come to skip over the inferior court. The royal courts in England prevailed over the local courts in part because of their willingness to allow litigation anew. Contrariwise, the contin-

ued thriving of state and federal courts in the United States is owing to a healthy doctrine of res judicata.

- On the level of *international law*, res judicata might not be absolutely necessary. The law of the jungle might work, because each nation has a zone of autonomous operation. But especially today, with ever-increasing globalization, a sensible international order requires an international law on the application of res judicata. The United States should and does respect the judgments of France, and vice versa.

Given that res judicata plays a key role in procedure, judicial operation, separation of powers, federalism, and international law, it is naturally a difficult subject. Moreover, like any policy, it has its costs as well as its benefits. As to obvious costs, one readily perceives that litigating about whether to relitigate is expensive, and some applications of the doctrine do seem outrageously unfair. Often frustrated students and other victims of res judicata, after realizing its difficulties and lamenting its costs, ask whether we would be better off without res judicata. Yet one must acknowledge that this question itself is nonsensical. Our legal system could not exist without res judicata. Sure, the system could lop off some extensions and some details of res judicata. But the essence of res judicata—its mission of defining adjudication—is nonoptional.

B. Sources

Res judicata is a classic common-law doctrine. *First*, responding to felt needs, every legal system has produced a body of res judicata law. "The doctrine of res judicata is a principle of universal jurisprudence forming part of the legal systems of all civilized nations."[1] But each jurisdiction generates its own distinctive body of law, as has been done independently by each of the states, by the federal system, and by other countries. American res judicata is distinctively a good deal more expansive than res judicata law in other countries. *Second*, American res judicata is an almost entirely judge-made body of law. Courts responded to the needs they most acutely felt by formulating, revising, and complexifying a doctrine. It is true that constitutions, legislation, and rulemaking can override the judicial doctrine. The U.S. Constitution has a real albeit limited impact on res judicata doctrine,

---

1. 2 A.C. Freeman, A Treatise of the Law of Judgments § 627, at 1321 (5th ed. 1925).

as this book will discuss. In many jurisdictions, statutes deal with small parts of the subject; Louisiana, indeed, has codified the subject, using quite general terms, in accordance with its civil-law traditions.[2] Most court rules, though, avoid most of the subject. The belief is that in general it is just too complex a subject for successful codification. *Third*, res judicata is policy-driven. Despite first impression, it comprises principles or standards as much as fixed rules and exceptions. As a result, it has been a surprisingly contentious and uncertain area of law.

We could suggest roots of Anglo-American res judicata going back pretty far.[3] Some other commentators find roots in Germanic, Roman, and other ancient systems. But in truth these are analogies rather than roots. Each legal system seems to produce its own res judicata law, often doing so independently in response to its own felt needs for finality and often ending up in a unique spot. At any rate, in the 1200s Bracton recognized the principle of res judicata in English cases. And from those beginnings our law has developed. In the ensuing centuries, the courts revised and complexified the doctrine. Progress has been pretty steady, although certainly some major doctrinal shifts have occurred in response to shifting policies behind res judicata.

The modern approach to res judicata in the United States finally emerged in the *Restatement (Second) of Judgments* (1982). As to its immediate sources, the Second Restatement drew on important works such as Allan D. Vestal, *Res Judicata/Preclusion* (1969), and *Developments in the Law—Res Judicata*, 65 Harv. L. Rev. 818 (1952). Of course, the Second Restatement built mostly on the great first *Restatement of Judgments* (1942). The latter in turn drew on such classic works in the area as Henry Campbell Black, *A Treatise on the Law of Judgments* (2d ed. 1902) (two volumes), and A.C. Freeman, *A Treatise of the Law of Judgments* (5th ed. 1925) (three volumes).

The American Law Institute's Restatements and the country's courts interact. The Second Restatement of Judgments tried to express and refine the recent efforts of the federal courts and the progressive state courts. Today those courts tend to follow the Second Restatement in further developing the doctrine of res judicata. As a consequence, a coherent modern law of res judicata has become perceptible and accepted. In fact, at one point Justice Rehnquist felt obliged to remind the other Justices that the Restatement of Judgments was not binding on the Supreme Court.[4] Even

2. La. Rev. Stat. Ann. §§ 13:4231-:4232 (West 1991).

3. See generally Allan D. Vestal, Res Judicata/Preclusion 17-42 (1969).

4. Montana v. United States, 440 U.S. 147, 164 (1979) (concurring in "the Court's opinion on the customary understanding that its references to...drafts or finally

if not binding, the Second Restatement merits careful study because it manages to bring much order to the field and because it has so influenced the courts. It is not perfect, as we shall argue here and there, but it is unarguably a work of the highest quality.

As a result of the Second Restatement and these courts' interaction, the United States today enjoys a semi-codification of most of res judicata law, fairly uniform albeit unofficial. Some big questions are settled. Certain pockets and details of this law, of course, remain unsettled. The best commentaries on the whole of this modern law of res judicata lie in particular volumes of the two wonderful multivolume works on civil procedure: 18 Charles Alan Wright, Arthur R. Miller & Edward H. Cooper, *Federal Practice and Procedure* (1981 & Supp. 1999), which is simply brilliant in many instances, and 18 Susan Bandes & Lawrence B. Solum, *Moore's Federal Practice* (3d ed. 1999).

Our primary emphasis in this book will be on this modern law of res judicata. There will be occasional references to contrasting older law and local variations, where appropriate. But the book will do more than convey the doctrine. And it will do more than supplement the doctrine with a discussion of practice, when especially Chapters 11 and 12 below describe how the doctrine actually works out in the real world. That is to say, the book will not avoid theory. It will in fact start with the theory of res judicata, especially in Chapters 3 and 4 below, because theory is what drives each jurisdiction's courts in creating the doctrine and molding the real-world practice of res judicata. Moreover, we believe that attention to the basic concepts and policies underlying res judicata—which the student usually does not perceive until the end of his or her study of the subject, if at all, and which a lawyer or researcher is all too likely to overlook—really helps to make sense of res judicata. It is the place to begin in reviewing the subject's doctrine and discussing its practice. Thus, the three major parts of the book sequentially cover theory, doctrine, and practice.

C. Contexts

Parties can invoke res judicata only after adjudication. Moreover, their locus for invocation must be outside the initial adjudicatory process and any direct review such as appeal. So, the usual discussion of res judicata

---

adopted versions of the Restatement of Judgments are not intended to bind the Court to the views expressed therein on issues not presented by the facts of this case").

contemplates the context of two actions, presuming an Action #1 that led to judgment and then addressing the judgment's effect on a pending Action #2, which may have begun before or after Action #1. For example, the plaintiff in Action #2 might invoke res judicata to preclude the defendant from defending on the underlying merits in an action upon a judgment rendered in Action #1 or might invoke res judicata to foreclose relitigation of certain issues decided in Action #1. Similarly, the defendant in a subsequent action might invoke res judicata as a defense by using a judgment to defeat a claim or preclude an issue.

This book begins its treatment of the theory, doctrine, and practice of res judicata with an even narrower context in contemplation. We at first consider only the subsequent effects, (1) when the parties to the subsequent litigation are the same as those to the initial action, (2) of a personal judgment rendered in an action seeking coercive relief in a civil court, (3) provided that the subsequent litigation is in the same court system as the initial action. We shall cover special situations later, when we turn to the effects on nonparties in Chapter 8 below, the effects of less ordinary kinds of judgment in Chapter 9 below, and the effects of nondomestic judgments in Chapter 10 below. Finally, in Chapter 13 below, we shall cover the special brand of res judicata called jurisdiction to determine jurisdiction, which can preclude an attack on the prior judgment.

D. Basics

So imagine a case within the narrow context of our opening contemplation. Take an Action #1 for damages resulting in a valid and final personal judgment, and then an Action #2 in the same civil court between the same parties.

If the plaintiff won Action #1, generally his claim is extinguished by, or *merged* in, the judgment. He cannot maintain Action #2 on the same claim in an effort to win a more favorable judgment.

If the plaintiff instead lost Action #1, generally his claim is extinguished, or *barred*, by the judgment. If he brings Action #2 to try again, the defendant may plead res judicata and thereby stop him in his tracks.

Of course, exceptions abound. What happens if, by virtue of an exception, the plaintiff can maintain Action #2 on the *same claim*? Or what happens in the more likely situation where the plaintiff and the defendant are involved in an Action #2 on a *different claim*, but a claim that involves some issues common to Action #1? These situations entail the effect in Action #2 of decisions on issues in Action #1. Generally, any such decision is conclusive on the same issue in Action #2 if it was actually litigated and determined in Action #1 and if its determination was essential to the judgment in Action #1. For example, if the judge in Action #1 found the plaintiff negligent in causing an accident, the former defendant could use that finding against him to preclude the issue's relitigation in Action #2, which was brought by the former defendant for her own injuries in the accident.

E. Terminology

Authorities categorize and label in various ways the rules of res judicata. (The whole doctrine is sometimes called, obsoletely and rather ungrammatically, *res adjudicata*.) Indeed, sometimes the term of res judicata is limited to the preclusive effect on claims, thus to the exclusion of the preclusive effect on issues. Adherents of this confusing terminology unfortunately have included the Supreme Court of the United States.[5]

Many authorities have recently made substantial progress toward a uniform terminology. Both of the Restatements used res judicata as a general term relating to the effects of a judgment either as completely extinguishing a claim or as conclusively determining particular disputed issues. But in going from the First to the Second Restatement, the American Law Institute adopted a new terminology to divide the general term into two subdoctrines tied to claim and issue effects: "claim preclusion" and "issue preclusion." This new terminology had gained favor over recent times, owing in large measure to the writings of Professor Allan Vestal.[6] Now, even the Supreme Court seems to be falling into line.[7]

Why use these new terms? The new terminology recognizes that the two most important subsets of the overall problem are those relating to a second suit for the same claim, on the one hand, and to the relitigation of specific issues, on the other hand. That is, claim preclusion and issue preclusion treat the two major settings where former adjudication has a preclusive impact, each in a distinctive way: where a former judgment works to fore-

---

5. See, e.g., Lawlor v. National Screen Serv. Corp., 349 U.S. 322, 326 & n.6 (1955). Accord 18 Susan Bandes & Lawrence B. Solum, Moore's Federal Practice § 131.10 (3d ed. 1999).

6. See, e.g., Allan D. Vestal, Res Judicata/Preclusion (1969).

7. See, e.g., Baker v. General Motors Corp., 522 U.S. 222, 233 & n.5 (1998). Accord 18 Charles Alan Wright, Arthur R. Miller & Edward H. Cooper, Federal Practice and Procedure § 4402 (1981 & Supp. 1999).

close a whole claim and where a former decision works to conclude a particular issue. (Both new terms incidentally resolved prior mini-disputes. "Claim" replaced the older usage of "cause of action," which carried plenty of connotative baggage loaded toward a narrower meaning. "Issue preclusion" replaced a plethora of older terms such as "estoppel by findings" or by "judgment," "record," or "verdict.")

The modern approach next proceeds to subdivide those two major subdoctrines of claim and issue preclusion:

- The extinguishment of a claim may be distinguished according to the setting: "merger" if the judgment in the first action was in favor of the claimant or "bar" if the judgment in the first action went against the claimant. Claim preclusion thus includes merger and bar.
- The effect of the prior judgment in conclusively determining disputed issues is still referred to in terms of estoppel: "direct estoppel" when the second action is upon the same claim as was the first or "collateral estoppel" when the second action is on a different claim. Issue preclusion thus covers both direct and collateral estoppel. (In fact, however, reference to direct estoppel is much less frequent than reference to collateral estoppel. The reason is that in most situations involving a second action on the same claim, the entire claim will have been extinguished by the first judgment through merger or bar and so the problem of estoppel never arises. Consequently, estoppel most often involves a second action on a different claim, and so the term collateral estoppel has all but displaced direct estoppel. That is, collateral estoppel has commonly come to describe the conclusive effect of a prior determination of particular issues without regard to whether the later action is on the same claim or on a different one. Following this usage, the Supreme Court has said that collateral estoppel "precludes relitigation of issues actually litigated and determined in the prior suit, regardless of whether it was based on the same cause of action as the second suit."[8] Still, the alternative, and preferable, generic term would be issue preclusion.[9])

This discussion sufficiently illustrates the sources of confusion that lurk in the terminology of the subject. A lawyer must be alert to possible ambi-

8. Lawlor v. National Screen Serv. Corp., 349 U.S. 322, 326 (1955).
9. See Baker v. General Motors Corp., 522 U.S. 222, 233 n.5 (1998).

guity, and always examine the context in which terms such as res judicata or collateral estoppel are used, to be sure of the intended meaning. In this book, we shall use res judicata to refer generally to the subject of conclusive effects of judgments in both claim-precluding and issue-precluding senses. The context or appropriate modifying language will make clear whether the meaning intended is that general subject or, more specifically, claim preclusion or issue preclusion or something else. We shall also employ the technical terms of merger, bar, direct estoppel, and collateral estoppel. So here, by way of summary, is how the basics of res judicata work out under our terminological scheme:

1. Claim Preclusion

Outside the context of the initial action, a party generally may not relitigate a claim decided therein by a valid and final judgment. The judgment extinguishes the whole claim, precluding all matters within the claim that were or could have been litigated in that initial action. Claim preclusion subdivides into merger and bar.

If the judgment in the initial action was in the *plaintiff's favor*, the plaintiff's claim is said to merge in the judgment. The plaintiff cannot bring a second action on the claim in the hope of winning a more favorable judgment. However, the plaintiff can seek to enforce the judgment, and the defendant cannot then raise defenses that were or could have been interposed in that initial action.

If the judgment in the initial action was in the *defendant's favor*, the plaintiff's claim is said to be barred by the judgment. The plaintiff cannot bring a second action on the claim in the hope of winning this time.

After treating the validity and finality prerequisites for res judicata in Chapter 5 below, this book in Chapter 6 below will examine the details of claim preclusion, before turning to issue preclusion in Chapter 7 below.

2. Issue Preclusion

Outside the context of the initial action, regardless of who won judgment, a party generally may not relitigate any issue of fact or law actually litigated and determined therein if the determination was essential to a valid and final judgment. Unlike claim preclusion, which reaches even matters that could have been but were not litigated, issue preclusion reaches only matters that were actually litigated and determined. Issue preclusion subdivides into direct estoppel and collateral estoppel.

If the second action is on the *same claim* as the initial action (the second action presumably falling within some exception to claim preclusion), then the applicable variety of issue preclusion is direct estoppel.

Much more commonly, the second action is on a *different claim*. Then the applicable variety of issue preclusion is collateral estoppel.

CHAPTER 2

Related Doctrines

Beyond the problems of terminology, further difficulties lie in the similarity between the matters falling under the rubric of res judicata and certain other well-established doctrines. The reader should, sooner rather than later, compare and contrast res judicata with the related but distinguishable doctrines. Together they constitute the subject of *former adjudication*. And together they reflect the determination that courts should not proceed as if writing on a blank slate. Former adjudication should and does affect future adjudication.

A. Stare Decisis[1]

Stare decisis, or the doctrine of precedent, is like res judicata in that it concerns the controlling influence on later cases of a decision rendered in an earlier one. It is different from res judicata in the function that it performs in our legal system, the manner in which the earlier case influences the later one, and the wider range of later cases that the earlier one may influence.

Basically stare decisis means that a court will stand by its decisions and by those of a higher court in a given judicial hierarchy. "Standing by a decision" means deciding a particular question of law the same way in each case that presents the question and, moreover, deciding so without serious reconsideration. *Stare decisis et non quieta movere*, or let the decision stand and do not disturb things that have been settled.

---

1. See generally 18 Susan Bandes & Lawrence B. Solum, Moore's Federal Practice §§ 134.01-.06 (3d ed. 1999).

Why? First, in deciding cases, courts must decide legal questions. Within the same jurisdiction, the law should give but one answer to a given legal question. To develop a law uniform over time and throughout the judicial system, courts must bow to a prior resolution. Second, even-handed and predictable justice means that like cases must be decided alike, regardless of who the parties involved may be. Third, if the practice were otherwise, prediction and planning in primary private ordering would be difficult. Fourth, stare decisis results in the appearance of reasoned, consistent, and impersonal opinions, which increases public support for the judiciary. Fifth, besides serving to unify the law, to foster even-handed and predictable justice, to facilitate private prediction and planning, and to augment public support, the existence of the doctrine of stare decisis improves the quality of judicial performance itself in a number of ways. It does this by encouraging more careful and thorough consideration than the initial judge might give to a new legal question if the determination had effect only in the case before the court and in no other cases; by causing later judges to rely and build on the past efforts of other judges; by inducing actual as well as apparent integrity as judges buy into the principle of impersonal judgment and thereby fight to overcome their own natural biases; and through easing the courts' burden by discouraging suits by litigants who would otherwise hope to get a different answer from a different judge. In brief, "no judicial system could do society's work if it eyed each issue afresh in every case that raised it."[2]

Therefore, decisions of a court are binding precedent on the legal question they involve: they must be followed by lower courts in later suits on undistinguishable facts and will ordinarily be followed by the rendering court itself. Stare decisis in our system applies to decisions interpreting constitutions and statutes as well as to decisions declaring common-law rules.

Stare decisis has limits, however. As a limit on the judiciary's making law, a function generally assigned to the legislature, stare decisis applies only to that part of a judicial decision that constitutes the holding of the court in an actual case, as contrasted to dicta contained in the court's opinion. On the one hand, declarations of law or of the meaning of laws made by the court have binding force as precedent for later cases only if the court made the declaration in resolving a question of law that was necessary to the decision of the case before the court. Only such declarations are holdings. On

2. Planned Parenthood v. Casey, 505 U.S. 833, 854 (1992).

the other hand, additional statements of law contained in the court's opinion are dicta that later cases may or not follow. The distinction between holding and dictum is not always easy to draw, particularly in cases where the legal proposition announced by the court as the basis for its decision is broader than would have been absolutely necessary but does cover the case to be decided. In any event, as the doctrine of stare decisis has developed flexibility in the United States (as contrasted to the stricter doctrine in England), the distinction has become more one of degree than of kind. Our legal system has generally recognized that even holdings are not absolutely binding in later cases. The rendering court can overrule them when clearly convinced they are wrong.

Stare decisis applies to all later cases that present the same legal question, without regard to who the parties are or were. Contrariwise, as we shall see, res judicata exerts no influence on later litigation unless at least one of the parties in the later action was a party, or in privity with a party, to the earlier action.

In summary, then, stare decisis, intended to give stability to the law, provides that a court's holding on a legal question will normally be followed, by the same court and any lower courts in that judicial hierarchy, in all future cases presenting undistinguishable facts. Contrasted with res judicata, stare decisis (1) applies only to decided issues of law, (2) permits courts to handle precedent much more flexibly, and (3) governs even in cases involving wholly new parties.

But if stare decisis is so different from res judicata, then why study it in conjunction with res judicata? The reason is that the doctrine of stare decisis carries two important lessons for the student of res judicata.

First, the existence of stare decisis might counsel against an extension of res judicata. Courts sometimes exaggerate the benefit of efficiency in preventing relitigation through issue preclusion. Even without extending res judicata, the background doctrine of stare decisis might serve to retrieve a good share of that efficiency for issues of law, while its flexibility would avoid the costs of needlessly inflicted unfairness.

Second, cutting the other way, the existence of stare decisis might prove the possibility of extending res judicata. Commentators sometimes raise constitutional objection to extending a judgment's binding effects to nonparties, arguing that limitation to parties and privies is the key distinction between adjudication, on the one hand, and legislation or administration, on the other. The simplest rebuttal is to observe that a judgment between parties *A* and *B* has stare decisis effect in a lawsuit between totally unrelated *C* and *D*, and that nobody questions the constitutionality of stare decisis.

B. Law of the Case[3]

Another doctrine that bears some resemblance to res judicata and to stare decisis is that known as law of the case. Despite its name, it now can apply to rulings on fact as well as on law. It is similar to stare decisis in that it applies rather flexibly, so that the rendering court or an equal-level court may revisit the ruling if convinced it was wrong. It is similar to res judicata in that it is narrow in application, so that it does not apply beyond the parties to the case in which the ruling was rendered. Indeed, the ruling is binding as the law of the case only during the later conduct of the very case in which the ruling was made, that is, within the context of the initial action. It will not bind the parties, or anyone else, in later proceedings that are not part of the same case.

Basically, the law of the case doctrine means that a question once resolved in the course of litigation will not be reconsidered at later stages in the same action, except by a higher court, even if the point was erroneously decided. This does not mean, of course, that the parties may not directly challenge rulings by regular procedures, such as by appeal or by motion for rehearing en banc. But if the ruling has withstood such direct challenges, as for instance when a case has been appealed and remanded, or if the challenge that might have been made was not, the ruling is said to have become the law of that particular case and is not subject to reexamination.

There are many exceptions to the application of the rule of law of the case, and some states profess to reject it altogether. One may question whether the interests of economy of judicial effort served by the doctrine are generally of such importance as to justify holding parties to erroneous rulings that could still be corrected within the framework of the same case. In view of the lesser justification of the law of the case doctrine, it is not surprising that courts have not applied it with as much rigor and consistency as they have shown in connection with res judicata. But if interpreted as mere maxims that a court will not lightly redo what has been done and

3. See generally 18 Charles Alan Wright, Arthur R. Miller & Edward H. Cooper, Federal Practice and Procedure §4478 (1981 & Supp. 1999).

that lower courts must obey higher courts, then law of the case only expresses the common sense of "protecting against the agitation of settled issues"[4] and does little harm.

In summary, then, law of the case, intended to foster judicial economy, provides that a court, and any coordinate or lower courts as well, will normally adhere to a ruling it has declared in a particular action if a party later raises the point again in the same action. Contrasted with res judicata, law of the case (1) applies traditionally but not exclusively to issues of law, (2) applies very flexibly, and (3) applies only in the one case at hand, usually before res judicata kicks in.

C. Former Adjudication as Evidence[5]

When a judgment does not receive conclusive effect in a subsequent action pursuant to res judicata, one might wonder whether it is admissible therein as probative evidence on a common issue. It is not. It is inadmissible on hearsay grounds, being a prior statement offered for its truth. Generally, then, a judgment either has conclusive effect under the rules of res judicata or has no effect at all.

However, the hearsay rule is relaxed in certain circumstances. The main statutory and judicial exceptions involve administrative findings, antitrust judgments, findings of patent validity, and criminal convictions. Thus, a felony conviction is usually admissible in a subsequent civil action.[6]

Indeed, civil-law countries heavily employ this evidential use rather than expand their doctrine of res judicata. One could argue that the United States should do the same. After all, this practice would give to all rulings an effect similar to the effect that stare decisis gives to legal rulings. The arguments against extending evidential weight to factual findings are that combining a past decision with new evidence is a bit like combining apples and oranges, that our jury system especially might have trouble in weighing a past decision, and that the evidential approach lacks res judicata's advantage of avoiding trial altogether.

---

4. Christianson v. Colt Indus. Operating Corp., 486 U.S. 800, 816 (1988) (quoting *Moore's Federal Practice*).

5. See Hiroshi Motomura, Using Judgments as Evidence, 70 Minn. L. Rev. 979 (1986).

6. See, e.g., Fed. R. Evid. 803(22).

D. Former Recovery[7]

Former recovery, intended to prevent double recovery, provides that an award by judgment will be diminished by the amount recovered on any earlier judgments for the same injury. This is only common sense.

E. Equitable Estoppel[8]

Equitable estoppel, sometimes called estoppel in pais, generally provides that a party may not take a position in litigation when that position is inconsistent with earlier conduct and the change would unfairly burden another party who has detrimentally relied. For an example of when this many-faceted doctrine might apply, consider the situation of a party having recovered worker's compensation for an accident and then in subsequent tort litigation unfairly trying to deny that she was an employee. Obviously, this loose doctrine presents a risk of expanding to punish merely unseemly behavior.

Contrasted with res judicata, the looser doctrine of equitable estoppel looks to the party's earlier out-of-court or in-court conduct, rather than to a prior judicial decision. Equitable estoppel can therefore play a role complementary to res judicata. For instance, failure to interpose a compulsory counterclaim in a proceeding that failed to end in judgment may nevertheless equitably estop the defendant from later pursuing the counterclaim.

F. Judicial Estoppel[9]

Another doctrine that some people confuse with res judicata is judicial estoppel. This controversial doctrine, which varies widely from jurisdiction to jurisdiction and which is even rejected outright in a good number of states and federal circuits, generally holds that a person cannot take factual positions in litigation that are directly inconsistent with positions previously taken by the person in a prior proceeding. Usually the doctrine ap-

---

7. See Restatement (Second) of Judgments § 32 cmt. c, § 50(2) (1982).

8. See generally 18 Charles Alan Wright, Arthur R. Miller & Edward H. Cooper, Federal Practice and Procedure § 4477 (1981 & Supp. 1999).

9. See generally 18 Susan Bandes & Lawrence B. Solum, Moore's Federal Practice §§ 131.13[6], 134.30-.34 (3d ed. 1999).

plies only to statements made under oath. Abuse of the court by violation of the oath seems to be the main justification for the doctrine, although sometimes courts give different rationales, some courts apply the doctrine even to statements that were not verified under oath, and a few courts use the term indiscriminately. It would seem better to do without the doctrine, while allowing use of the prior statements, whether or not under oath, as evidence in the later action under the normal rules of evidence.

Judicial estoppel differs from equitable estoppel in that it does not require detrimental reliance. It differs from the issue-precluding effect of res judicata in that it does not require the prior rendering of a decision.

G. Election of Remedies[10]

Election of remedies, like estoppel, focuses on party conduct. Election of remedies provides that a party who ordinarily would have a choice among alternative remedies can disentitle himself to one or more of those remedies by knowingly engaging in conduct deemed inconsistent therewith. For a *first* example, alteration of a purchased chattel may foreclose rescission as a remedy for fraud, leaving damages as the only available remedy. A *second* example commonly described in terms of election of remedies arises when a party to a voidable transaction manifests her election to affirm or disaffirm it by bringing a lawsuit. A person who has been induced to enter into a contract by another's false representations has, upon discovering the fraud, an election to affirm the contract and insist upon her rights under it or to disaffirm and rescind it. Any act plainly manifesting her election to affirm it precludes her from later rescinding. One such act of affirmance might be the initiation of an action for specific performance or for damages for breach of the contract. The initiation of the action to enforce the contract in such a case is arguably an election between two conflicting substantive rights, and then only remedies appropriate to the elected right should be available to the plaintiff. For a *third* example, which represents an increasingly outmoded view that generalizes the second example, some courts hold that mere commencement of an action seeking a particular remedy forecloses other formally inconsistent remedies.

It is that third sort of merely "procedural" election of remedies that some people confuse with res judicata. But under procedural election of reme-

10. See generally 18 Charles Alan Wright, Arthur R. Miller & Edward H. Cooper, Federal Practice and Procedure § 4476 (1981 & Supp. 1999).

dies, it is the choice of one among alternative remedies that prevents resort to other inconsistent remedies for the same wrong. It is the initiation of the action, not its conclusion, that triggers the operation of the rule. The doctrine does not require a judicially rendered decision. In this respect, of course, it plainly differs from the doctrine of res judicata.

In earlier times, it did not seem so anomalous to hold a plaintiff bound by a choice once made. It was a general characteristic of the common-law system to require the parties to stick by the positions taken in their pleadings. Under the prevailing system of pleading, the doctrine of election of remedies may have served some desirable purpose in checking the number of successive suits for the same wrong. Because a plaintiff who had once sued and lost often was not barred by res judicata from suing again for the same wrong, either by bringing a different form of action or by switching between law and equity, the election of remedies rule served to limit the opportunities for repetitive litigation. The rule was not really directed to that end, however, as it applied whether or not the first suit resulted in a judgment. Moreover, it applied whether or not the plaintiff's change of position detrimentally affected the defendant.

In today's law, procedural election of remedies probably has no proper place. Res judicata has expanded in application. Moreover, the doctrine of election of remedies seems inconsistent with modern pleading reforms, which de-emphasize the role of the pleadings and which tolerate joinder of alternative and inconsistent claims in the same action. A party who pleads alternatively inconsistent claims may be required by practicality to choose one or the other at some later stage of the proceeding, but this is not because of any general rule of election of remedies.

In most cases that still purport to apply the doctrine of procedural election of remedies, there are grounds that would bar the second suit without resort to that doctrine. If the initiation of the plaintiff's first suit induced the defendant to rely in such a way that she would now be unfairly prejudiced if he were allowed to change the nature of his action, ordinary principles of equitable estoppel can prevent the plaintiff from changing theories. No need in such a case exists to talk of election of remedies as a separate rule.

In the relatively few cases in which procedural election of remedies is the only explanation for the outcome, the outcome has usually been an unfortunate one. A common situation is that of the victim of a conversion of chattels. Several common-law theories are available at his election. He can sue in a tort action to recover the value of the goods or to recover them in specie. Or he can waive the tort and sue in quasi-contract for their value or sue for the proceeds of their sale if they were sold by the tortfeasor. Some cases have held that the initiation of suit on a quasi-contract theory precludes a later suit on a tort theory, even if the first suit was terminated by voluntary dismissal rather than judgment on the merits. Some courts have even applied election of remedies in cases where the plaintiff's successive suits were both on a tort theory, say, first suit for damages for conversion and second suit for replevin. The justification for these results, in a case where the defendant has not detrimentally relied, is not obvious. Little justification for such results can exist unless the doctrine of res judicata or equitable estoppel would be applicable. All in all, then, the doctrine of procedural election of remedies would seem to be an appropriate candidate for extinction.

H. Other Action Pending[11]

Dealing with the same problems as does res judicata but taking a very different route to their solution, the doctrine of other action pending tries to stop repetitive litigation in its tracks, well before any troublesome rendition of judgment. This affirmative defense, sometimes called prior pending action, is rather narrowly applicable. It will result in dismissal without prejudice if another action on the same claim between the same parties was pending in the same state, or in the same federal district, when the instant action was commenced and if that other action is still pending.

This defense seems a sensible way to reduce repetitive litigation. But its very limited scope of application serves powerfully to underscore that the usual approach is to allow a second court to proceed toward judgment despite earlier-instituted litigation. The pendency of a lawsuit is normally no impediment to another, related suit. Although the first action to go to judgment should be res judicata in the other, the pendency of parallel proceedings is a commonplace with no ready, general cure.[12]

Besides other action pending, other inroads on the usual approach exist, but they too are minor. One court, usually the first to acquire jurisdiction, might enjoin proceedings in the other court. Alternatively, one court, usually the second, might stay its own hand in deference to the other court. A little more detail on these two approaches is appropriate.

---

11. See generally 1 C.J.S. Abatement and Revival §§ 16-84 (1985).

12. See generally James P. George, Parallel Litigation, 51 Baylor L. Rev. 769 (1999).

An *antisuit injunction* by one court against proceedings in another jurisdiction, within the United States, generally is prohibited or at least will be discretionarily refused. On the international level, however, some American courts are more willing to enjoin a party subject to its personal jurisdiction from participating in specified foreign proceedings, equitably balancing interests but still weighting the balance against interference.[13]

Nevertheless, one court may stay its own proceedings in deference to the other's, if the other related proceedings are in a more appropriate forum. This discretionary power, constituting a vague doctrine called *lis alibi pendens* ("suit elsewhere pending") or lis pendens, has been judicially created as an incident to the courts' inherent power to control their own dockets. It is, in a sense, an interjurisdictional version of the other action pending doctrine. When a court stays itself under lis pendens, it is exercising self-restraint in the exercise of its jurisdiction. Indeed, this doctrine is very similar to forum non conveniens.[14]

I. Double Jeopardy[15]

Another doctrine that bears considerable resemblance to res judicata is the proposition that a criminal defendant should not be prosecuted twice for the same offense. This principle is embodied in the Fifth Amendment of the Constitution of the United States—"nor shall any person be subject for the same offence to be twice put in jeopardy"—and has been held applicable to the states through the Fourteenth Amendment.[16] But double jeopardy differs from res judicata in various ways. First, double jeopardy becomes operational even if the prosecution short-circuits, as in the case of a mistrial. An accused criminal defendant comes into jeopardy as soon as the jury is sworn or, if the case is tried to the judge, as soon as evidence is offered by the prosecution. Res judicata thus is narrower, because its operation requires a decision on the merits. Second, double jeopardy precludes another criminal prosecution only for the same offense. Thus in some re-

---

13. See generally Edward Dumbauld, Judicial Interference with Litigation in Other Courts, 74 Dick. L. Rev. 369 (1970).

14. See generally Gary B. Born, International Civil Litigation in United States Courts 461-74 (3d ed. 1996).

15. See generally 5 Wayne R. LaFave, Jerold H. Israel & Nancy J. King, Criminal Procedure ch. 25 (2d ed. 1999) (double jeopardy); 4 id. § 17.4(a) (collateral estoppel).

16. Benton v. Maryland, 395 U.S. 784 (1969).

spects double jeopardy is narrower than res judicata, because several offenses each with some different elements may arise from the same act, just as the same crime pursued by different sovereigns constitutes separate offenses. Third, unlike res judicata, the rationale for the double jeopardy protection rests on preventing governmental oppression.

After jeopardy attaches, the government cannot again prosecute the accused for the same offense, regardless of the outcome of the prosecution, except in certain situations. If the defense itself willingly consents to a mistrial or obtains a dismissal, it waives the double jeopardy protection. If a convicted defendant obtains a reversal on appeal on grounds other than insufficiency of the evidence, the government may prosecute him again for the same offense. If the prosecution has proceeded past the point when jeopardy attaches, but the case terminates by "manifest necessity," such as the death or incapacity of the judge or some other exigency beyond the control of the parties, a second prosecution for the same offense is permissible. Further, if the first prosecution results in a hung jury, a second prosecution for the same offense is permissible, although this and some other exceptions might seem anomalous. The result is a complex thicket of law.

At any rate, the double jeopardy doctrine serves to prevent prosecution of a criminal defendant more than once for the same offense. Because jeopardy attaches even before judgment, any judgment that would be valid, final, and on the merits for purposes of merger and bar would also be one covered by double jeopardy. The existence of the double jeopardy protection thus has retarded the independent application of the claim preclusion aspects of res judicata in repetitive criminal cases.

Put claim preclusion aside now, and consider instead issue preclusion. The same historical facts and other common issues may arise in a later prosecution for a different offense. A single act may violate more than one criminal statute or affect more than one victim—or involve more than one defendant. Issue preclusion may foreclose the relitigation of issues, previously determined favorably or even unfavorably to the defendant, in a later prosecution for a different offense—but normally not in a later prosecution of a different defendant. Furthermore, in criminal prosecutions, issue preclusion may apply in rare circumstances to essential issues actually litigated and decided in earlier civil cases. The applicable brand of issue preclusion is collateral estoppel. In some of these applications, indeed, collateral estoppel is constitutionally imposed as part of the double jeopardy prohibition, according to the Supreme Court of the United States[17]—and as explained just below.

Criminal cases may have collateral estoppel effects in later civil cases too. But for a variety of reasons, this carryover presents particular problems. The carryover also brings us back into the main focus of this book, namely, the preclusive effects of former adjudication in subsequent civil litigation. Consequently, we shall delay treating the subject of criminal judgments' effects on civil litigation until Chapter 9-C below, and stick here to the subject of former adjudication in the context of subsequent criminal litigation. Separate treatment here of res judicata in criminal cases is, moreover, justifiable because the context is so different from civil cases that the criminal doctrine has developed quite independently into a very different form.

1. Collateral Estoppel from Criminal Judgment to Subsequent Criminal Prosecution of Same Defendant

a. Collateral Estoppel Asserted by Acquitted Defendant

In *Ashe v. Swenson*,[18] the Supreme Court held that collateral estoppel was a feature of the Fifth Amendment's double jeopardy protection, which applies to state as well as to federal prosecutions by way of the Fourteenth Amendment. A defendant who has won a judgment of acquittal may rely upon that judgment to establish certain issues conclusively if the prosecutor later pursues him for a different crime to which some of the same issues are material. That is, if the second prosecution is not for the same offense, the double jeopardy protection will not preclude the prosecution as such, but it may preclude the litigation of common issues. Thus, if the defendant pleads an alibi defense in a prosecution for felony-murder, and wins acquittal on the basis of that defense, he can rely upon that finding to establish the alibi in a later prosecution for the underlying felony of robbery.[19] Most cases hold, however, that an acquittal of criminal charges does not preclude parole revocation based on the same charges, because of the lesser standard of proof applicable in the parole revocation proceeding.[20]

On the one hand, the collateral estoppel effect of an acquittal in a criminal prosecution may be somewhat broader than the effect of a civil judg-

---

17. Ashe v. Swenson, 397 U.S. 436 (1970).

18. 397 U.S. 436 (1970).

19. Turner v. Arkansas, 407 U.S. 366 (1972).

20. See, e.g., Standlee v. Rhay, 557 F.2d 1303 (9th Cir. 1977); Standlee v. Smith, 518 P.2d 721 (Wash. 1974).

ment. In connection with civil judgments, the party asserting collateral estoppel in the second action has the burden of showing that the issue was actually litigated and determined in the first action. This can be a serious obstacle to invoking the issue preclusion effect of a judgment that was based upon a general verdict. Although a general verdict of conviction in a criminal case entails an adjudication of all the elements of the crime, a general verdict of acquittal may rest on the prosecution's failure to prove any one of the elements. If the burden were fully on the defendant to show just which issue the acquittal rested on, the value of *Ashe*'s double jeopardy extension would be rather limited. Accordingly, the Supreme Court ruled that when the defendant invokes the collateral estoppel effect of a prior judgment of acquittal based on a general verdict, the court must actively consider all circumstances in determining "whether a rational jury could have grounded its verdict upon an issue other than that which the defendant seeks to foreclose from consideration."[21]

On the other hand, other bounds on the usual rule of collateral estoppel apply. Thus, this rule of constitutional collateral estoppel in criminal cases applies only between the same parties. Therefore, a *federal* court will not accord collateral estoppel effect to issues litigated in a *state* prosecution that resulted in an acquittal of the same defendant. The United States, not being a party to the state action, is not collaterally estopped from litigating any issue.

Although the opinion in *Ashe v. Swenson* did not indicate that the incorporation of the collateral estoppel rule into the double jeopardy protection was subject to any exceptions, it is likely that some exceptions exist. For example, when an acquitted criminal defendant is later prosecuted for perjury in connection with the defendant's testimony in the first case, arguably the accused should not be able to invoke collateral estoppel. Permitting an accused first to avoid conviction by perjuring himself, and then to avoid conviction of perjury by invoking collateral estoppel, would positively encourage and reward perjury.

b. Collateral Estoppel Asserted Against Convicted Defendant

Now consider whether the prosecution can rely upon the collateral estoppel effect of issues litigated in an earlier criminal proceeding in a later prosecution of the same defendant for a different offense. This is a differ-

21. 397 U.S. at 444 (quoting Daniel K. Mayers & Fletcher L. Yarbrough, *Bis Vexari*: New Trials and Successive Prosecutions, 74 Harv. L. Rev. 1, 38-39 (1960)).

ent question, one that does not involve double jeopardy, because this is a use against the defendant rather than a protection of the defendant.

Here the Supreme Court has not applied collateral estoppel. Instead, the Court considers that collateral estoppel on the elements of a crime would violate due process.[22]

Between the pro-defendant collateral estoppel required by the Double Jeopardy Clause and the anti-defendant collateral estoppel prohibited by the Due Process Clause, there is some room for the governing law, state or federal, to shape a supplementary extension of collateral estoppel. This extension would constitute common-law res judicata, rather than constitutional doctrine. Thus, a court might allow the prosecution to preclude the defendant on a matter not going to guilt or innocence on an element of the crime, an example being an issue decided in the first criminal case that arises on a pretrial motion to suppress evidence in the second criminal case.[23] The norm, however, is for the governing law in criminal cases not to extend res judicata this way, but instead to stick pretty closely to the minimum of res judicata required by the double jeopardy protection.

2. Collateral Estoppel from Criminal Judgment to Subsequent Criminal Prosecution of Different Defendant

The government cannot use collateral estoppel to establish any points in a prosecution against a new defendant who never had a day in court on those issues. Therefore, a judgment convicting one defendant of a particular crime would not even establish the fact that the crime was committed in a later prosecution of an accessory, accomplice, or co-conspirator.

On the other side of the coin, the Constitution does not dictate that a judgment of acquittal can be used to preclude issues in favor of a different defendant in a later prosecution. Double jeopardy applies only between the same parties.[24] So, an alleged accomplice, accused in the second action, was not allowed to rely on a judgment acquitting the principal defendant to establish that no crime had been committed.[25] Again, however, a court might, but most do not, choose to extend its nonconstitutional law of collateral

22. See Simpson v. Florida, 403 U.S. 384, 386 (1971) (dictum).

23. See, e.g., United States v. Thoresen, 428 F.2d 654 (9th Cir. 1970); People v. Scott, 405 N.Y.S.2d 169 (N.Y. Sup. Ct. 1978).

24. See Standefer v. United States, 447 U.S. 10 (1980).

25. United States v. Musgrave, 483 F.2d 327 (5th Cir. 1973).

estoppel in the direction of allowing the accomplice to preclude the prosecution.[26]

3. Collateral Estoppel from Civil Judgment to Subsequent Criminal Prosecution

Instances in which issues litigated in a civil action will receive preclusive effect in a later criminal suit are rare indeed. If the government was not a party or privy to the civil action, it cannot be bound by anything adjudicated in it. On the other side of the coin, the government will not be able to claim the benefit of issues decided in an earlier civil suit to establish any element of the crime because of the different standard of proof.

Occasionally, however, those rare instances occur. For example, sometimes the government will initiate a civil action against a defendant and, after losing, prosecute the defendant for a crime involving some of the same facts. Failure of the government to establish its case under the preponderance of the evidence standard of the civil law would indicate that it could not meet the criminal standard of beyond a reasonable doubt. In such a case, the defendant should be able to rely upon the civil judgment as conclusive on the common issues.[27] This application of res judicata does not, however, rest on double jeopardy, because the first case was not a criminal proceeding. So, this is another instance of the governing law slightly extending collateral estoppel as part of the common-law doctrine of res judicata that supplements the constitutional core called double jeopardy.

26. See, e.g., People v. Taylor, 527 P.2d 622 (Cal. 1974).
27. See, e.g., United States v. Rogers, 960 F.2d 1501 (10th Cir. 1992).

CHAPTER 3

Policies Underlying Rules and Exceptions

Let us return to the basic context of civil litigation. There we find behind res judicata the fundamental idea that at some point the pursuit of truth should and must cease. Justice demands an end. Otherwise, litigants could inflict great oppression and harassment. As Sir Edward Coke put it long ago, "*interest reipublicœ ut sit finis litium*," or it concerns the state that there be an end to litigation.[1]

Today an economist would put that fundamental idea into more modern terms. For a court to readdress the same matter inflicts some direct costs, i.e., the additional out-of-pocket costs to all of running the legal system. As no general reason exists to suppose that a second try will be more accurate, readjudication on average will avoid no error costs, i.e., the costs to social goal-maximization caused by mistaken outcomes. Given relitigation's increased direct costs and neutral error costs, the law-and-economics adherent would come out in general favor of res judicata.[2]

Under either way of looking at the topic, an elaboration of the fundamental idea would run along the following lines. The primary objective of most judicial proceedings is the rendition of a judgment—an authoritative determination of the legal relations of the parties with respect to some particular subject. The subject may be the liability vel non of one person on an obligation claimed by another. It may be the domestic status of parties, or the ownership of specific property, or the duty to do or refrain from doing certain specified acts, or any one of many other subjects. Whatever

1. Ferrer's Case, 77 Eng. Rep. 263, 266 (C.P. 1599).

2. See Richard A. Posner, An Economic Approach to Legal Procedure and Judicial Administration, 2 J. Legal Stud. 399, 444-45 (1973).

the subject involved in judicial proceedings, its resolution will normally turn on the legal significance of certain historical facts, events that have, or are alleged to have, already taken place. The parties may disagree about what happened. They may disagree as to what the law is. They may disagree upon the significance of admitted facts in the light of what they agree to be the law. Disputes, or potential disputes, of one or more of these types are involved in all judicial proceedings, and the adjudicator must authoritatively resolve them before rendering a judgment. This costs time, energy, and money. Litigation is troublesome and expensive, not only for the litigants themselves but also for society in general.

The legal system designs the institutional processes of courts to resolve such disputes, that is, to determine facts, to find the applicable law, and to apply the law to the facts. Different tribunals may have different procedural mechanisms for identifying and resolving the disputed issues of fact and/or law—subject to the fundamental requirement that the process, whatever its mechanical details, must comply with the minima of due process. The requirements of due process in this context aim at ensuring that the parties have had a full and fair opportunity to present their positions on the issues in dispute. If the procedures of the tribunal afford them that opportunity, then the judgment of that tribunal resolving the disputed questions is about as likely to be accurate as the judgment of any other tribunal. Given the costliness of relitigation, the same parties should not be allowed to present the same matter for resolution to a court again. One full and fair day in court is enough. There must be an end to litigation, even if the first judgment was actually erroneous.

So runs the usual justification of res judicata. It is true to an extent, but it is a gross simplification. In the first place, this explanation conflates issue preclusion, which reaches only matters actually litigated and determined, with claim preclusion, which blocks "relitigation" of matters never even litigated. In the second place, this explanation fails to predict the considerable complexity of res judicata doctrine, constructed as it is of fine rules and peppered as it is with fuzzy exceptions. In the third place, this explanation has managed to pervert res judicata on recent occasions, because its simplistic emphasis on judicial economy can blind courts to other relevant policies that would argue against expanding res judicata.

A fuller explanation of the policies that detail res judicata would recognize that efficiency factors can counsel not only for but also against preclusion. Moreover, although some arguments that draw instead on fairness do favor preclusion, powerful fairness concerns cut the other way, counseling either to stop the rule of res judicata short of the particular case or to create an exception to the rule of res judicata for the particular case. Finally, res judicata does not exist in a procedural vacuum, but responds to specific substantive policies as well.

A. Res Judicata Rules

1. Procedural Factors Favoring Preclusion

Some major efficiency factors push for a rule of preclusion, but so do some minor fairness factors. A basic categorization follows (along with some parenthetical notes about the categorization process itself):

- E_w or the efficiency of avoiding *wasteful* litigation: Society, including all litigants, has an interest in avoiding the expenditure of time, energy, and money on repetitive litigation and in providing court access to the others waiting in line. That seems obvious enough, but it entails some nonobvious corollaries. Most importantly, the lawmaker must not restrict attention to short-run considerations. A significant efficiency consideration is the long-run deterrent effects of res judicata. Claim preclusion's harsh result in the case at hand might encourage many future litigants to dispose of their whole dispute, optimally defined, in a single lawsuit. Issue preclusion might encourage the litigants, and the court, to treat that first lawsuit seriously and carefully. (Admittedly, this long-run consideration is more powerful in connection with justifying claim preclusion than issue preclusion. This observation serves to make the general point that all these factors apply somewhat differently to those two major subdoctrines.)
- E_i or the efficiency of avoiding possibly *inconsistent* adjudications: Society has an interest in avoiding inconsistent adjudications. At best, inconsistency would erode faith in our system of justice and diminish acceptability of its output. At worst, inconsistency would also put a party into an impossible situation of conflicting obligations. (Avoidance of inconsistency is powerful in justifying many rules of issue preclusion and some of claim preclusion, but not all. For example, no risk of inconsistency lies behind the rule that losing a claim because of failure to prosecute bars that whole claim forevermore. In brief, all these factors are but factors, being neither necessary nor sufficient conditions for any provision of res judicata.)

- E_r or the efficiency of avoiding any decrease in the certainty and stability of *repose*: Society has a strong interest in increasing certainty for the purposes of primary conduct. Once a court determines legal relations, we all need to be able to act in the world with assurance that the relations are indeed fixed to some known extent. Society also has an interest in increasing stability in the judicial system. We all benefit when courts treat prior decisions, from the same or other courts, with respect and comity. (These interests of certainty and stability call for a clear doctrine, without too many fuzzy exceptions. Moreover, the interest in saving costs of administering the res judicata law argues for a straightforward doctrine, without too many complicated rules. Indeed, simple clarity seems a prerequisite to the doctrine's realizing almost any of its promised benefits, be they the avoidance of wasteful litigation or inconsistent adjudications or be they the achieving of repose or the doctrine's fair application.)
- F_{er} or the preclusion *equities* of the "*invoker*" of res judicata, especially the burden of conducting new litigation: Fairness supports the use of res judicata to protect the party invoking the doctrine from the burdens of repetitive litigation. A litigant should not have to struggle to reestablish that litigant's adjudicated rights. (Many ways exist to categorize reasons behind legal rules. A strict distinction between efficiency and fairness reasons is common in res judicata cases, but it has logical flaws that make it ultimately untenable. Fairness may indeed be no more than an obfuscatory term for ultimately instrumental objectives, similar to efficiency. The present listing intends no strict distinction between the two terms. Here, instead, efficiency suggests primarily the pursuit of the social goal of minimizing economic costs, while fairness references the process's treatment of the litigants.)
- F_{ie} or the preclusion *inequities* of the "*invokee*," especially any fault in causing new litigation: Fairness also supports the use of res judicata to prevent a party's profiting from abusively repetitive or otherwise undesirable litigation tactics. That litigant was entitled to a day in court, but not to inflict a repetition of it. (In considering whether or not to establish a rule of claim or issue preclusion, the court would focus on the equities and inequities of the run of persons who might come within the reach of the rule. In considering whether or not to create an exception to preclusion, as opposed to a rule, the court's focus would be more individualized, turning on the equities and inequities of the particular parties in the instant case. So again, all these

factors are of broad relevance to res judicata, but courts weighing them must remain sensitive to the specifics of the doctrinal inquiry at hand.)

- F_{rs} or the fairness of a broad but rigid preclusion doctrine's furtherance of *reliance* interests and *similar* treatment: Fairness further argues for the predictable and consistent application of relatively wooden preclusion rules without overly sizable or flexible exceptions. Such a scheme enables a person to rely on prior adjudication, while ensuring even-handed treatment by the doctrine. Society also has an interest in the appearance of fairness, as well as in the reality of fairness. Although similar, these fairness concerns are distinguishable from the efficiency interest in repose, in that these concerns focus on the litigants' fair treatment rather than society's economic cost. (This fair-doctrine factor is another that highlights the formal aspects of the res judicata doctrine itself. The form of the res judicata law has consequences on fairness, and on efficiency too.)

2. Procedural Factors Favoring Nonpreclusion

Some major fairness factors push against a rule of preclusion, but so do some minor efficiency factors:

- F_{ee} or the nonpreclusion *equities* of the *invokee*, especially the unfairness of forfeiting a fresh look at the matter: Life can be complex, and litigation often is as well. The realities of a case can mean that an otherwise sound rule of res judicata yields an unforgivably harsh result for persons in the invokee's situation.
- F_{ir} or the nonpreclusion *inequities* of the *invoker*, especially any misbehavior in putting the opponent into a res judicata bind: Res judicata can be a fatal weapon. The reports are brimming with cases in which the invoker was trying to pull a fast one, all too often successfully.
- F_{mt} or the fair-outcome value of deciding on the *merits* rather than on technicalities and of refusing to curtail society's search for *truth*: It is well to remember that res judicata is not an end in itself—it merely plays a role in a larger system of justice. Unfortunately, remembering this truism, as usual, advances the ball only a little. It does, however, serve to remind the lawmaker both that getting the disputed matter ultimately right is a value and also that fairness, as well as efficiency, demands this value enter onto the balance.

- E_a or the direct costs of *administering* this extension of the res judicata doctrine: The lawmaker must not forget the costs of administering the res judicata doctrine itself. The costs of litigating about whether or not to relitigate are a negative. And those costs mount as res judicata rules become broader and more complicated, just as they do when res judicata exceptions proliferate and soften.
- E_o or the direct costs of stimulating *overlitigation* in the initial action: The simplistic approach is to assume that res judicata, at least if effortlessly applied, always saves costs by foreclosing additional litigation. But a moment's thought reveals countervailing effects. A broad rule of claim preclusion will encourage a claimant to put everything before the first court, while a narrower rule might result in unasserted matters never having to be litigated at all. A broad rule of issue preclusion, which establishes an outcome for all purposes in all contexts for all times, may produce litigation to the death over that issue in the initial action. Obviously, every res judicata problem requires the weighing of net savings: adding up the savings of avoided later litigation, but subtracting the costs of fighting over res judicata's application and also the costs of intensified initial litigation.
- E_t or the error costs of not seeking *truth* by reaching the merits and trying to correct any initial mistake: Because legal rules have goals—be they the maximization of economic value or other substantive goals—and because realization of modern goals requires accurate application of the law to the facts, mistakes by the judicial branch distance society from those goals. Judicial mistakes thus impose social costs, and the procedural system should strive to reduce those costs. Procedure should frown on any impediment to correcting mistake. So the possibility of initial mistake is a factor favoring nonpreclusion. Although commentators frequently observe that existence of error in the prior judgment is irrelevant to res judicata, this is not really true. It is true that often res judicata can apply preclusion based on an erroneous judgment. But it is certainly not true that error is irrelevant to the formulation of res judicata. In shaping the rules and exceptions of res judicata law, the lawmaker must remain aware that the possibility of error is relevant to efficiency, as well as to fairness. Consequently, the lawmaker will be wary of allowing a small-claims court's judgment to bind a court of general jurisdiction, for example, or of enshrining a jury verdict as res judicata if it obviously resulted from compromise.

3. Combining All Factors

Strictly as a procedural matter, res judicata should apply where the net efficiency of preclusion outweighs the net fairness of nonpreclusion. The lawmaker—usually the courts, for res judicata—must find a way to balance the various factors. Most courts proceed intuitively. A more rigorous approach would require converting the factors into costs, measured in some common currency. Whether proceeding intuitively or rigorously, the courts must then mold res judicata to minimize the sum of those costs.

Regardless of the method of combining the factors, the courts must consider all relevant factors. Our list of factors thus far is incomplete, as we have listed only the policies that are procedural, in the sense of their being transsubstantive rather than focused on specific substantive goals. To demarcate a sound doctrine of res judicata, the balance must also contain any relevant substance-specific policies—ranging from market conditions to attorney-client relations. These substantive policies can either favor preclusion or, more likely, favor nonpreclusion, and they can be several on either side. For example, in matters of title to land, the law should be fierce about res judicata to promote an effective market. But when a fiduciary like an attorney tries to wield res judicata against a beneficiary like a client, the law should become wary. We can represent the sum of substantive policies favoring preclusion as $\sum S_p$ and the analogous substantive policies favoring nonpreclusion as $\sum S_n$.

A major insight, then, is that res judicata is merely the algebraic sum of various policies directed to various private and public ends. The lawmaker must consider all relevant policies, procedural and substantive. Obviously, the weights of these policies are subjective and debatable.

Another insight lies in observing that res judicata is highly sensitive to the prevailing legal and social system. Policies can appear and disappear. The weights of policies can change, for example, as the procedural and institutional system evolves. Moreover, the implications of those policies can change. Thus res judicata may have long preferred a plaintiff to join related grievances in one complaint to the extent procedurally permissible. But this policy implied that when the Federal Rules of Civil Procedure came to expand dramatically the plaintiff's permission to present a whole transaction in one shot, res judicata's scope in requiring joinder would undergo a gigantic expansion. The bottom line is that no eternal or universal doctrine of res judicata exists. Instead, res judicata is very much the child of its time and place.

B. Res Judicata Exceptions

The same considerations, especially those resting on individualized fairness, support departures from the principle of preclusion. That is, over the run of past and future cases, all the factors might support a general rule of preclusion. But in an individual case before a court, these same factors might call for nonpreclusion and thus justify a special exception to the rule.

The *grand trend* in the development of the modern doctrine of res judicata has been expanding the theoretical applicability of the preclusion rules while at the same time recognizing more and more exceptions of considerable scope and discretionary nature.

This trend's desirability is questionable. On the one hand, even the many existing exceptions do not remove all the bite from the sometimes harsh doctrine of res judicata. The exceptions have not kept up with the rapid expansion of the rules. On the other hand, as exceptions continue to multiply, the question arises whether a broad but marginally narrowing and increasingly discretionary doctrine of res judicata is really preferable to an absolutely bare but clear minimum of preclusion. It must be conceded that if the law elects to assign a substantial role to res judicata, its courts must apply the doctrine with some breadth and woodenness in order not to defeat its purposes.

The *bottom line* is a perhaps questionable, but doubtless considerable, net expansion of the scope of res judicata in modern America.

C. Summary

The factors pushing for preclusion, P, are represented by this sum:

$$E_w + E_i + E_r + F_{er} + F_{ie} + F_{rs} + \sum S_p = P$$

The factors cutting the other way, in favor of nonpreclusion, N, are represented by this sum:

$$F_{ee} + F_{ir} + F_{mt} + E_a + E_o + E_t + \sum S_n = N$$

The law should preclude what our society sees as a person's normal right to seek adjudication when $P > N$. Contrariwise, preclusion should not prevail—that is, a rule of res judicata should not extend—when $P \leq N$. If society is somewhat more risk averse as to intrusions on fairness by its courts than as to losses of efficiency, then the argument becomes stronger for the allocation of the burden of persuasion that is represented by those two different inequality symbols.

If the case falls within an established rule of res judicata, the lawmaker should create an exception when a more particularized inquiry shows that in the instant case $P < N$.

Admittedly, although pretty simple and comprehensible, this formulaic schema looks a little silly. But do not be fooled by appearances. It is not intended to suggest precision of analysis. It is meant only to recall the complex policy-driven nature of res judicata, while emphasizing the need for inclusive and thorough thought about all those varying procedural and substantive policies.

Many persons intuitively react strongly against such a formulaic approach. They say that no one can think in such a complex, multi-factored fashion. No one can assign weights to these policies in an objective manner. No one can convert these policies—so many apples and oranges, like efficiency and fairness—into a common currency for weighing them against one another.

Well, it would be fine to believe all that, except for the unavoidable fact that society has already given just those tasks to its res judicata lawmaker, which is usually the courts. The courts must, and implicitly do, distill all those conflicting policies. If a court does not think of a policy, it implicitly sets its value at zero. If a court thinks that lessening its docket in this age of overburdened courts is critically important, it is subjectively overvaluing E_W. If the court recognizes that preclusion will inflict great hardship and so elevates F_{ee}, but nevertheless feels that in the long run the benefits of preclusion are worth the costs, it is simply saying $E_W > F_{ee}$.

Thus, the choice lies between (1) the usual opaque brand of decisionmaking, whereby the judge lazily takes a stab at the outcome, but thereby unavoidably performs a complex calculation shielded from appellate scrutiny and academic criticism and perhaps even hidden from the judge's own consciousness, and (2) a perhaps silly-seeming rigorous form of decisionmaking, which serves to remind the judge of what is at stake and forces the thought process into the open by requiring complete explanation.

More sophisticated critics of that second route fall back to maintaining that its mathematical air dehumanizes the judicial process. The counterargument is that incomplete consideration of undefined policies combined in an unspecified way makes the judicial process all too human, too pervasively subject to mistake and bias. Again, the formulaic approach has the simple purpose of reminding all persons of how ideally to proceed and encouraging them to do the best job possible. Of course, in the hands of humans, its calculation remains subject to miscalculation and even manipulation—but less so than the obscurity and obfuscation of a lawmaker's stab.

CHAPTER 4

Jurisprudence of Rules and Exceptions

The competing policies, described in the preceding chapter, determine the scope of preclusion, and hence the complementary realm of nonpreclusion. But there is a separate question of form. How should the lawmaker—usually the courts, for res judicata—formulate the doctrine into rules and exceptions?

This very question implies perhaps that some intrinsic difference exists between rules and exceptions. But ultimately the contents of rules and exceptions are logically interchangeable. Any proposition of preclusion or nonpreclusion could appear either as a rule or as an exception. For example, the law could say that a particular preclusion provision applies only to prior judgments regarding land, or that it applies to all prior judgments except ones not regarding land. Another way of expressing the structure of such a two-staged doctrine of rules and exceptions is in terms of "if" clauses and "unless" clauses. If A and B, then res judicata, unless C or D. As a logical matter, any condition can be stated as an if clause or negatively restated as an unless clause. In brief, any distinction between rules and exceptions would seem to have a shaky foundation.[1]

Nevertheless, we can define rules and exceptions in terms of content so that the two expressions have meaning at least as a matter of degree. Here, then, "rules" mean a series of statements constituting a *general formulation of inclusion* that establishes the prima facie reach of the doctrine, and "exceptions" remain exceptional in *excluding only certain special situations* from

1. For some of the further involvements of the jurisprudential problem, see Richard A. Epstein, Pleadings and Presumptions, 40 U. Chi. L. Rev. 556 (1973).

the doctrine's application. Moreover, as long as rules and exceptions differ at least as a matter of degree, the policies behind a doctrine will not be indifferent to the allocation of the contents of rules and exceptions. The policies will call for an optimal phrasing of the doctrine.

A. Res Judicata Rules and Exceptions

Res judicata presents a truly classic struggle between the need for clear, simple, and rigid law and the desire for its sensitive application. Such a struggle never has a perfect resolution, but can have a best one. Careful attention by the lawmaker as to when to cast a rule and when to create an exception can aid mightily in shaping the best res judicata law possible.

With a sense of the meaning of rule and exception, and with a knowledge of the relevant policies, we can make general statements about the optimal phrasing of res judicata doctrine. The following three precepts as to the nature and scope of res judicata rules and exceptions, and their ideal jurisprudential relationship, should assist in the task of resolving res judicata's classic struggle. (These precepts apply specifically to res judicata, and so do not apply necessarily to the phrasing of other legal doctrines.)

- **Clear, simple, and rigid rules should approximate the outcome of the balance of the efficiency, fairness, and substantive policies behind res judicata.**

  Chapter 3 above showed how some of the policies behind res judicata call for a clear, simple, and rigid doctrine. The lawmaker should pursue these formal virtues through the rules rather than through the exceptions of res judicata.

  The doctrine's overall aim is to distinguish preclusion situations from nonpreclusion situations in accord with the tiltings of the policy balance. Rules should represent a good-faith stab at approximating that ultimate reach of the doctrine. That is, the rules should get the prima facie results pretty close to the desired endpoint. And in still other words, most results given by the rules alone, without the help of exceptions, should be right. But the specific interests in clarity, simplicity, and rigidity dictate that the rules can do no more than approximate the desired endpoint. The rules cannot embody the infinitely fine adjustments that would yield individualized precision. Instead, the rules must draw a limited series of lines that only approximate the myriad of desired outcomes.

As the lawmaker draws the rough lines by rules, there will be conscious overinclusion and underinclusion. That is, the preclusion rules will reach situations that they ideally should not, and they will fail to reach situations that they ideally should. Arguably, these two kinds of failing are not of equal gravity, overpreclusion being the greater danger. Preclusion intrudes on what our society sees as a person's normal right to seek adjudication. In appearance and in reality, overpreclusion entails an undesirable departure from that norm. Precluding someone who should not be precluded will inflict net fairness costs, and although nonpreclusion might be inefficient in net terms, society would rather tread on efficiency by relitigating cases on the margin than tread on fairness by precluding. Society may be more risk averse as to intrusions on fairness by its courts than as to losses of efficiency.

Maybe society is right, in that the marginal cost of overpreclusion could conceivably exceed the marginal cost of underpreclusion. But if the lawmaker has properly measured and balanced the relevant policies, then the difference at the margin should be small. Moreover, overinclusion has a cure. Exceptions to preclusion can exist, despite the defensible desire to keep them to a minimum, and they do work to cure any overinclusion.

In sum, the rules perhaps should reflect somewhat greater concern with overinclusion of res judicata than with underinclusion. Yet more subtle consideration of this intuitive stance suggests that any differential fear of overinclusion on the part of the lawmaker should be slight, at most. The lawmaker's principal aim should be making the rules carry most of the load, by approximating the outcome of the policy balance.

- **Flexible or even ad hoc exceptions should work to remedy any remaining overinclusion of res judicata in particular circumstances, but the exceptions should be small in scope even if necessarily considerable in number.**

Chapter 3 above showed how some of the other policies behind res judicata call for precise and individualized application of the doctrine. The lawmaker should pursue these formal virtues through the exceptions rather than through the rules of res judicata.

These precise and individualized exceptions can comprise a flexible list of factors compiled by the lawmaker for later use by the lawapplier. Or the exceptions can be frankly ad hoc, so that the court as applier of the doctrine decides on an all-things-considered basis whether to lift preclusion. At any rate, such exceptions are applied ex post, while any rules are formulated ex ante. Flexible or ad hoc, such exceptions will be fuzzy relative to the woodenness of the rules.

Fuzzy exceptions do create a gray zone where res judicata's applicability will be uncertain and unpredictable, being more or less up to a court's ex post discretion. The doctrine should aim to minimize that gray zone. Making the rules themselves more fuzzy would maximize the gray zone. But broad and wooden rules with small fuzzy exceptions manage to minimize, in appearance and in reality, the extent of the gray zone of res judicata's applicability. Res judicata not only looks more fixed, but also is more fixed.

Clear, simple, and rigid rules that establish an outer boundary of preclusion, with exceptions only cutting back on preclusion, additionally serve certainty and predictability by delineating definitely a zone where res judicata will *not* apply. Maybe the unit cost of not knowing whether the res judicata law reaches one's case does not exceed the unit cost of not knowing whether someone can wiggle out. But unidirectional confusion seems preferable to bidirectional confusion. At least the outer bound of res judicata can remain fixed.

- **There should be no exceptions to exceptions, because so extending preclusion is costly with few benefits.**

Although rules and exceptions can reach, as closely as is humanly possible, the doctrine's desired endpoint, the law's approach toward that endpoint might be more elegant or easier if the doctrine also contained exceptions to exceptions. That is, a formulation of "if A and B, then res judicata, unless C or D, except res judicata nevertheless applies when the exceptional situation E prevails" may be neater to draft than the alternative of narrowing C or D. So exceptions to exceptions could work to re-extend preclusion back into the nonpreclusion realm of an exception.

But the complexities of exceptions to exceptions are not only unnecessary but costly. With exceptions to exceptions, the doctrine would become more complicated to apply, and hence more expensive to administer. These costs would come in return for the small benefit of neatly curing underinclusion. Concededly, without the technique of exceptions to exceptions, the lawmaker sometimes may not bother to narrow an exception and thus may fail to preclude. But so what? When the lawmaker focuses on particular cases, as opposed to

> the run of all cases relevant to rulemaking, preclusion truly can become outrageously unfair. Exceptions therefore must exist. Contrariwise, nonpreclusion in a particular case exacts only the steady but not outrageous costs of relitigation. Exceptions to exceptions therefore need not exist. The law can survive and prosper without picking up every last case where preclusion would on balance be appropriate.
>
> Consequently, the modern doctrine of res judicata does not in fact feature exceptions to exceptions.

In sum, such a threefold approach to form best serves efficiency and fairness. These three precepts should be the lawmaker's primary guides in choosing between the forms of rule and exception. But they are not the only guides. The lawmaker might also consider the specific consequences that would follow from narrowing the rule rather than creating an exception.

Most prominently, the lawmaker might consider that the burden of proof for the invoker/invokee of res judicata very much tends to follow the rule/exception distinction. Almost always, the party invoking res judicata must show that the requirements of the rule are met, and the party resisting res judicata must show that the conditions of any exception exist. If for some substantive policy reason a particular allocation of burden is desirable, the lawmaker might take account of the judicial practice to allocate the burden on formal grounds and therefore cast the law accordingly into a rule or an exception.

Moreover, in particular circumstances, the effectiveness and ease of law formulation might influence the lawmaker's choice between narrowing the rule and creating an exception. If the current rule is unusually workable and effective as is, the lawmaker might incline toward changing the law by creating an exception. If instead an appropriate exception would be very difficult to formulate, the lawmaker might choose to skirt the difficulty by surgically reducing the rule itself.

B. Claim and Issue Preclusion Doctrine

All this theory has a tangible impact on fleshing out the doctrine. For example, given general res judicata rules approximating the policy balance, issue preclusion should entail more exceptions to carve out individualized situations than does claim preclusion.[2] The differential arguments for and

2. See Federated Dept. Stores v. Moitie, 452 U.S. 394 (1981) (rejecting exceptions to claim preclusion); Spilker v. Hankin, 188 F.2d 35 (D.C. Cir. 1951) (embracing excep-

against exceptions emerge from a grid of exceptions' effects on the policies behind the two major subdoctrines (see grid, page 45).

Claim preclusion therefore tends to be rigid, while issue preclusion tends to be flexible. But taking the approach of many individualized exceptions to an extreme would raise anew the ultimate desirability of the rules. Is the issue preclusion subdoctrine by now so limited in extent and mushy in meaning that the law would be better off just abolishing most of it? No, as long as the courts retain some restraint in creating exceptions.

Finally, with all this theory in mind, we are now ready to describe the details of the rules and exceptions of claim preclusion and issue preclusion. We turn to that project in this book's next part.

tions to issue preclusion); 18 Charles Alan Wright, Arthur R. Miller & Edward H. Cooper, Federal Practice and Procedure §§ 4415, 4426 (1981).

Policies from Chapter 3	**Claim Preclusion** arguments against exceptions	**Issue Preclusion** arguments for exceptions
Fairness to Invoker of Res Judicata	exceptions mean that invoker, often a repeat defendant, must face a whole new lawsuit, not merely relitigate an issue: therefore, exceptions are especially undesirable	exceptions mean that invoker, often a repeat plaintiff who is getting to choose the forum, loses opportunities for abuse, which here are multifold: therefore, exceptions can be desirable, for example, where an invoker tries to use a prior determination of a common legal issue by an inferior court in an inconvenient forum on a less significant claim
Fairness to Invokee of Res Judicata	less need for exceptions, because invokee often could protect against claim preclusion's effects: for example, where a fairly warned invokee could have put the whole claim before the prior court	more need for exceptions, because invokee often could not protect against issue preclusion's effects and so would innocently forfeit the opportunity to relitigate: for example, where an invokee had a relation of trust with the invoker, could not appeal the prior determination, and could not foresee the issue arising again
Other Fairness Concerns: fair doctrine and fair outcome	claim preclusion is susceptible to a broad and wooden formulation; claim preclusion's one-bite-at-the-apple notion can fairly apply to almost all claimants and has intuitive appeal, even without exceptions	issue preclusion resists being reduced to a simple and clear rule; society's sometimes unfairly shutting its eyes to the truth by means of issue preclusion, regardless of circumstances, has little intuitive appeal and so calls for exceptions
Direct Expenditures	exceptions mean that society must handle a whole new lawsuit, as well as bearing the expense of litigating over the reach of the exception	exceptions mean that society avoids overlitigation in the prior action, while incurring the expense of relitigating only a single issue
Other Efficiency Concerns: inconsistency, decreased repose, and error costs	exceptions would diminish the considerable possibilities for consistency and repose that come from foreclosing a whole claim	exceptions would avoid the error costs that would multiply as issue preclusion's effects ripple from one claim to different claims
Substantive Policies	less need for exceptions to effectuate substantive policies, because claim preclusion forecloses only a particular grievance that has already undergone adjudication	more need for exceptions to effectuate substantive policies, because fixing a legal issue for all purposes in all contexts for all times can really impede substantive policies

PART II

DOCTRINE

Res judicata facit ex albo nigrum; ex nigro, album; ex curvo, rectum; ex recto, curvum.

A thing adjudged makes white, black; black, white; the crooked, straight; the straight, crooked.

(Civilian maxim)

CHAPTER 5

Prerequisites for Res Judicata

A thing adjudged is powerful stuff, obviously, but we should start getting nervous when it makes straight the crooked, as the old maxim puts it. Do we not have to limit such magic to certain judgments? Yes, before a judgment enjoys res judicata effects, it must be valid and final.

A. Validity

For a judgment to have res judicata effects, it must be "valid." To be treated as valid, the judgment must be of sufficient quality to withstand an attack in the form of a request for relief from judgment.

Validity needs to be considered in connection with relief from judgment. Therefore, validity and late post-judgment requests for relief from judgment are together the subject in depth of Chapter 12 below. Nevertheless, it can be said here that the later chapter produces a rough but useful convention on the characteristics of a valid judgment. The gist of that coverage is this:

A judgment generally will survive an attack seeking relief from judgment if and only if the rendering court satisfied the requirements of (1) subject-matter jurisdiction, (2) territorial jurisdiction, and (3) adequate notice.

A judgment generally is valid for res judicata purposes if the court rendering the judgment had jurisdiction over the subject matter and over the defendant or other target of the action and complied with the basics of procedural due process. It may be valid in this sense even though other errors were committed that would warrant reversal on appeal. An erroneous judgment thus can be valid for res judicata purposes and will bind the parties unless and until it is reversed on appeal.

Even with its scope limited to these very basic defects, validity is an enormously deep subject, with an incredible amount of law filling the depths of jurisdiction and due process. Being a prerequisite condition for res judicata, validity can arise during attempts to defeat the doctrine's application. Accordingly, the study of validity and the doctrine of res judicata are intrinsically linked together.

B. Finality

For a judgment to have res judicata effects, it must be "final." The rendering court must have uttered its last word on the claim or issue to qualify the ruling as final.

There is no general doctrine of *res litigiosæ*, or thing being litigated, just *res judicata*, or thing adjudged. The law is not terribly concerned with the pendency of multiple lawsuits.[1] But once one lawsuit goes to judgment, the law gets very serious about its binding effect. Consequently, the effective date of a judgment is its date of rendition, having nothing to do with the date of the action's commencement.[2]

Once the trial court renders judgment, that judgment is usually deemed final. Although some states have held that pendency of an appeal or other procedure to set aside the judgment renders it nonfinal for res judicata purposes, the law in most jurisdictions today does not postpone finality pending review. Thus, in most jurisdictions, it makes no difference if the right to execute or otherwise enforce the judgment is delayed or stayed during review. Indeed, it makes no difference if the unhappy party in fact takes the steps to get review or does not. The law does not wait until the time for taking appeal expires, or even until the time expires to try to set aside the judgment in the trial court by motion for new trial or the like. The judgment is final upon its rendering, and it stays final unless and until it is actually overturned.

Similarly, judgments that seek to control future activity—such as injunctions, specific performance decrees, support orders, custody determinations, and the like—are commonly subject to modification, even retroac-

---

1. But see supra Chapter 2-H (other action pending doctrine, antisuit injunctions, and lis pendens).

2. See Restatement (Second) of Judgments § 14 (1982).

tively, by the court that rendered them. Still, such judgments are sufficiently final for res judicata purposes. The claims and issues to which preclusive effect may apply, however, are those as existing at the time of the judgment. A change in circumstances could create different claims and issues. For example, a determination in a custody contest that the mother of the child is a fit parent does not, of course, preclude relitigation of the question of her fitness in a later proceeding when conditions have changed.

1. Meanings of Finality

So when exactly is a judgment deemed finally rendered by the trial court? The meaning of finality has come to vary between claim preclusion and issue preclusion. The desirability of this bifurcation remains quite debatable.

a. Claim Preclusion

For the purposes of claim preclusion, a judgment becomes final when the trial court has concluded all regular proceedings on the claim, other than award of costs and enforcement of judgment.

A judgment does not have the effect of merger or bar unless it is final.[3] The law does not want to preclude on the basis of the tentative, contingent, or provisional. The law wants the rendering court to have uttered its last word on the claim. A judgment is final when all the issues on which it turns have been decided and judgment has been entered for the winning party. It matters not that time for attack in the trial or appellate court remains, or even that the loser has launched such a direct attack. It matters only that the trial court has concluded the regular proceedings in adjudicating the claim. Thus, for instance, a judgment is final even though a motion for new trial or an appeal is pending, but a determination of liability is not final if damages remain to be determined.

Finality in its claim preclusion sense means roughly, but not exactly, the same as it does when the term "final decision" is used to describe those orders that may be immediately appealed. The two senses do somewhat differ. Finality for claim preclusion can be both narrower and broader than finality for appealability.

On the one hand, in recent times, courts have allowed appeals by fashioning a number of refinements to finality. Collateral orders are now im-

3. See generally Restatement (Second) of Judgments § 13 (1982).

mediately appealable,[4] as are a rare set of orders for which on an ad hoc basis the benefits of immediate appeal strongly outweigh the costs.[5] Such refinements have not carried over to claim preclusion, which sticks closer to the traditional definition of final decision. In this regard, then, finality for claim preclusion is narrower than modern appealability's final decision rule.

On the other hand, under the common law, a judgment in an action involving multiple claims or parties was not final for appealability purposes until all claims had been decided. A final determination of one claim in a multiclaim or multiparty action could be final for claim preclusion purposes, however, as long as the court had clearly terminated its proceeding on that part of the action. In this regard, finality for claim preclusion is broader than appealability's final decision rule. Note, however, that under Federal Rule of Civil Procedure 54(b) and similar state procedural rules, an order finally determining one claim in a multiple claim or multiple party suit can now be declared appealable even though other claims remain to be decided. In such a procedural system, then, finality for appeal and finality for res judicata more closely mean the same thing.

b. Issue Preclusion

For issue preclusion, an adjudication is sometimes treated as a final judgment at an earlier stage than for claim preclusion. According to some authorities, the court in the subsequent action has discretion cautiously to treat a prior determination as final if after adequate hearing and full deliberation the initial court made a firm decision on the issue, even though in that initial action there is as yet no final judgment on the claim.

Traditionally, issue preclusion has been regarded as applying only to determinations embodied in a judgment, and only to such judgments as are final. The test of finality for these purposes has generally been assumed to be the same as the test used to fix finality for purposes of claim preclusion.

Yet when the preclusive effect of the initial action is invoked not to extinguish an entire claim, but to prevent relitigation of a particular issue or issues, the importance of postponing the preclusive effect of the initial action until *all* issues have been resolved is not obvious. Of course, a truly

4. See Cohen v. Beneficial Indus. Loan Corp., 337 U.S. 541 (1949).
5. See Gillespie v. United States Steel Corp., 379 U.S. 148 (1964).

tentative determination of an issue should not have preclusive effect. If, however, it is clear that the issue has been solidly determined after active litigation and that the other requisites of issue preclusion are met, the determination of that issue would seem sufficiently final to warrant preclusive effect. That is, if the particular issue sought to be precluded in the subsequent action has been actually, fully, fairly, and finally determined in the initial action, issue preclusion would seem appropriate even if there has not yet been a final judgment disposing of all issues in the initial action. Postponement of the preclusive effect of some issues that have been really resolved pending the resolution of other issues would seem to generate either unnecessary relitigation or undue delay in the subsequent action. Moreover, the relaxation of the traditional notion of finality in the context of issue preclusion would seem especially desirable in view of the tendency of modern civil procedure to foster complex and multifaceted lawsuits, huge sprawling lawsuits involving numerous issues and lasting for years.

Several well-considered authorities have taken this position. In *Lummus Co. v. Commonwealth Oil Refining Co.*,[6] Judge Friendly commented: "'Finality' in the context here relevant may mean little more than that the litigation of a particular issue has reached such a stage that a court sees no really good reason for permitting it to be litigated again." That case, however, involved a situation particularly appropriate for preclusion, because the earlier ruling on an issue of fact had been definitively made *by a court of appeals* on interlocutory reversal of a preliminary injunction.

The Second Restatement adopted and generalized this position, declaring that "for purposes of issue preclusion (as distinguished from merger and bar), 'final judgment' includes any prior adjudication of an issue in another action that is determined to be sufficiently firm to be accorded conclusive effect."[7] The Restatement does, however, modify Judge Friendly's words by putting the burden on the invoker of res judicata to show finality. The Second Restatement thereby ends up with a fuzzy rule that requires the subsequent court to measure whether the prior adjudication was litigated and deliberated adequately and was expressed with adequate firmness. In addition to the obvious difficulties of a fuzzy rule, giving issue preclusion effect to a decision that may yet evolve opens up a number of potentially undesirable complications.

6. 297 F.2d 80, 89 (2d Cir. 1961).

7. Restatement (Second) of Judgments § 13 (1982).

The Second Restatement's approach permits issue preclusion effect to be given to decisions that are not appealable at the time, because interlocutory decisions commonly are not appealable until a final judgment for the whole action is entered. Because issue preclusion so extends to decisions that may be reviewed and reversed on appeal much later, inconsistent judgments become possible. Admittedly, this same possibility would exist, albeit for a shorter period, even if issue preclusion were limited to rulings embodied in judgments that are final in the strict sense, because preclusive effect is not denied to such judgments that are, or may be, appealed. Thus, the mere fact that the ruling was not ripe for immediate appeal should not automatically prevent preclusion of the issue in the subsequent action. Nevertheless, the fact that the interlocutory ruling was not ripe for appeal should at least be a factor that inclines the subsequent court to view the ruling as nonfinal for issue preclusion purposes.

Another problem with the Second Restatement's watering down of finality is that the initial trial court itself could revisit the issue in the course of the initial proceedings and change its mind. Early finality simply increases the chances that later events will make issue preclusion undesirable after all.

A third problem even more troubling, or at least more frequent, lies in the very real possibility of the initial case's turning out in a way that makes the issue's determination not essential to the final judgment, and hence not ultimately entitled to issue preclusion effect. For example, the loser on the interlocutory issue might win the case. Or the case might just settle, with the parties' agreeing against issue preclusion effect. In brief, the Second Restatement extends issue preclusion in the interim to determinations that do not ultimately deserve issue preclusion effect.[8]

Therefore, one could persuasively argue that the Second Restatement's extension of issue preclusion causes some major complications with correspondingly big costs. True, the extension is relatively minor in scope, but that means it has correspondingly small benefits. In other words, this development is just not worth the trouble. Instead, for issue preclusion the law should return to the same strict standard of finality that it applies for claim preclusion.

Nevertheless, the weight of recent authority follows the Second Restatement, ascribing issue preclusion effect to rulings that are not final for claim preclusion purposes. Still, that power should be exercised cautiously, that

---

8. See Avondale Shipyards v. Insured Lloyd's, 786 F.2d 1265, 1269-71 (5th Cir 1986).

is, only where the propriety and advantage of issue preclusion are clear, as in the *Lummus* case itself.

2. Complications of Finality

a. Effects of Reversal

If a judgment is reversed or modified by appeal (or by other means), its preclusive effects will henceforth be in accordance with its new terms. If in the meantime some other judgment has been based on that earlier judgment before its overturning, then relief from the other judgment normally may be had by appropriate proceedings.[9]

The usual rule is that a judgment is final for res judicata purposes even though it is attacked or appealed. If it is actually set aside or otherwise overturned, it no longer has the same res judicata effects, of course.

This approach can produce an anomalous situation if a later judgment has been based on the earlier judgment that gets overturned. For example, a plaintiff sues upon a judgment that is still on appeal and gets a new judgment upon the first judgment while the appeal is pending. If the first judgment is eventually reversed on that appeal, what effect does that have on the second judgment based on it, assuming that the second proceedings are now all over?

The Supreme Court has held that the reversal of the first judgment does not automatically affect the second judgment based on it.[10] Although the fact of the reversal of the first judgment is ground for relief in some form from the second judgment based on it, the aggrieved party must follow appropriate procedure to set it aside. Federal Rule of Civil Procedure 60(b)(5) authorizes, on motion to the court that granted the second judgment, the granting of relief from that judgment when, inter alia, "a prior judgment upon which it is based has been reversed or otherwise vacated." In states not having a comparable rule, the proper procedure to avoid the second judgment might be an independent action to enjoin its enforcement. Restitution, if necessary, would also be available.

b. Inconsistent Judgments

If by failure to invoke or apply res judicata two inconsistent judgments are rendered, then the judgment later rendered has the controlling preclu-

9. See generally Restatement (Second) of Judgments § 16 (1982).
10. Reed v. Allen, 286 U.S. 191 (1932).

sive effects. This somewhat arbitrary practice is called the last-in-time rule.[11]

One of the purposes of res judicata is to minimize the possibility of inconsistent judgments on the same claim or issue. However, the doctrine cannot eliminate that possibility completely. First, res judicata must be raised in the subsequent action by the party who seeks to take advantage of it. If that party fails to assert the preclusive effect of the former adjudication, a judgment may be rendered in the subsequent action that is inconsistent with the judgment rendered in the initial one. Second, inconsistent judgments can also result when the party entitled to rely upon the initial judgment does assert it, but the subsequent court erroneously refuses to give it preclusive effect. The subsequent court may believe that some requirement of res judicata is lacking or some exception applies, and the resulting relitigation may produce a different outcome.

So when inconsistent judgments do come about, how should the law handle them? Under the rule generally followed, when there are two valid and final but inconsistent judgments, it is the later one that is entitled to res judicata effects.[12]

For a claim preclusion example, a plaintiff who won a judgment may be dissatisfied with the amount of damages awarded. So instead of seeking enforcement of the judgment, she may sue again on the original claim. Although a claim merges in a judgment in favor of the claimant, the subsequent court will not ordinarily raise the defense of res judicata on its own motion. If the defendant does not raise the defense of merger, another trial on the merits of the original claim may be held. The judgment reached in this second action may be for the defendant. Hence, inconsistent judgments can come into existence.

- If the same claim is presented in a third action, the question will arise as to which, if either, of the now two valid and final but inconsistent judgments is to be given preclusive effect in the third action. That is, if the originally successful plaintiff were now to bring a third action, either an action on the original claim or an action upon the first judgment, could the defendant invoke the second judgment as a defense? Yes, the second judgment is entitled to res judicata effect.

11. See generally Restatement (Second) of Judgments § 15 (1982); Ruth B. Ginsburg, Judgments in Search of Full Faith and Credit: The Last-in-Time Rule for Conflicting Judgments, 82 Harv. L. Rev. 798 (1969).

12. See, e.g., Treinies v. Sunshine Mining Co., 308 U.S. 66 (1939); Donald v. J.J. White Lumber Co., 68 F.2d 441 (5th Cir. 1934).

- If the defendant had raised the defense of res judicata in the plaintiff's second action but the court had erroneously refused to consider or uphold it, the result would be the same as if the defense had not been raised, unless the second judgment is appealed and reversed.
- If, in the example, instead of the defendant's winning the second action, the plaintiff had won a judgment for a greater amount than had been awarded in the first action, the second judgment would still be the one entitled to res judicata effect.

Now, for an issue preclusion example, a fact issue may go in favor of *A* over *B* in Forum #1. If the same issue arises in a second action on a different claim in Forum #2, and *A* fails to raise collateral estoppel, another trial on the merits may produce a determination on the issue in favor of *B*. Again, then, inconsistent judgments can come into existence.

- If the common issue is presented in a third action on yet a different claim in Forum #3, and *B* raises collateral estoppel, what happens in the face of two valid and final but inconsistent judgments? F-3 must accept the determination of F-2.
- If F-3 and F-1 were in fact the same court, the result would still be that the determination of F-2 prevails. So even though F-1 acted first, and even though the proceeding in F-2 should have been precluded, the court in F-1 must ignore its own previous determination of the issue.
- If, finally, the third proceeding were an appeal in F-1 from the first judgment, even then the determination of F-2 should govern the disposition of the appeal, subordinating the earlier trial court determination in F-1 to the later determination of F-2. Although the appellate court in F-1 would naturally tend to resist this astounding application of the last-in-time rule,[13] the best approach is indeed for the F-1 courts to respect res judicata and its latest effects, at least during the regular course of proceedings in the trial and appellate courts of F-1.[14] If, however, those regular trial and appellate proceedings in F-1 were complete when F-2 made its determination, the first judgment normally would not be undone or otherwise overturned, but it

13. See, e.g., American Postal Workers Union Columbus Area Local v. United States Postal Serv., 736 F.2d 317, 319 (6th Cir. 1984).

14. See Parsons Steel, Inc. v. First Ala. Bank, 474 U.S. 518 (1986); 18 Charles Alan Wright, Arthur R. Miller & Edward H. Cooper, Federal Practice and Procedure §4404, at 30-31, §4433, at 314 (1981).

would stand shorn henceforth of its preclusive effects. F-2's later determination would be the one entitled to res judicata effects.

The rationale of this last-in-time rule may not be overwhelming, but does exist. One of the inconsistent judgments must prevail in order to avoid theoretically endless relitigation. Perhaps the second judgment is more apt to be right, as it resulted from relitigation and redetermination. At any rate, the party entitled to the benefit of res judicata in the second action was in a position to avoid the possibility of inconsistent judgments. If he failed to avail himself of the opportunity to invoke res judicata, and so allowed the matter to be relitigated, he is not in a position to complain when the second determination is treated as conclusive in a third action, unless there were elements of unfairness in the second action that caused him to waive his right. If he did assert his right, but the second court erroneously denied it, he should have sought correction of the error by appeal from the second court, as with any other error by a trial court.

Some exceptions to the last-in-time rule have been suggested. The most plausible one relates to the case in which the second action is brought in a different state from the state of the first judgment's rendition; the court in the second action erroneously refuses to accord preclusive effect to the first judgment, in contravention of the Full Faith and Credit Clause of the United States Constitution; and the appellate courts of the second state affirm. If the party claiming the benefit of the first judgment is unable, without fault, to obtain review of the second judgment by the Supreme Court of the United States, should the last-in-time rule still govern when the matter is presented in a third action? It is arguable that the party should not be bound by the preclusive effect of the second judgment, because the party could have done nothing more to avoid an inconsistent judgment.[15] But res judicata frequently enshrines erroneous judgments, including those to which the Supreme Court has denied certiorari. To be consistent, res judicata should protect the second judgment here by the usual last-in-time rule. Although this hypothetical scenario works well to expose, on peculiarly wrenching facts, the somewhat arbitrary nature of the last-in-time rule, the remaining reasons behind the rule push toward its application even in this

15. See Ruth B. Ginsburg, Judgments in Search of Full Faith and Credit: The Last-in-Time Rule for Conflicting Judgments, 82 Harv. L. Rev. 798 (1969); cf. Restatement (Second) of Conflict of Laws § 114 cmt. b (1971) (raising the problem without taking a position).

extreme scenario. One judgment should prevail, and the second is more apt to be right on the merits.[16]

16. See 18 Charles Alan Wright, Arthur R. Miller & Edward H. Cooper, Federal Practice and Procedure § 4404, at 28-29 (1981 & Supp. 1999); cf. Parsons Steel, Inc. v. First Ala. Bank, 474 U.S. 518 (1986) (strong support for the last-in-time rule in the federal-state setting).

CHAPTER 6

Claim Preclusion

A. Requirements of Rule

Once a claim has been presented for adjudication and then a valid and final judgment has been rendered, the same claim cannot be asserted in a subsequent suit. The judgment has extinguished the claim, however that claim is to be defined. This is the claim preclusion doctrine of res judicata, with its subdoctrines of merger and bar.

One consequence of this doctrine is the prohibition against splitting a claim. Any plaintiff who asserts only a part of a claim is said to have split the claim, and claim preclusion prevents subsequent assertion of the claim's remainder. For example, *P* sues *D* for personal injury resulting from an automobile accident. After valid and final judgment on the merits, *P* sues *D* for property damage in the same accident. *D* pleads res judicata. If and only if personal and property damages from the same accident constitute the same claim under the applicable res judicata law, *P* has impermissibly split the claim, and so claim preclusion would preclude the second action.[1] Thus, claim preclusion can reach not only matters actually asserted in the prior action but also matters within the scope of the claim that might have been but were not presented for decision.

The doctrine of claim preclusion could be viewed as a common-law rule of compulsory joinder. A judgment precludes a later action on any grievances that were required to be joined in that action, whether they were or not. However, claim preclusion has not traditionally been described in terms of compulsory joinder. The plaintiff is not seen as having several

1. See Restatement (Second) of Judgments §24 cmt. c, illus. 1-2 (1982).

grievances that must be joined, but rather as having one claim that cannot be split. The problem of determining what must be included in a single lawsuit thus becomes a problem of defining the scope of that single claim that cannot be split.

In sum, claim preclusion prohibits repetitive litigation of the same claim. If the claim in the first action was identical to a claim in the second action, claim preclusion normally applies. This formulation makes identity of claim into the doctrine's key requirement. This requirement necessitates knowing what a claim is. The claim-splitting prohibition, in particular, reveals that to understand claim preclusion, it is necessary to define claim—in terms of the dimensions of a claim.

1. Dimensions of Claim

"Claim" has replaced the older usage of "cause of action," which carried plenty of connotative baggage loaded toward a narrow meaning. What do these terms mean? These terms have significance in several contexts other than res judicata, a fact that compounds the difficulty of defining them for any one given purpose. So, what do these terms mean for res judicata purposes?

The old view, to which some jurisdictions still adhere, defined cause of action more narrowly in terms of a single legal theory or a single substantive right or remedy of the plaintiff. The modern view is that a claim includes all theories' bestowal of rights on the plaintiff to remedies against the defendant with respect to the *transaction* from which the action arose.

The modern, or so-called transactional, view of res judicata dictates that the plaintiff *should* in a single lawsuit fully litigate all grievances arising from a transaction, just as the plaintiff *may* do under the modern rules of procedure. The rationale is that this view increases efficiency, with an acceptable burden on fairness.

a. Evolution of Transactional View

Forms of Action. Under the common-law procedural system, it seems clear that the determination of the range of claim preclusion, like most other matters, was a function of the forms of action.[2] The defense of res judicata could be asserted when the plaintiff had previously won or lost a

2. See Robert Wyness Millar, The Historical Relation of Estoppel by Record to Res Judicata, 35 Ill. L. Rev. 41 (1940); Robert Wyness Millar, The Premises of the Judgment as Res Judicata in Continental and Anglo-American Law (pts. 1-2), 39 Mich. L. Rev. 1, 238 (1940).

judgment in an action alleging the same basic facts and brought in the same form of action. Also, it was generally said that the plaintiff could not avoid res judicata by merely changing the form of action, and this was said to be true whether the plaintiff had won or lost the first action.[3] But actually, whether a second action alleging the same basic facts could be brought in a different form of action depended in part on whether the plaintiff had won or lost the first action.[4]

If the plaintiff had won the first action, another action would not lie against the same defendant for the same injury through the mere expedient of changing forms of action. The law generally will not allow a plaintiff more than one recovery for the same injury.

If the plaintiff had lost the first action, however, the matter was not so clear. If the first action had failed because the plaintiff had chosen a form of action that did not fit the facts, a later action brought in the proper form would lie. The reason for this was not that the second action was based on a different cause of action, but that the first judgment was not "on the merits." Even in other situations, however, a later action would usually lie in a different form. It was recognized that the same event could give rise to two or more different causes of action. For the most part, if the facts relating to the event could fit into a different form of action that involved a different legal theory, a different cause of action existed for res judicata purposes. By and large, then, in spite of the so-called general rule that res judicata could not be avoided by changing the form of action, a judgment against the plaintiff in the first action usually did not have claim-preclusive effect in a later action in a different form of action, even when the same basic event was involved.

Primary Right. The abolition of the forms of action by the nineteenth-century procedural reforms led to more careful analysis of the rules relating to merger and bar. Although it seems to have been assumed at first that an analytically definable concept of cause of action did exist, no unitary definition of it ever gained universal acceptance, and eventually it came to be recognized that the term could mean different things in different contexts. The Field Code alluded to "the facts constituting a cause of action" in prescribing what a complaint had to contain. This suggested that a cause of action is a group of facts, but it did not tell what facts were to be included in

3. See 2 Henry Campbell Black, A Treatise on the Law of Judgments 1091, 1095 (2d ed. 1902); Charles E. Clark, Handbook of the Law of Code Pleading 473-74 (2d ed. 1947).

4. See Restatement (Second) of Judgments § 25 cmt. l (1982).

the group, particularly not for res judicata purposes. Several different approaches have been used by courts to resolve that question.

One test, often associated with the nineteenth-century scholar John Norton Pomeroy, focused on the violation of a primary right. It saw the cause of action as "the facts from which the plaintiff's primary right and the defendant's corresponding primary duty have arisen, together with the facts which constitute the defendant's delict or act of wrong."[5] The two sets of facts together constituted the cause of action for res judicata purposes.

Under this view, to use a simple illustration, a land contract purchaser would have but one cause of action for the defendant's breach in refusing to convey. Although the plaintiff in such a situation might have two alternative remedies—damages or specific performance—the plaintiff would have but one cause of action, because the plaintiff's primary substantive right (to the promised conveyance) and the defendant's delict or wrong (refusal to convey) were the same regardless of which remedy the plaintiff sought.

By contrast, because the rights to bodily integrity and the rights in personal property were analytically separate primary rights, the single negligent act of a defendant driver that caused injury to both the person and the property of the plaintiff would give rise to two different causes of action. This result shows the disturbingly narrow scope of cause of action under the primary right theory.

Likewise, two separate causes of action would seem to exist under this theory when two separate wrongs of the defendant contributed to the same invasion of the plaintiff's primary right. For an extreme example, if the defendant was negligent both in operating a vehicle with defective brakes and in failing to keep a proper lookout, and both factors were causally connected to hitting the plaintiff, this theory would seemingly identify two different causes of action. Nevertheless, the cases generally did not carry this theory to that extreme, as virtually all cases treated different acts of negligence by the defendant causing a single injury to the plaintiff as parts of a single cause of action.[6]

Remedial Right. This theory viewed the cause of action as being composed of a single remedial right.[7] Unlike the primary right theory just dis-

---

5. John Norton Pomeroy, Remedies and Remedial Rights by the Civil Action 488 (Boston, Little, Brown 1876).

6. See Ernst Schopflocher, What Is a Single Cause of Action for the Purpose of the Doctrine of Res Judicata?, 21 Or. L. Rev. 319, 329-33 (1942).

7. See O.L. McCaskill, Actions and Causes of Action, 34 Yale L.J. 614 (1925).

cussed, this approach treated a request for damages and one for specific performance based upon the same breach of contract as two separate causes of action, because the plaintiff sought two different remedies. Likewise, a breach-of-contract claim seeking as damages the agreed price of goods or services given by the plaintiff to the defendant was a different cause of action from one seeking their reasonable value in quantum valebant or quantum meruit on an unjust enrichment theory.[8]

Another way in which this approach could authorize two separate actions for essentially the same wrong is illustrated by a case of trespass to real estate that led only to an injury to fixtures thereon. At common law, the injuries might be recoverable as matters in aggravation in an action of trespass q.c.f., or they might be recoverable in an action on the case. Even after the abolition of the forms of action, these two were regarded as alternative remedies, in spite of the fact that the same measure of recovery was used. Thus, two separate actions might be brought for the injury to the fixtures (but, of course, only one recovery could be had). Incidentally, here the same result would be reached in courts following the primary right theory, because the right to exclude entry and the right to avoid injury were theoretically separate.

Same Evidence. In view of these older theories' obvious difficulties and narrowness, most modern courts have defined cause of action in terms of a functionally related group of facts, without direct reference to whether those facts might involve one or more rights or remedies. Still, the question of what facts are to be considered in the group has received variant answers.

One approach has focused upon the evidence necessary to make out a prima facie case. If the evidence required to support the second action is the same that would have supported the first, the same cause of action is involved in each, regardless of the legal theory underlying the two actions, and regardless of different allegations in the pleadings. If the evidence to support the second action would not have supported the first, the causes of action are separate, and the second action is not precluded.

Actions for damages to person and to property stemming from the same negligent conduct would be separate causes of action under this approach, because proof of damage is necessary to establish a prima facie case, and proof of damage to property would not support a claim for injuries to the

---

8. See, e.g., Smith v. Kirkpatrick, 111 N.E.2d 209 (N.Y. 1953), overruled, O'Brien v. City of Syracuse, 429 N.E.2d 1158, 1160 n.1 (N.Y. 1981) (adopting transactional view).

person. This result of separate causes of action is troubling in this situation.

Thus, although often referred to as an all-purpose test, the same evidence test works better as a test for inclusion than as a test for exclusion. It is a good means of telling when two suits *do* involve the same cause of action, but not of telling when they *do not.* Identity of evidence supporting the two causes can show that the second action is so closely related to the first that only one lawsuit should be permitted. The lack of identity of evidence, however, does not necessarily mean that the second action should be allowed. Many cases recognized this,[9] and this is the view reflected in the Restatements.[10] Accordingly, other criteria have to be used to determine whether a second action should be precluded when it did not depend upon the same evidence that would have supported the first action.

Transactional View. All the foregoing approaches try to subdivide a transaction into a number of causes of action. None include more than a transaction. All involve huge definitional difficulties. So why not make transaction itself the unit for claim preclusion? This would make application of the doctrine simpler. Such breadth would enhance the efficiency benefits of the doctrine. And once procedural rules for pleading, discovery, and amendment have become liberal enough to permit the parties to litigate fully the whole transaction in one lawsuit, such breadth would not be unfair.

Of course, such a transactional view still requires definition of transaction, but modern procedure is used to defining that term functionally rather than analytically, and flexibly rather than rigidly. Its definition in this context turns pragmatically on the efficiency/fairness rationale of res judicata. The pragmatic approach that seems most consistent with modern procedural philosophy is one that looks to see if the claim asserted in the second action should have been presented for decision in the earlier action, taking into account practical considerations relating mainly to trial convenience and fairness. Modern procedure seeks to maximize the efficiency of judicial proceedings by encouraging the presentation of all grievances that can conveniently and fairly be tried together in the framework of a single lawsuit.

---

9. E.g., Williams v. Jensen, 408 P.2d 920 (Nev. 1965).

10. See Restatement (Second) of Judgments §24 cmts. a-b, §25 cmt. b (1982); Restatement of Judgments §61 (1942).

Federal Rule of Civil Procedure 18, for instance, allows a plaintiff to join as many claims as the plaintiff has against the defendant in a single action. The judge may separate claims or issues for separate trials when the joined claims do not constitute one convenient and fair trial unit, and the criteria for ordering separate trials (or for consolidating actions) under Federal Rule of Civil Procedure 42 are highly pragmatic. The same sort of pragmatic considerations should be taken into account in defining the scope of a plaintiff's claim that cannot be split into more than one suit or, to phrase the same point differently, in deciding when a plaintiff should be compelled to join grievances in a single suit through the operation of res judicata.

Federal Rule of Civil Procedure 13(a) does require a defendant to assert as a counterclaim any claim the defendant may have against the plaintiff that "arises out of the transaction or occurrence that is the subject matter of the" plaintiff's claim. There is, however, no express requirement that a plaintiff join all grievances arising out of the same transaction or occurrence in the first instance. The compulsion that exists to force joinder is whatever is embodied in the doctrine of claim preclusion. The pragmatic approach would use considerations like those developed in construing the compulsory counterclaim rule to determine when the plaintiff's grievances are so closely related that they can be the subject of only one action—that is, to determine the dimensions of the plaintiff's claim.

The Second Restatement endorses this pragmatic approach. It abandoned the First Restatement's unsuccessful attempt to rationalize the old tests. Indeed, in the attempt to thwart any inclination to read the old tests back into the new approach, the Second Restatement avoids the use of "cause of action" and casts the black-letter rule in terms reminiscent of the Federal Rules of Civil Procedure:

> **§ 24. Dimensions of "Claim" for Purposes of Merger or Bar—General Rule Concerning "Splitting"**
>
> **(1) When a valid and final judgment rendered in an action extinguishes the plaintiff's claim pursuant to the rules of merger or bar..., the claim extinguished includes all rights of the plaintiff to remedies against the defendant with respect to all or any part of the transaction, or series of connected transactions, out of which the action arose.**
>
> **(2) What factual grouping constitutes a "transaction," and what groupings constitute a "series," are to be determined pragmatically, giving weight to such considerations as whether the facts are related in time, space, origin, or motivation, whether they form a**

> **convenient trial unit, and whether their treatment as a unit conforms to the parties' expectations or business understanding or usage.**

To make its rejection of the older theories unmistakable, the Second Restatement in its elaborative § 25 declares that the transactional view may:

> **extinguish a claim by the plaintiff against the defendant even though the plaintiff is prepared in the second action**
> **(1) To present evidence or grounds or theories of the case not presented in the first action, or**
> **(2) To seek remedies or forms of relief not demanded in the first action.**

That is, the plaintiff must be careful to put any asserted claim entirely before the court, because judgment will not only preclude actual relitigation but also preclude later pursuit of the claim's unasserted portion. Under the transactional view, a claim is big enough to include: (1) different harms; (2) different evidence; (3) different legal theories, whether cumulative, alternative, or even inconsistent; (4) different remedies, whether legal or equitable; and (5) a series of related events.

Although in its early years the transactional approach was vigorously criticized as being too vague and leaving too much to the whim of the judge, in recent times it has come to be recognized that much of the certainty of application supposedly possessed by other tests, such as the primary right or remedial right tests, was illusory. Judges can and will find ways to ameliorate the rigors of any test when the interests of justice seem to require it. The transactional test has the advantage of recognizing this fact of legal life and of focusing the inquiry upon factors that are really relevant to the administration of justice, rather than masking them under some largely artificial analytical concept. Also, the transactional view clearly is more consonant with present-day legal reasoning than the other tests. Accordingly, the trend of decisions is toward ever wider acceptance of it.[11]

Nevertheless, the transactional view has not yet completely displaced the older approaches. At the very least, the older definitions of cause of action

11. E.g., Williamson v. Columbia Gas & Elec. Corp., 186 F.2d 464 (3d Cir. 1950); O'Brien v. City of Syracuse, 429 N.E.2d 1158 (N.Y. 1981).

continue to be quoted by courts. Often, however, in such cases the same decision would have followed under the transactional view.

b. Application of Transactional View

In some common types of cases, decisions are sufficiently numerous to permit generalization about the dimensions of the claim under the transactional view. In fact, courts tend to reach the same conclusion in these cases whatever the approach to the definition of claim that they may follow, but not always.

Multiple Parties. Traditionally, claims of several plaintiffs arising from the same conduct of a defendant have been analyzed as separate claims for res judicata purposes. A judgment for or against one such plaintiff in an action in which the others were not parties generally has no effect of precluding the claims of the others. The same is true in cases when the multiple parties are defendants.

Nevertheless, there are some situations in which a judgment may have claim-preclusive effects in later actions involving nonparties. Such situations might be present in connection with in rem proceedings or class actions, or other situations in which the nonparty's interests are represented by one who is a party. These situations are more easily understood if viewed as applications of privity,[12] rather than as situations in which the scope of a single claim includes grievances by or against multiple persons, although some cases do analyze the problem as one of the scope of the claim.

Another such situation is present when the obligation sued on is characterized as joint on the part of the obligors. Joint obligors had to be sued in the same action at common law. If the plaintiff brought an action against fewer than all of the joint obligors and proceeded to judgment, the judgment would normally preclude a later action against an unjoined obligor. It thus could be said that the scope of the claim in such a case encompassed the obligations owed by more than one person. Instances of obligations that are truly joint in this sense are much rarer today than was true at common law.[13] Still there remains a narrow realm for claim preclusion in favor of the nonparty, especially in cases of indemnity. However, these situations are

---

12. See infra Chapter 8-A.

13. Compare Restatement (Second) of Judgments § 49 cmt. b (1982), with Restatement of Judgments § 101 (1942).

best analyzed as nonmutual claim preclusion,[14] rather than as involving a big claim including grievances by or against multiple parties.

In sum, even under the transactional view, the typical claim involves only a single plaintiff and a single defendant. So, multiple parties on either side typically mean multiple claims.

Legal and Equitable Grievances Resting on Same Basic Facts. Before the merger of law and equity, the judgment in an action at law was said to preclude a later suit in equity on the same cause of action. However, the equitable suit was often found to involve a different cause of action, in spite of general factual similarities. Or for some other reason, no claim preclusion resulted. One such reason rested on a general exception to claim preclusion: when part of the relief the plaintiff might seek is beyond the jurisdiction of the court in which the action is brought, a judgment in that action does not preclude a later one seeking the relief that could not have been obtained.[15]

When the first suit was in equity, however, that general exception was normally not available, because the equitable clean-up principle generally permitted the award of legal-type relief in conjunction with the equitable suit. In some courts, this meant that legal relief obtainable through the clean-up principle was precluded by the equitable suit.[16] In other courts, however, res judicata persisted in treating the two forms of relief as different causes of action and so allowed a later law action, unless the legal relief had in fact been requested in the earlier suit.[17]

With the merger of law and equity and the growing acceptance of the pragmatic fact-grouping view of the scope of a claim, the confusion of two different claims sometimes arising from the same basic facts no longer seemed justified. Consequently, most jurisdictions today view actions for legal and equitable relief on the same basic facts as parts of the same claim for res judicata purposes.[18]

---

14. See infra Chapter 8-B-2-c.

15. See infra Chapter 6-B-2.

16. E.g., Gilbert v. Boak Fish Co., 90 N.W. 767 (Minn. 1902); Pruitt v. Hammers, 292 P.2d 157 (Okla. 1955).

17. E.g., Chanute Brick & Tile Co. v. Gas Belt Fuel Co., 130 P. 649 (Kan. 1913); Citizens Tel. Co. v. Anderson, 291 S.W.2d 527 (Ky. 1956).

18. E.g., Hennepin Paper Co. v. Fort Wayne Corrugated Paper Co., 153 F.2d 822 (7th Cir. 1946); see Restatement (Second) of Judgments § 25 cmt. i (1982).

Contract Claims. The commonest types of problem cases are those involving a single contract but (1) multiple breaches or (2) multiple remedies.

Multiple Breaches. A given contract may encompass several undertakings, and failure on any of them may constitute a breach. If after a breach, either party to the contract repudiates it, the contract is at an end. The plaintiff then must seek all remedies with respect to the contract in one lawsuit.[19]

In the absence of repudiation, each breach of the contract is generally regarded as a separate claim, and a separate action can be brought for each breach as it occurs. Each breach does not remain a separate claim, however, if the injured party does not soon sue on it individually. The scope of the claim for breach of an entire, as opposed to a divisible, contract normally includes all grievances for breaches that occurred before the initiation of the action and that have not been the subject of a prior judgment.[20]

On the one hand, in an unrepudiated contract calling for periodic payments of money, like a lease, the claim includes all installments that are due and unpaid at the time of commencing the action, except those that have been sued to judgment in a prior action. Judgment on a claim for fewer than all the due and unpaid installments will preclude a later claim for the others.[21]

On the other hand, if the installment obligations were embodied in negotiable instruments, like notes, the contract is said to be divisible. Nonpayment of each instrument constitutes a separate claim, and a judgment on one will not preclude a claim on others, even though they were due and unpaid at the time of commencing the action.[22] Parties' expectations and business understandings thus enter into the definition of a claim, given the functional flexibility of the transactional view.

Multiple Remedies. A remedy of damages and a remedy of specific performance arising from the same breach are usually regarded as within the scope of the same claim for res judicata purposes in modern courts where law and equity have been combined. Likewise, although the traditional

19. See Restatement (Second) of Judgments § 26 cmt. g (1982).

20. See Restatement (Second) of Judgments § 24 cmt. d (1982)

21. See Fox v. Connecticut Fire Ins. Co., 380 F.2d 360 (10th Cir. 1967); Le John Mfg. Co. v. Webb, 91 A.2d 332 (D.C. 1952); Jones v. Morris Plan Bank, 191 S.E. 608 (Va. 1937).

22. See Cromwell v. County of Sac, 94 U.S. 351 (1877).

practice permitted a second suit for reformation of a written agreement on ground of fraud or mistake after an unsuccessful action for breach of contract, in modern courts where law and equity have been merged, a suit for reformation is usually regarded as part of the same claim as an action for breach.[23]

What is the scope of the claim when as part of a single business transaction, both a personal obligation was incurred and a security interest in property was created? Such arrangements of debt and lien are common, of course, in sales of both real and personal property.

The traditional approach has been to treat the debt and the lien as separate claims for res judicata purposes. Debts are interests in personam; liens are in rem. Judgments of different courts might be necessary to effectuate both claims because of jurisdictional limitations. However, even if jurisdiction to adjudicate both debt and lien were present in a single court, the traditional view has been that separate actions are permitted. A judgment in an action based on the personal obligation would not preclude a later suit to foreclose upon the encumbered property. If the plaintiff won on the debt and the judgment was satisfied, the lien would be discharged, of course, but the mere rendition of the judgment would not preclude a later suit to realize upon the security. Collateral estoppel might preclude some issues in the later suit, but the claim itself would not be merged or barred. Likewise, a judgment as to foreclosure did not preclude a later action on the personal obligation, unless the property obtained through the foreclosure was sufficient to satisfy the debt.

The ascendant pragmatic fact-grouping conception of the scope of a claim might suggest that only one claim should exist for personal and nonpersonal remedies. It is accordingly sometimes argued that if the plaintiff can acquire both personal jurisdiction over the debtor and nonpersonal jurisdiction over the res subject to the security interest, the plaintiff should not be permitted to bring two different actions for the debt and the lien.[24] But the cases generally have not accepted this argument. The traditional view of separate claims for debt and lien continues to be generally followed today, with occasional exceptions.[25]

---

23. See Massari v. Einsiedler, 78 A.2d 572 (N.J. 1951); Restatement (Second) of Judgments § 25 cmts. f, i (1982).

24. See Restatement (Second) of Judgments § 30 cmt. b (1982) (setting out the argument).

25. E.g., In re Wilson, 390 F. Supp. 1121 (D. Kan. 1975) (holding that a judgment on a note merged the security claim, so that the claimant was denied secured-creditor

Tort Claims. The commonest types of problem cases are those (1) where a single wrongful act injures more than one identifiable right of the plaintiff; (2) where the defendant may have been guilty of more than one identifiable tortious act causing the plaintiff's injury; or (3) where the tortious act or its effects extend over a relatively long span of time.

Single Wrongful Act Injuring More Than One Right. Typical of the first class of cases is the aforementioned situation where the plaintiff has suffered injury to both person and property as a result of the defendant's single act of negligence. Cases following different theories as to the scope of a claim have reached different conclusions on the question of whether in such a situation the plaintiff has one claim or two. The ever-growing majority of cases effectively follow the transactional view, treating the situation as one claim.[26]

Single Injury Caused by More Than One Wrongful Act. Where two or more tortious acts of the defendant concur to produce injury to the plaintiff, the same kinds of differences can be seen in the cases. Some courts, emphasizing the analytical definitions, treat distinguishable torts as separate claims in spite of common factual elements. Other courts, focusing upon pragmatic considerations such as the degree of factual overlap in the proof of the different torts, treat the whole matter as one claim.

On the one hand, the older authorities state that "distinct trespasses or other torts, although they be more or less connected, will give rise to distinct causes of action."[27] They therefore support the proposition that a judgment in an action for the trespassing by the defendant's cattle on the plaintiff's land does not preclude a later action for similar trespasses occurring before those on which the prior action was based.[28] An early Kansas case held that where a mare and her colt both got onto a railroad right-of-way, and a train struck and killed them about 165 yards apart, two separate

---

status in the debtor's bankruptcy proceedings). But see Bank of Okla. v. Fidelity State Bank & Trust Co., Dodge City, Kan., 623 F. Supp. 479 (D. Kan. 1985) (rejecting *Wilson* as "dead wrong").

26. See Dearden v. Hey, 24 N.E.2d 644 (Mass. 1939) (one cause of action); Rush v. City of Maple Heights, 147 N.E.2d 599 (Ohio 1958) (same); Restatement (Second) of Judgments § 24 cmt. c (1982). But see Clancey v. McBride, 169 N.E. 729 (Ill. 1929) (two causes of action). See generally Andrea G. Nadel, Annotation, Simultaneous Injury to Person and Property As Giving Rise to Single Cause of Action—Modern Cases, 24 A.L.R.4th 646 (1983).

27. 2 Henry Campbell Black, A Treatise on the Law of Judgments 1116 (2d ed. 1902).

28. See De La Guerra v. Newhall, 55 Cal. 21 (1880).

causes of action existed, and judgment for the plaintiff for the value of the colt did not bar a later action for the value of the mare.[29]

On the other hand, the Second Restatement follows the transactional view. It declares that when one person has trespassed daily on the land of another for a week, it is the series of trespasses that constitutes the claim—although the owner could have sued separately for each trespass as it occurred, as in the case of installment payment obligations.[30] Likewise, a single action only can be brought if the defendant breaks into the plaintiff's house, assaults the plaintiff, and steals the plaintiff's goods.[31]

As noted above, even under the older views, courts generally do not treat separate negligent acts or omissions that contribute to one accident or injury as separate claims. Thus, when a defendant was negligent both in driving a vehicle with defective brakes and in failing to keep a proper lookout, and both were causally connected to the accident in which the plaintiff was injured, the plaintiff would have only one claim for res judicata purposes.[32]

Tort Extending for a Period of Time. A plaintiff may suffer injury from the defendant's act for a long period of time. What influence does this factor have on the scope of the claim?

If the tort is a simple impact tort—an act that occurs once and then is over, but has enduring effects—only one claim exists. The plaintiff may suffer a disability that prevents working for 1000 days as a result of a single negligent act by the defendant. But the plaintiff has only one claim for that injury, and so only one day in court to recover all the damages suffered to that date and all to be suffered in the future caused by that one negligent act. This principle of "one sum recovery" acts to prevent a later action, even for consequences of the original tort that do not manifest themselves until after judgment.[33]

If the tort involves the creation or maintenance of a more or less permanent condition that constitutes an actionable violation of the plaintiff's rights every moment that it exists, the res judicata situation is more com-

29. Missouri Pac. Ry. v. Scammon, 21 P. 590 (Kan. 1889).

30. See Restatement (Second) of Judgments § 24 cmt. d (1982).

31. See Restatement (Second) of Judgments § 24 cmt. d, illus. 6 (1982); Restatement of Judgments § 62 cmt. f (1942).

32. See Ernst Schopflocher, What Is a Single Cause of Action for the Purpose of the Doctrine of Res Judicata?, 21 Or. L. Rev. 319, 329-33 (1942).

33. See Restatement (Second) of Judgments § 25 cmt. c (1982). But see Note, Claim Preclusion in Modern Latent Disease Cases: A Proposal for Allowing Second Suits, 103 Harv. L. Rev. 1989 (1990).

plicated. This situation of an ongoing tortious act is typified by cases of nuisance, as well as by cases of trespass in the form of an encroaching construction. These are cases in which the plaintiff may have both a right to compensation for injuries suffered up to the time of the action (enforceable by an award of damages, which might even cover future damages) and a right to be free of the condition in the future (enforceable by an injunction to abate the nuisance or end the trespass or by an ejectment to compel the removal of the trespassing condition). Conflicting results in such cases have been reached on the scope of the claim for res judicata purposes.

It is generally recognized that the claim in an action for damages caused by the continuing nuisance or trespass includes at least all of the damages sustained up to the time the plaintiff sues.[34] Beyond this, generalization is more difficult, and requires consideration not only of the definitional approach to the scope of a claim followed in the jurisdiction in question, but also such matters as, first, the details of the "permanent injury" doctrine in cases of continuing nuisance or trespass; second, the extent to which the common-law action of ejectment has been modified by statute, rule, or decision; and, third, the degree to which law and equity have been merged in that jurisdiction.

First, many jurisdictions follow the view that if the nuisance or trespassing structure is of such a durable nature that it will continue unabated indefinitely in spite of a judgment finding its existence to be a tortious interference with the plaintiff's rights, then the plaintiff has a present right of action for damages for the permanent injury, measured by the diminution in the total value of the plaintiff's land attributable to the nuisance or trespass. That is, if the condition is deemed permanent,[35] the plaintiff has but one claim for damages. A judgment rendered for or against the plaintiff in an action for damages caused by such a condition precludes a later action for damages based on the same condition, even if the plaintiff fails to request any damages other than those suffered before the action was brought.

If the nuisance or trespass is deemed temporary, the usual view is that the plaintiff must bring successive damage actions so long as the condition remains. The claim in each such action would include all damages sustained since the last suit that went to judgment, up to the time of the new action's

---

34. See Henegar v. International Minerals & Chem. Corp., 354 S.W.2d 69 (Tenn. 1962); Restatement (Second) of Judgments § 26 cmt. h (1982).

35. See 1 Dan B. Dobbs, Dobbs Law of Remedies 822-25 (2d ed. 1993) (giving criteria for permanence in this context).

filing—or, rather, the subset of those damages within the statute of limitations.

Some courts, however, have established as a matter of substantive law that the plaintiff has an election to treat the nuisance or trespass either as permanent or as temporary. The law of res judicata would then adjust accordingly, to respect the plaintiff's election.[36]

Second, at common law, the action of ejectment lay for the recovery of possession of land. Damages resulting from the dispossession of the plaintiff—such as the value of the defendant's use of the land—could not be sought in ejectment, but rather had to be sought in a separate action of "trespass for mesne profits" after possession had been recovered. In modern practice, however, possession of the land and damages for mesne profits are generally recoverable in the same action if jurisdiction over the person of the defendant as well as over the property itself is acquired.[37] When recovery in the same action is possible, the logic of the rule applicable to damage actions for nuisance or trespass—that the plaintiff must recover in one action all damages accrued to the time of commencement of suit—yields the view that the remedy for possession of the land and the remedy for damages for the dispossession should be sought in one action, and thus constitute a single claim for res judicata purposes.[38] Nevertheless, a few courts following one of the older approaches to the definition of the scope of a claim have indicated that the actions for possession and damages remain distinct claims, and thus that separate suits are permissible.[39]

Third, before the merger of law and equity, a judgment in an action brought to recover damages for injuries already sustained did not preclude a later equitable suit to enjoin future injuries. The reason given for this result might be that a damages action and an injunction suit were separate causes of action for res judicata purposes or that part of the relief was beyond the jurisdiction of the court. Thus, the plaintiff could sue at law for damages accrued as a result of the nuisance or trespass, and then sue again to enjoin the continuance of the condition in the future.

---

36. See Reynolds Metals Co. v. Wand, 308 F.2d 504 (9th Cir. 1962); Spaulding v. Cameron, 239 P.2d 625 (Cal. 1952); Restatement (Second) of Judgments § 26(1)(e) cmt. h (1982).

37. See Fed. R. Civ. P. 18(b).

38. See Restatement (Second) of Judgments § 25 cmt. j (1982).

39. E.g., Clay v. Field, 115 U.S. 260 (1885).

If the plaintiff brought a *first suit in equity solely for an injunction*, however, some courts held that a judgment did preclude a later action for damages, because a plaintiff could obtain both injunction and damages in the same equity suit by virtue of the equitable clean-up principle. Some other courts, however, persisted in the view that suits for injunctions and damages were different causes of action. Today the better view, in the light of modern procedural philosophy, would be that the request for damages is precluded by the decree granting or denying an injunction, as part of the same claim, wherever both forms of relief are available in the same suit. As that availability exists almost everywhere today in this post-merger country, preclusion ordinarily follows a suit for injunction.[40]

Nevertheless, it is not clear that the converse is true, i.e., that a judgment rendered in a *first action at law solely for accrued damages* should preclude a later suit for injunction against future continuance of the nuisance or trespass. As already observed, the older cases generally did not find the injunction suit precluded in this situation, and there is probably good reason for not doing so even today. First, injunctions are still viewed as remedies of a sterner nature than damages. Not only do they subject the defendant to contempt sanctions that may operate more harshly than a damages judgment, but also they may require continuing attention by the court to administer relief and possibly require later litigation over the question of compliance. If a damages judgment will adequately protect the plaintiff's interests, the court will therefore not issue an injunction. Second, it is at least arguable that the objective of economy of judicial effort, which underlies the whole subject of res judicata, is furthered by encouraging a plaintiff to seek only damages for the continuing nuisance or trespass. Unnecessary judicial effort would have to be expended if the plaintiff has to join the injunction request with the damages request, as some separate issues would have to be litigated in the first action that otherwise might not have to be litigated at all. A plaintiff may believe at the start of litigation that a damages judgment will both compensate for past injuries and cause the defendant to cease the nuisance or trespass out of self-interest to avoid future liability. In fact, a judgment for the plaintiff in such a case may well induce the defendant to cease. Even if it does not, the major issue of nuisance or trespass vel non will have been litigated and should be conclusive by issue preclusion in the event of a later suit for an injunction. And, of course, a

40. See Restatement (Second) of Judgments § 25 cmt. i(2), illus. 19 (1982).

judgment for the defendant in the damages action may well end the dispute.

Therefore, in these continuing nuisance and trespass cases, when the question of whether a remedy remains available is posed as a question of the scope of the claim, then the scope would appear to depend upon whether the first suit sought an injunction or damages only. A suit for an injunction will preclude a claim that encompasses damages. But an action seeking accrued damages for temporary nuisance or trespass should not preclude a later claim for an injunction, just as it does not preclude a claim for later-accrued damages. This malleability of the claim concept is a further showing of the functional flexibility of the transactional view.

The distinction suggested is based upon the difference between the kind of relief sought in the first suit—whether the relief is forward or backward looking—and not on the technical question of whether the first suit is characterized as equitable or legal. Legal actions that seek forward-looking relief will preclude a later injunction suit. For example, in a continuing trespass case, the plaintiff may have a legal remedy to bring about specific relief, namely, ejectment; if the plaintiff in the first action seeks an order directing the specific discontinuance of the trespassing condition, the claim for res judicata purposes should include both ejectment and also injunction as an alternative remedy, as well as damages; if the plaintiff seeks only ejectment or only injunction in the first action, the resulting judgment should preclude a later suit for the omitted relief.[41] Likewise, if the plaintiff seeks future damages in a permanent trespass case, the resulting judgment should preclude a later suit for specific relief.[42]

Federal and State Grievances Resting on Same Basic Facts. The same basic group of facts may give rise to a right of action under both state and federal law. For instance, the same conduct may contravene both state and federal antitrust laws, giving rise to rights under each. Or the same conduct may be involved in an ordinary state-law tort claim and a claim under the Federal Civil Rights Act in 42 U.S.C. § 1983. This sort of overlap is the source of some interesting res judicata questions. Is there only one claim for res judicata purposes in such cases, or are there two? The primary right approach to the definition of claim would indicate two, but the transactional view only one. Cases can be found exhibiting each approach.

---

41. See Hahl v. Sugo, 62 N.E. 135 (N.Y. 1901).

42. See generally 18 Charles Alan Wright, Arthur R. Miller & Edward H. Cooper, Federal Practice and Procedure § 4409, at 77-80 (1981 & Supp. 1999).

Because the cases we are referring to are cases in which the state and the federal grievances rest on basically the same facts, one day in court could suffice for the adjudication of both. When both the state and the federal grievances could be adjudicated in either state or federal court, one judgment, whether state or federal, could thus be conclusive of the rights deriving from both sources. Consider the three possible situations. First, if the federal grievance could not be heard in the federal court (e.g., because of an insufficient amount in controversy or the like), the state judgment could encompass both the state and the federal grievances. Second, if the federal grievance could be heard in the federal court, the state grievance could ordinarily be entertained there too, either by virtue of diversity jurisdiction under 28 U.S.C. § 1332 or by virtue of supplemental jurisdiction under 28 U.S.C. § 1367. Both grievances could also be adjudicated in the state court, unless the federal grievance is one of those that by statute lies exclusively in the jurisdiction of federal courts. Third, if the federal grievance is one over which federal courts have exclusive jurisdiction (e.g., where the federal grievance arises under the antitrust laws), a state court would not be competent to adjudicate the federal grievance directly.

If both state and federal grievances are within the rendering court's jurisdiction, the modern transactional view of the scope of a claim would indicate that the judgment, whether of the state or the federal court, should preclude a later action in the other forum, even if the full claim was not in fact asserted in the prior action. The law should not countenance such splitting of the claim.[43]

If the plaintiff sues in federal court, when independent subject-matter jurisdiction for the state grievance is lacking, still under the transactional view the federal judgment should normally preclude a later state action, because the federal court ordinarily could have exercised supplemental jurisdiction. But an exception should apply if the federal court declined, or would clearly not have exercised, supplemental jurisdiction.[44]

If the plaintiff sues in state court on the state grievance, when the federal grievance is within the federal courts' exclusive jurisdiction, can the plaintiff sue later in federal court on the federal grievance? If so, the policies of res judicata are subverted to some extent. The plaintiff had a forum choice, having been able to pursue both state and federal grievances in the

43. See Restatement (Second) of Judgments § 25 cmt. e, illus. 11 (1982).

44. See Belliston v. Texaco, Inc., 521 P.2d 379 (Utah 1974); Restatement (Second) of Judgments § 25 cmt. e, illus. 10 (1982).

federal court, and so arguably the plaintiff waived the federal grievance by choosing to litigate in the state court. However, the legal system is reluctant to force a plaintiff to surrender the right of access to the state court. Moreover, even if a later federal action is permitted, issue preclusion would ordinarily apply to retrieve lost efficiency. Finally, giving the state judgment a claim-preclusive effect would greatly undermine the purpose of exclusivity of federal jurisdiction embodied in the act of Congress. In sum, this is a close question, but most courts have allowed the plaintiff to sue later in federal court on the exclusively federal grievance. They have reached that result either by finding that the federal and state grievances are separate claims for res judicata purposes or, better, by invoking the exception to claim preclusion applicable when the relief sought in the second action was beyond the jurisdiction of the first court.[45]

Choice of Law. Now, what we are describing throughout these early chapters is the res judicata law of a typical American jurisdiction, which would govern in subsequent litigation in the same court system as the initial action. But here we have wandered into hypotheticals involving successive actions in two different court systems. Later, in Chapter 10-B below, we shall cover the nature of the res judicata law that applies to such nondomestic judgments. The gist of that coverage is that the law of the sovereign rendering the initial judgment generally governs in the subsequent action elsewhere. Thus, even in our last hypothetical concerning a state judgment's effect on exclusively federal relief, the state's res judicata law generally governs. So, what we are saying in this chapter is that typical state law would in effect allow the plaintiff to sue later in federal court on the exclusively federal grievance, because the state's res judicata law would not apply claim preclusion when the relief sought in the second action was beyond the jurisdiction of the first court.

Illustration. To review this whole problem area, grievances under state and federal securities legislation are illustrative. The plaintiff cannot bring the federal grievance in state court because federal jurisdiction of such claims is exclusive. Moreover, unless there is diversity of citizenship, the plaintiff may possibly be unable to bring the state grievance in federal court. Of course, under supplemental jurisdiction, the federal court could entertain a state grievance arising from the same transaction.

---

45. See Cream Top Creamery v. Dean Milk Co., 383 F.2d 358 (6th Cir. 1967); Restatement (Second) of Judgments § 26(1)(c) cmt. c(1), illus. 2 (1982); Note, The Effect of Prior Nonfederal Proceedings on Exclusive Federal Jurisdiction over Section 10(b) of the Securities Exchange Act of 1934, 46 N.Y.U. L. Rev. 936, 943-47 (1971) (citing cases).

In view of that, if the first securities action is in the federal court, a judgment would normally preclude the state grievance as well, whether or not the plaintiff chose to present it in the federal action. Still, the exercise of supplemental jurisdiction is discretionary with the trial judge. If the plaintiff did present the state grievance, but the federal court refused to entertain it, the judgment would not preclude a later state action. The reason is that if a plaintiff cannot present both grievances to the court, the judgment of the court should not preclude the part of the claim arising under the other law.

Likewise, if the first securities action is in the state court, the judgment would not preclude a later action on the federal grievance. The state court could not hear the federal grievance, and unless the plaintiff could be said to have waived the right to the federal grievance, there is no rule requiring the plaintiff to proceed on the federal grievance before suing on the state grievance.

If the defendant removed the state securities action to the federal court on the basis of diversity of citizenship, however, the plaintiff could there amend the complaint to add the federal securities grievance. If the plaintiff does not amend, the res judicata question is close. Because the court could have adjudicated the federal grievance in the removed action, the resulting judgment should probably preclude it, whether or not the plaintiff asserted that federal grievance.[46]

Summary. When all is said and done, a simple scheme emerges under the transactional view:

Federal and state grievances resting on the same basic facts constitute a single claim. But if the plaintiff jurisdictionally cannot assert both, an exception applies to allow a later action in the other forum.

Abstention. Still, federal and state relations are undeniably complex, so that some special problems will arise. Consider the example generated by the abstention doctrine. If the plaintiff with federal and state grievances resting on the same basic facts chooses federal court, the court may abstain from deciding a federal constitutional grievance before a determination by the state court on uncertain questions of state law.[47] The plaintiff then must initiate some sort of proceeding in the state court after all. Whatever the nature of the proceeding under state procedure, the plaintiff must present the state grievance in light of the federal grievance, although he may reserve

46. See Engelhardt v. Bell & Howell Co., 327 F.2d 30, 35 & n.2 (8th Cir. 1964).

47. See Railroad Comm'n v. Pullman Co., 312 U.S. 496 (1941).

the federal grievance for later determination in federal court. Not surprisingly, res judicata law allows the plaintiff after state judgment to return to federal court to pursue the reserved federal grievance.[48] This is in the nature of the general exception to claim preclusion that recognizes the court can authorize the plaintiff to split a claim.[49] The plaintiff may, however, in the interest of economy or for some other reason, decide to present both the state and federal grievances unreservedly to the state court for adjudication. In that case, the resulting judgment will have normal claim preclusion effect on the whole claim.

If the plaintiff's lawyer desires a federal forum for the federal grievance but is relatively sure that the federal court would abstain if the action were commenced there first, she may decide to proceed in the state court first, presenting the state grievance while reserving the federal grievance for assertion later in a federal action. This otherwise reasonable strategy is very risky from a res judicata viewpoint, however. The lawyer will likely find that the state judgment precludes the federal grievance even though she expressly refused to assert it in the state court. The two grievances, in other words, will be regarded as constituting a single claim for res judicata purposes, and there was no judicial permission to split the claim.[50]

2. Extinguishing Claim by Judgment

Outside the context of the initial action, a party generally may not relitigate a claim decided therein by a valid and final judgment. The judgment extinguishes the whole claim, precluding all matters within the claim that were or could have been litigated in that initial action. This doctrine of claim preclusion subdivides into merger and bar.

The doctrine of claim preclusion applies as well to judgments by default or dismissal as to judgments rendered after a full trial. Also, the cases usually hold the doctrine applicable to judgments based on an agreement or settlement by the parties, such as consent judgments, in the absence of some stipulation indicating that the parties contemplated a possible later suit on part of the claim. A few courts, however, take the position that because by a general exception to claim preclusion the parties can agree to splitting a

---

48. See England v. Louisiana State Bd. of Med. Exam'rs, 375 U.S. 411 (1964); Restatement (Second) of Judgments § 86 cmt. f (1982).

49. See infra Chapter 6-B-3.

50. See generally 18 Charles Alan Wright, Arthur R. Miller & Edward H. Cooper, Federal Practice and Procedure § 4471.1 (Supp. 1999).

claim,[51] such agreement will be presumed in the absence of a contrary stipulation, at least when the consent judgment does not cover all of the claim.[52]

a. Merger

If the judgment in the initial action was in the plaintiff's favor, the plaintiff's claim is said to merge in the judgment. The plaintiff cannot bring a second action on the claim in the hope of winning a more favorable judgment. However, the plaintiff can seek to enforce the judgment, and the defendant cannot then raise defenses that were or could have been interposed in that initial action.

A judgment in favor of the claimant precludes a later suit on the underlying claim.[53] The original claim merges in the judgment so that no other suit on that claim is permitted. This is true even if the claimant did not seek all the relief available in the first suit. One judgment on a claim is all to which a claimant is entitled. The claimant cannot split the claim into two or more suits.

Although a second suit on the original claim is not permitted, the successful claimant can bring a new action upon the judgment. At common law, a judgment for money was viewed as a cause of action in itself. It was a debt, being an obligation to pay a certain sum of money, which would support an action in the form of "debt on a record." The idea that a judgment is itself a claim, distinct from the original one on which it was based, has persisted to this day. The subdoctrine of merger is indeed sometimes explained in terms of a lower right (the original claim) being displaced by a higher one (the claim upon the judgment).

When an action is brought upon a judgment, the object is merely to obtain another judgment, which still must be enforced through execution or other process if the defendant does not comply. What, then, is the point of suing upon a judgment? Why not simply seek enforcement of the first judgment? The answer is that the first judgment may not be enforceable by normal procedures at the time and place when and where some property of the defendant can be found, seized, and sold to satisfy the judgment or the person of the defendant is found. First, the original judgment may have become "dormant" by the passage of time and need reviving, and an action

---

51. See infra Chapter 6-B-4.

52. See E.H. Schopler, Annotation, Res Judicata As Affected by Fact That Former Judgment Was Entered by Agreement or Consent, 2 A.L.R.2d 514, 562 (1948).

53. See generally Restatement (Second) of Judgments § 18 (1982).

upon the judgment may be one way of accomplishing that. Or the statute of limitations on enforcing the original judgment might be about to expire. Second, the original judgment may have been obtained in a state other than the one in which enforcement is now sought. A local sheriff normally will not enforce a judgment issued by another state, and a local judge may not be empowered to enforce a judgment that is not a matter of record in that state. The traditional process by which judgments of one state become enforceable in another is through this device of bringing an action in the enforcement state upon the obligation represented by the other state's judgment, producing a regularly enforceable local judgment.

If an action is brought upon the judgment, none of the issues going to the merits of the original claim that were or might have been presented for decision in the original action can be reexamined. This includes matters of the defendant's defense to the original claim as well as elements of the plaintiff's claim itself.

As noted above, a judgment is considered itself a claim that will support a lawsuit for a new judgment. Logic might lead one to conclude that when a new judgment is obtained in an action upon a previous judgment, the claim upon the previous judgment disappears—merged in the new judgment—so that any further action upon the previous judgment would be precluded. But logic would mislead one as to the prevailing law here. To illustrate, assume that *A* obtains a judgment for money against *B* in State X. Being unable to obtain satisfaction of the judgment in State X, *A* sues upon the judgment in State Y and gets a State Y judgment that can then be executed in State Y. If complete satisfaction cannot be obtained in State Y, *A* may want again to seek a writ of execution in State X. Can *A* obtain it, or has the State X judgment merged in the State Y judgment so that an action upon the State Y judgment is now necessary in State X? Most courts have held that the earlier judgment retains its vitality. Insofar as enforcement of the earlier judgment in State X is concerned, the State X judgment did not merge in the State Y judgment, and so it is not necessary to sue in State X to turn the State Y judgment back into a State X judgment. Similarly, if *A* now seeks enforcement in State Z, *A* may sue upon the judgment of either State X or State Y. *A* can seek to enforce any or all of these judgments, but of course is limited to one satisfaction.[54]

54. See Moore v. Justices of the Mun. Court, 197 N.E. 487 (Mass. 1935); Restatement (Second) of Judgments § 18 cmt. j (1982).

b. Bar

If the judgment in the initial action was in the defendant's favor, the plaintiff's claim is said to be barred by the judgment. The plaintiff cannot bring a second action on the claim in the hope of winning this time.

A judgment against a claimant precludes a later suit on the same claim.[55] In this case, the claim does not merge in the judgment. Rather, the judgment bars the claim and any further suit on it, both as to elements that were asserted in the first suit and those that might have been. Thus, the rule of bar, like that of merger, serves to deter the splitting of a single claim into more than one lawsuit.

Indeed, most of the principles of merger are applicable to a judgment against the claimant. There are, however, some distinctive features of the bar aspect of claim preclusion. The most notable of these is the concern that the judgment against the claimant be "on the merits," which is discussed next.

B. Exceptions to Rule

Predictably, the broad transactional conception of claim preclusion has generated several significant, generally recognized exceptions. In some situations, a valid and final judgment will not preclude a later action on the original claim, so that the plaintiff may bring a second action on part, or all, of the same claim.

1. Adjudication Not on the Merits

Formerly, claim preclusion operated only if the judgment was rendered "on the merits." Today that requirement has broken down to give preclusion wider application, but still certain threshold dismissals that are not based on evaluation of the substance of the action are treated as exceptions to claim preclusion.

Every judgment for the plaintiff is a judgment on the merits. Such a judgment officially determines the substantive validity of the claim, even if it is entered by default or otherwise without trial. It has a merger effect. A judgment against the plaintiff, however, may be given for various reasons

55. See generally Restatement (Second) of Judgments § 19 (1982).

that may have nothing to do with the substantive validity of the claim. A claim may be dismissed for certain procedural defects in the form or manner of its presentation. A claimant should not be penalized to the extent of losing the right to a fair day in court on the substantive merits of the claim just because of a technical error. Accordingly, there are some judgments against the claimant, although they are valid and final judgments, that do not have bar effect.[56] A good example of this type is a dismissal for improper venue, which has no bar effect.

One term that is commonly used in distinguishing judgments that do have bar effect from those that do not have bar effect is "prejudice."[57] If the judgment was with prejudice, it bars a later action; if without prejudice, it does not. But this term by itself does not help identify which judgments have bar effect.

"On the merits" at least suggests some in the class of judgments that have bar effect. The First Restatement so used that term.[58] The use of the phrase on the merits to describe those judgments has been criticized as misleading, however, because it does not accurately describe the class. A judgment entered after a determination of the substance of the claim usually does have bar effect, but not all judgments that have bar effect are based on such substantive determinations. In reality, then, bar applies to judgments that may logically be described as on the merits and, increasingly in recent times, also to other judgments that cannot be so described without indulging in fiction. A good example of the latter type is a dismissal for failure to prosecute, which has bar effect.

The Second Restatement in its rule of bar abandons the traditional phrase of on the merits;[59] it deals with the problem of separating the kinds of judgments that do and do not have bar effect by first declaring bar to be applicable to all valid and final judgments but then excepting a list of judgments that covers most of the kinds of cases traditionally characterized as not on the merits, while still avoiding the phrase of on the merits.[60] Its approach should help to eliminate some of the confusion that stemmed from the necessity under the traditional approach of classifying some rulings as

---

56. See generally Restatement (Second) of Judgments § 20 (1982).
57. See, e.g., Fed. R. Civ. P. 41(a).
58. See Restatement of Judgments § 48 (1942).
59. See Restatement (Second) of Judgments § 19 (1982).
60. See Restatement (Second) of Judgments § 20 (1982).

on the merits for bar purposes even though they actually never reached the substantive issues of the case.[61]

Still, many cases continue to use the traditional terminology. Many statutes and rules likewise employ the terms of "with prejudice" and "on the merits" to describe rulings that have bar effect. So, the reader should not forget the old ways, as we sketch the details of the Second Restatement's exception to the general rule of bar.

a. Dismissal for Lack of Jurisdiction

Certain threshold defenses are so obviously off the merits, in any sense, that no court would view them as generating a bar. Thus, dismissals for lack of subject-matter jurisdiction or territorial jurisdiction, improper venue, inadequate notice, or nonjoinder or misjoinder of parties do not have bar effect.[62]

b. Dismissal for Insufficiency of Complaint

Older Approach. Is a judgment sustaining a demurrer based on insufficiency of the complaint, or sustaining the more modern motion to dismiss for failure to state a claim upon which relief can be granted, a judgment on the merits? Historically, some judgments sustaining demurrers to the plaintiff's pleading did have bar effect and some did not. The cases sought to explain this discrepancy by declaring that some demurrers went to the merits of the cause of action and some did not. The First Restatement endorsed this usage but failed to clarify it.[63]

In general, under the old case law, if the demurrer was based on any threshold defect other than failure to state a cause of action, the judgment on the demurrer did not act as a bar, because it was not a judgment on the merits. Such matters as jurisdiction over the person or subject matter, nonjoinder and misjoinder of parties, and other dilatory matters could be raised by demurrer, and judgments based on the sustaining of demurrers on those grounds did not bar a subsequent suit on the same cause of action.

A demurrer truly for failure to state a cause of action might or might not go to the merits. On the one hand, if the defect challenged by the demurrer merely related to the form of pleading, the merits were not implicated, and no bar resulted. On the other hand, if the facts alleged in the

---

61. See Restatement (Second) of Judgments § 19 cmt. a (1982).

62. See Fed. R. Civ. P. 41(b); Restatement (Second) of Judgments § 20(1)(a) (1982).

63. See Restatement of Judgments § 50 (1942).

complaint revealed the existence of a valid defense, such as the statute of frauds, the complaint was demurrable, and a judgment on such a demurrer would bar a later action. Also, if the facts alleged showed that the plaintiff was seeking a remedy for a wrong that the law simply did not recognize—a so-called entire failure to state a cause of action—a judgment on a demurrer to the complaint would be a bar; therefore, it would block a new action on the same claim (say, for mental distress) even if the substantive law had since altered to provide a remedy for the wrong in question.

One common situation was particularly troublesome. When the plaintiff's complaint alleged facts suggesting the existence of a legally cognizable cause but omitted one or more essential allegations, was this a defect in the form of pleading, which did not go to the merits? Or was it more like the case in which the plaintiff pleaded a cause that the law did not recognize, a defect that did go to the merits? Of course, if the plaintiff realleged basically the same facts, then direct estoppel would defeat a new action. But what if the plaintiff added the missing allegations to the complaint? The general approach was that a dismissal for an inadequately stated cause rested on a formal defect not on the merits, and thus such a judgment did not bar a later action based on the same cause of action.[64] In other words, the first judgment determined merely that the facts there alleged were insufficient; it did not determine that those facts plus one or more others were insufficient; and the plaintiff should have a day in court to test the legal sufficiency of the latter group of facts. This approach served to protect a plaintiff from losing a cause of action through improper pleading or through the lawyer's ignorance or inattention. It also, however, provided a device that could be used vexatiously. Subsequent actions were not barred by a judgment on a demurrer based on the omission of essential allegations, so the plaintiff could bring repeated actions after such judgments, as long as each new complaint supplied additional facts.

Some courts approached the same troublesome situation by declaring that a judgment sustaining a demurrer for omission of an essential allegation was just as much a judgment on the merits as one on any demurrer for entire failure to state a cause of action. Under this approach, however, the barred cause of action still could be regarded as merely the one alleged in the first action. A pleading alleging those facts plus the missing one could be regarded as stating a different cause of action. The result, then, would

64. See Keidatz v. Albany, 249 P.2d 264 (Cal. 1952).

be the same as that reached under the general approach: the dismissal for omission of an essential allegation did not bar a later action in which the plaintiff pleaded the missing allegation.

Other difficulties lay in the background of these old views, which were based on antiquated conceptions of pleading and motion practice. If the first pleading actually alleged all the essential elements, but the trial judge erroneously ruled that an additional allegation was necessary, a curious situation resulted. The addition of an immaterial allegation in a second action would not supply anything truly missing from the first, and so the second complaint would not be materially different from the first. Should the plaintiff be permitted to plead what is essentially the same case again? Or should the plaintiff be barred and thus forced to appeal the erroneous ruling? It is arguable that the plaintiff should be able to start a new lawsuit without the necessity of appeal in such a case. However, some courts ruled otherwise.[65]

One means of limiting these potentialities for abuse and lurking difficulties of application was to permit the plaintiff to amend the pleading in the first action by adding the omitted allegation. If the plaintiff thus amended the complaint, judgment on the sustained demurrer would be avoided. If the plaintiff could not, or would not, or in any event did not amend the pleading under those circumstances, judgment would be entered on the demurrer. Some courts then held that this judgment barred any later action, even a later action in which the missing allegation was pleaded. Other courts, however, did not follow this approach, so that the plaintiff still could choose between amending the old complaint and starting a new action.[66]

Modern Approach. Even this amendment cure did not go far enough for modern tastes.[67] The transactional view of a claim rejects, of course, the approach of viewing the successive actions as being on different claims. Moreover, the policy-driven tendency toward expanding res judicata chafed at the old view of a dismissal on demurrer as not being on the merits. Accordingly, most jurisdictions today hold that a judgment for insufficiency of the complaint operates as a bar to the existing claim that the plaintiff ap-

---

65. E.g., Wade v. Peters, 173 P. 567 (Or. 1918).

66. Compare Elfman v. Glaser, 47 N.E.2d 925 (Mass. 1943) (second action barred if plaintiff refused to amend after leave to amend granted), with Rost v. Kroke, 262 N.W. 450 (Minn. 1935) (second action not barred).

67. See Osserman v. Jacobs, 339 N.E.2d 193 (Mass. 1975); Developments in the Law—Res Judicata, 65 Harv. L. Rev. 818, 836-37 (1952).

peared to be trying to state.[68] The rendering court could specify no bar when the particular circumstances warranted, by providing that its judgment was without prejudice to a new action. But in the absence of such a specification, any dismissal for failure to state a claim is a bar.

Admittedly, not all modern cases hold that way. Some still hold that a second action alleging new facts is not precluded.[69] It has been suggested that in view of the limited effort required of the defendant, it is unfair to require the plaintiff to be prepared to have the whole case determined finally on a motion to dismiss, especially on formal grounds. However, modern procedure can probably avoid any unfairness to the dismissed plaintiff, by affording leave to amend, a specification of no prejudice, or at least the opportunity for appeal. Thus, the unmistakable trend in the case law is toward bar effect.

Indeed, for a federal judgment based on a dismissal under Federal Rule of Civil Procedure 12(b)(6), some have argued that the question is no longer an open one. Federal Rule of Civil Procedure 41(b), while dealing specifically with involuntary dismissal of actions for failure to prosecute or obey rules, provides more generally as follows:

> Unless the court in its order for dismissal otherwise specifies, a dismissal under this subdivision and any dismissal not provided for in this rule, other than a dismissal for lack of jurisdiction, for improper venue, or for failure to join a party under Rule 19, operates as an adjudication upon the merits.

Dismissals under Federal Rule 12(b)(6) for failure to state a claim upon which relief can be granted would seem to be within the literal scope of the quoted passage. They are a "dismissal not provided for in" Federal Rule 41. The phrase "adjudication upon the merits" seems obviously to imply that such judgments should have bar effect, unless the rendering court specifically declares otherwise. The task of determining which dismissals for failure to state a claim have claim-preclusive effect is thus apparently committed to the judge in the first action, rather than being left up to the judge in the second action as under the normal operation of res judicata.

---

68. E.g., Rinehart v. Locke, 454 F.2d 313 (7th Cir. 1971); see Restatement (Second) of Judgments § 19 cmt. d (1982); 18 Charles Alan Wright, Arthur R. Miller & Edward H. Cooper, Federal Practice and Procedure § 4439 (1981 & Supp. 1999).

69. See 9 Charles Alan Wright & Arthur R. Miller, Federal Practice and Procedure § 2373, at 407-08 (2d ed. 1995) (citing cases).

However, the Supreme Court of the United States, in *Costello v. United States*,[70] did not interpret Federal Rule 41(b) that way. In that case, a judgment dismissing a denaturalization proceeding on the ground that the government had failed to file with the complaint an affidavit of good cause—an essential precondition of the statutory action—was held not to bar a later suit seeking denaturalization on the same facts, in spite of the absence of any specification in the earlier judgment that it was not on the merits. The Court ruled that a dismissal for failure to satisfy the affidavit precondition was a dismissal "for lack of jurisdiction," which the Court ruled does not have a technical or narrow meaning for Federal Rule 41(b) purposes. That reading devastates most of the definitiveness of Federal Rule 41(b). The Court effectively read the provision's exception to bar—"other than a dismissal for lack of jurisdiction, for improper venue, or for failure to join a party under Rule 19"—not to be an exhaustive listing. A dismissal on jurisdiction, venue, or joinder will not have bar effect, but other dismissals also may have no bar effect. By Federal Rule 41(b)'s express terms, a dismissal for "failure of the plaintiff to prosecute or to comply with these rules or any order of court" will have bar effect unless otherwise ordered, but other unmentioned dismissals also may have bar effect. It is thus up to case-by-case adjudication to decide which other dismissals will lack or will have bar effect. The case law has since established that truly threshold dismissals lack bar effect, while other dismissals such as those for insufficiency of the complaint have bar effect.[71] These cases have looked to the policies underlying res judicata, rather than mechanically applying Federal Rule 41(b).

In sum, looking to res judicata policies, most courts today hold that dismissals, by whatever procedural vehicle, for failure to state a claim constitute a bar to a new lawsuit.

c. *Dismissal for Prematurity in Bringing Action*

If an action is dismissed because a fact essential to recovery has not yet occurred, the judgment of dismissal does not bar a later action after the occurrence.[72] Thus, in an action for breach of contract, if it appears that the time for performance by the defendant has not arrived, or if some other condition precedent has not been satisfied, a judgment of dismissal on that

---

70. 365 U.S. 265 (1961).

71. See generally 18 Charles Alan Wright, Arthur R. Miller & Edward H. Cooper, Federal Practice and Procedure § 4435, at 332-38 (1981 & Supp. 1999).

72. See Waterhouse v. Levine, 65 N.E. 822 (Mass. 1903); Restatement (Second) of Judgments § 20(2) (1982).

ground will not bar a later action after the condition has been satisfied. This is the usual approach even when the prematurity is not disclosed until the case has been tried, or when an amended or supplemental pleading could have cured the prematurity.

This approach operates in federal courts, as well as in most states whether or not they have an equivalent of Federal Rule of Civil Procedure 41(b). Under that provision, a judgment of dismissal on any ground, except lack of jurisdiction, improper venue, or absence of an indispensable party, would literally seem to be an adjudication upon the merits unless the rendering court otherwise specifies. However, as just explained, the Supreme Court in *Costello* read Federal Rule 41(b) not to be an exhaustive listing of such exceptions to the rule of bar, and the subsequent case law establishes that most dismissals for prematurity of suit, or for failure to satisfy some precondition to suit, do not have bar effect.

Perhaps there should be room for a general fairness exception to this usual exception from bar for a judgment of dismissal for prematurity. If the circumstances are such that it would be very unfair to subject the defendant to a later action, the second suit should arguably be barred. An instance of such unfairness would be a case in which the issues were fully tried in the prior action, and the precondition rendering the action premature was within the plaintiff's control to satisfy during the prior action. If, for example, the action was premature merely because the plaintiff failed to demand relief before bringing suit, the refusal to make a formal demand after the court made it clear that one was required hurts the plaintiff's equities. Nevertheless, the defendant could have raised the precondition before trial, or could have waived satisfaction of the precondition. Also, if the defendant's equities were so strong, the defendant could have sought a specification from the trial court that its judgment was with prejudice to a new action, and appealed any denial. All things considered, then, there should be no exception to the exception, and the result of no bar accepted for any unqualified dismissal for prematurity.[73]

d. Dismissal for Statute of Frauds

Although there was some waffling in older authority as to a dismissal based on the statute of frauds—the view being that such a dismissal might

---

73. See John E. Eichhorst, Symposium Note, Res Judicata Effects of Involuntary Dismissals: When Involuntary Dismissals Based upon Prematurity or Failure to Satisfy a Precondition to Suit Should Bar a Second Action, 70 Cornell L. Rev. 667 (1985); supra Chapter 4-A.

be somehow only denying a remedy rather than denying the substantive validity of a right under a contract or other instrument falling within the statute's coverage—today a judgment of dismissal based on the statute of frauds should be and is regarded as on the merits. It bars a later action on the same claim, both within and without the forum of rendition.[74]

e. Dismissal for Statute of Limitations

If the statute of limitations is viewed as cutting off the plaintiff's substantive right, as is frequently the case in connection with statutes applicable to actions to recover real or personal property, a judgment of dismissal based on the statute is a judgment on the merits in the same sense that any other judgment declaring the nonexistence of an asserted right would be. It bars a later action on that claim in the same jurisdiction or in a different one.

Most statutes of limitations, however, are regarded as denying merely the remedy rather than the right. Nevertheless, if the subsequent action is brought in the same jurisdiction, a judgment of dismissal based on such a statute results in preclusion. Even if the prior judgment were to lack bar effect because it was not on the merits, it did preclusively determine the issue of the statute's application to that particular claim: the determination that the statute for that claim had expired was litigated in the first action and was essential to the dismissal, so relitigation of that issue would be foreclosed by the rule of direct estoppel. Thus, if the second action is just a rehash of the first action, preclusion results.

But what if the plaintiff recasts the theory of the action to fit within a longer period of limitations? A second action in the same jurisdiction is still precluded. One could continue to conceive of this, with an effective amount of clarity, as entailing direct estoppel—an estoppel that broadly defines the issue in question to be the whole statute's application to that claim, however the claim is pleaded.[75] The cases, however, tend to invoke claim preclusion, holding that the earlier dismissal was on the merits and bars any second action on the same claim in the same jurisdiction.[76] Either way, the plaintiff, if proceeding in the same jurisdiction, must pursue the new theory by amendment in the first action, or not at all.

---

74. See Restatement (Second) of Judgments § 19 cmt. f, reporter's note (1982).

75. See Restatement (Second) of Conflict of Laws § 110 (1971).

76. E.g., Williamson v. Columbia Gas & Elec. Corp., 186 F.2d 464 (3d Cir. 1950); see Restatement (Second) of Judgments § 19 cmt. f (1982).

If the plaintiff brings the second action in a different jurisdiction that would apply a different and sufficiently long statute of limitations, the result differs. As already stated, a judgment based on a limitations statute that denies the substantive right is considered to be on the merits barring a second action on the same claim, not only in the jurisdiction where it was rendered but also elsewhere. If, however, the first judgment is based on a statute that does not deny the right, but merely denies a judicial remedy for the enforcement of the right, it has supposedly determined only that no remedy is available in the courts of the first jurisdiction; and so a second action may be brought on the claim in a different jurisdiction, in spite of the fact that a second action would be precluded in the first jurisdiction. A leading case on this point is *Warner v. Buffalo Drydock Co.*,[77] in which Judge Augustus Hand expressed the proposition as follows:

> A decision that the Ohio statute of limitations barred the remedy was not res judicata in an action to assert plaintiffs' rights in another forum. If the Ohio statute had extinguished the plaintiffs' rights, as in case of adverse possession of real property beyond the statutory period of limitation, the situation would be different. The decisions of the Supreme Court and the English cases all indicate that the judgment of the court of a foreign state which dismisses a cause of action because of the statute of limitations of the forum is not a decision upon the merits and is not a bar to a new action upon the identical claim in the courts of another state.

The permissibility of a second action prevails only in a second jurisdiction that would apply a different statute of limitations. Thus, if the choice-of-law rule or a borrowing statute in the second jurisdiction calls for the application of the same jurisdiction's statute of limitations as was applied in the first action, res judicata will prevent a second action.

The Second Restatement restates this traditional doctrine, while questioning the soundness of the part of the doctrine permitting a second action in another jurisdiction after a judgment of dismissal based on the statute of limitations.[78] In fact, some courts are willing to accord bar effect

---

77. 67 F.2d 540, 541 (2d Cir. 1933); see Restatement (Second) of Judgments § 19 cmt. f (1982).

78. See Restatement (Second) of Judgments § 19 cmt. f, reporter's note (1982).

to all nondomestic judgments based on the statute of limitations.[79] Their reasons are many. The plaintiff has had a day in court, and the defendant should not have to suffer another. The limitations defense is indistinguishable in nature from many defenses that are unquestionably on the merits, especially as the realm of bar has expanded to reach failure to state a claim and the statute of frauds. The different effect of the limitations dismissal in the second forum from its effect in the rendering court is at least anomalous, if not actually in conflict with the principles of full faith and credit. Seemingly, if the dismissal is a bar in the first jurisdiction, then it should be a bar in the second. It appears, then, that the wave of the future will be to treat dismissals on the basis of the statute of limitations like other dismissals on the merits, that is, as creating a bar.

In getting to this law of tomorrow, some courts look to Federal Rule of Civil Procedure 41(b) when deciding whether a judgment of a federal court dismissing an action because of the statute of limitations will preclude a second suit. It has been argued that Federal Rule 41(b) supersedes the doctrine of *Warner v. Buffalo Drydock Co.* and makes every federal dismissal on statute of limitations grounds a judgment on the merits, unless the judge makes the saving specification that Federal Rule 41(b) allows.[80] Other authorities, however, argue that Federal Rule 41(b) does not settle this difficult point and, as already explained, they are correct.[81]

In sum, the courts have developed a special exception for dismissals on limitations grounds, which is applicable when the plaintiff later recasts the action in the same court or brings a new action elsewhere in an attempt to circumvent the statute of limitations. Such a dismissal acts as a bar in courts applying the same jurisdiction's statute of limitations, but for reasons difficult to fathom it may not act as a bar to suit elsewhere on the same claim.

How much farther does this special exception extend? Not far. There is some case authority concerning dismissals based on public policy. A claim may be dismissed because recovery would be contrary to the public policy of the jurisdiction in which the action is brought. Such a dismissal is re-

---

79. E.g., Semtek Int'l Inc. v. Lockheed Martin Corp., 736 A.2d 1104 (Md. Ct. Spec. App. 1999), rev'd on other grounds, 2001 WL 182650 (U.S.).

80. See Bertha Bldg. Corp. v. National Theatres Corp., 248 F.2d 833 (2d Cir. 1957).

81. See 18 Charles Alan Wright, Arthur R. Miller & Edward H. Cooper, Federal Practice and Procedure § 4441, at 372-73 (1981 & Supp. 1999).

garded as on the merits, and so a bar to a later action on the same claim, if the forum's public policy denies the existence of the substantive right, but not necessarily if it merely denies a judicial remedy. That is, relevant here is the same basic distinction between judgments denying the existence of the right and judgments denying enforcement to such right. A judgment dismissing a claim on grounds of public policy is a bar to a new action in the same jurisdiction. But this judgment may not bar a new action in a different jurisdiction if it denied only a remedy.[82]

f. Summary Judgment

A summary judgment may be granted under Federal Rule of Civil Procedure 56, or a state equivalent, if the court is convinced that there is no genuine issue as to any material fact and that the moving party is entitled to a judgment as a matter of law. Such a judgment for the defendant is typically on the merits and bars a later suit on the same claim.[83] However, if the true basis for the summary judgment is jurisdictional defect, prematurity, or statute of limitations, the judgment goes not enjoy increased preclusive effect merely by its summary judgment label.[84]

g. Voluntary Dismissal

Through the device of a voluntary nonsuit, the common law allowed a plaintiff as a matter of right, at any time before a verdict or judgment was rendered, to terminate the lawsuit without prejudice to later suit on the same cause of action, although the plaintiff was liable for costs. Such a device is difficult to reconcile with the policies underlying the doctrine of res judicata, and consequently a statute, rule, or decision has modified it in most states. Federal Rule of Civil Procedure 41(a)(1) permits voluntary dismissal without prejudice as an unqualified matter of right if the right is exercised before the adverse party serves an answer or a motion for summary judgment. So generally, under modern law, the plaintiff still has a right to terminate the case voluntarily without prejudice, but the right must be exercised at an early stage in the proceedings. The right today may be subject to other limitations as well.[85]

Although today's plaintiff in given circumstances cannot voluntarily dismiss the case without prejudice as a matter of right, the trial court has the

---

82. See Restatement (Second) of Judgments § 19 cmt. f (1982).

83. See Restatement (Second) of Judgments § 19 cmt. g (1982).

84. See 18 Charles Alan Wright, Arthur R. Miller & Edward H. Cooper, Federal Practice and Procedure § 4444 (1981 & Supp. 1999).

85. See Restatement (Second) of Judgments § 20(1)(b) (1982).

power to order dismissal on the plaintiff's motion, if the judge deems proper such an order with or without terms and conditions. Such a dismissal will have no bar effect, unless the judge otherwise specifies. Courts typically allow dismissal without prejudice unless the defendant faces special disadvantage, other than the prospect of having to defend a later action. Also, a voluntary dismissal will have no bar effect if all the parties to the action stipulate to the dismissal, unless they otherwise specify as part of a settlement.

The plaintiff can use voluntary dismissal in successive lawsuits on the same claim. But the second such dismissal may have bar effect. Federal Rule 41(a)(1) provides that a "notice of dismissal operates as an adjudication upon the merits when filed by a plaintiff who has once dismissed in any court of the United States or of any state an action based on or including the same claim." This two-dismissal rule of Federal Rule 41(a)(1) apparently does not apply unless both of the dismissals were solely by the plaintiff's act, rather than the court's order or the parties' stipulation.[86] Moreover, this particular two-dismissal rule operates only when the second dismissal is in a federal court. If the second dismissal occurs in a state court, the state rule rather than Federal Rule 41(a)(1) governs the question of its bar effect, even if the first dismissal occurred in a federal court.

Of course, even if the plaintiff has a right to dismiss the action without prejudice, the dismissal will have bar effect if the plaintiff intends that result. This was true at common law, as the plaintiff could renounce the suit in open court and obtain a judgment referred to as a retraxit rather than a nonsuit. It remains true under modern law. Judgments voluntarily dismissing an action after a settlement agreement generally specify that the judgment is with prejudice or on the merits. Federal Rule 41(a) allows the notice of dismissal, order, or stipulation to provide that the dismissal will have bar effect.

h. Involuntary Dismissal

Each state may provide that involuntary judgments of dismissal, other than those already discussed, are or are not on the merits, or may grant to the rendering judge control over the matter of the res judicata effect of such judgments. In federal courts the matter is governed by Federal Rule of Civil Procedure 41(b), and such judgments will have bar effect unless the rendering judge specifies that they are not on the merits. Dismissals for failure to prosecute the claim, or penalty dismissals for failure to comply with the

86. See Cornell v. Chase Brass & Copper Co., 48 F. Supp. 979 (S.D.N.Y. 1943).

rules or orders of the court, are prime examples of such judgments in state or federal court.[87]

The trend toward applying bar to such penalty dismissals shows the inadequacy of the phrase of on the merits. In such a case, there may have been no consideration whatsoever of the merits, and yet the dismissal will preclude a second action. This harsh result for the plaintiff is necessitated by the court's interests in controlling its docket and enforcing its rules, to say nothing of the defendant's interests.[88]

i. Dismissal for Insufficiency of Evidence

Many different terms have been applied to devices for raising at trial the issue of the sufficiency of the plaintiff's evidence: the motion for involuntary (or compulsory) nonsuit, the demurrer to the evidence, the motion for involuntary dismissal, the motion for judgment on partial findings, the motion for a directed verdict, the motion for judgment notwithstanding the verdict, and the motion for judgment as a matter of law. The involuntary nonsuit was a later development from the common-law voluntary nonsuit and, like it, was held not to preclude a later suit on the same cause of action. By contrast, the demurrer to the evidence at common law did lead to a judgment on the merits that had bar effect, as did all the other, more modern motions.

The justification for attributing different res judicata effects to judgments based on the same basic decision, but with different names, is not obvious. And by now in this sketch, we have moved solidly into decisions on the substantive merits of the case. The common-law involuntary nonsuit is largely obsolete today.[89] At any rate, the modern approach is to treat as a bar any judgment rendered on the basis of the plaintiff's failure to adduce sufficient evidence, unless the rendering judge otherwise specifies.[90]

j. Summary

Certain dismissals *not on the merits* remain *exceptions* to the rule of bar, namely: (1) dismissals for lack of subject-matter jurisdiction or territorial

---

87. See Restatement (Second) of Judgments § 19 cmt. e (1982).

88. See 18 Charles Alan Wright, Arthur R. Miller & Edward H. Cooper, Federal Practice and Procedure § 4440 (1981 & Supp. 1999).

89. See Restatement (Second) of Judgments § 20 cmt. g (1982).

90. See Restatement (Second) of Judgments § 19 cmt. h (1982).

jurisdiction, improper venue, inadequate notice, or nonjoinder or misjoinder of parties; (2) most dismissals for prematurity of suit or failure to satisfy a precondition to suit; and (3) most voluntary dismissals. Moreover, unless prohibited by statute or rule, the court in the first action can specify that its dismissal is not to act as a bar; and the court in the second action will defer to that specification.

Other dismissals and judgments, which are perhaps not in any real sense on the merits but which were preceded by an ample opportunity for the plaintiff to litigate the claim, have of late come within the rule of bar, at least in the view of many courts and legislatures. Examples include: (1) a dismissal for failure to state a claim; (2) a summary judgment, judgment on partial findings, or judgment as a matter of law and other decisions squarely on the merits; and (3) a dismissal for failure to prosecute or to obey a court order or rule, even though it is not in any real sense on the merits.

2. Jurisdictional or Procedural Limitation

Whenever the plaintiff is unable in the first action to present the entire claim because a jurisdictional or procedural limitation prohibits asserting a certain legal theory or demanding a certain remedy, the plaintiff can bring a second action on that theory or for that remedy.

Allusion has previously been made to the exception to claim preclusion applicable when the claim includes different kinds of relief, not all of which are recoverable in the court.[91] A prime example came during the discussion of how federal and state grievances constitute a single claim. Say *P* sues *D* for fraud in state court. After judgment, *P* sues *D* on the same transaction in federal court under the Federal Securities Exchange Act, an action within the exclusive federal jurisdiction. *D* pleads res judicata. The result generally is no claim preclusion as to the federal part of the claim.

Important to note here is that this exception allows the plaintiff to preserve only the part of the claim that the first court would clearly not have entertained. Thus, if in the preceding example *P* had chosen first to sue in federal court, *P* would there have had to assert both federal and state grounds in order to avoid losing them to claim preclusion.

---

91. See Restatement (Second) of Judgments §26(1)(c) (1982); 18 Charles Alan Wright, Arthur R. Miller & Edward H. Cooper, Federal Practice and Procedure §4412 (1981 & Supp. 1999).

Moreover, this exception allows the plaintiff to preserve only the part of the claim that the plaintiff could not have joined with the rest of the claim by selecting some other court in the same court system. Thus, if the plaintiff voluntarily chooses to sue in a state court of limited jurisdiction and recovers all that the court can award, but a state court of general jurisdiction was available, claim preclusion will prevent suing for additional relief in a court of general jurisdiction. To be more specific, monetary limits on the jurisdiction of inferior courts are common, and a plaintiff may be unable to get a judgment in such a court for all of the damages suffered. Given that usually a court of general jurisdiction in the same system of courts is available to entertain the entire claim, a plaintiff who chooses to sue in an inferior court in which full recovery is unavailable cannot thereby escape the consequences of claim preclusion. Although res judicata does not force the plaintiff to abandon the state court system for the federal court system, it does effectively force the plaintiff into an appropriate state court.

Another situation in which jurisdictional limitations may give rise to an exception to the application of merger or bar is when long-arm service can reach the defendant for only part of the claim. For instance, the plaintiff may have both tort and contract theories for recovery on the same basic facts. The long-arm statute may subject the defendant to personal jurisdiction on the tort theory but not reach the contract theory,[92] and personal jurisdiction may not be attainable by virtue of the defendant's appearance or otherwise.[93] In such a case, the plaintiff must either sue on the tort theory only or else take the lawsuit to a state where the defendant can be served for all purposes. The plaintiff should have a right to choose the former alternative, and so the resulting judgment should not subject the contract grievance to claim preclusion.

3. Judicial Permission

Unless prohibited by statute or rule, the court in the first action can specify that its judgment is without prejudice to bringing a second action on a portion or all of the same claim, or so provide in other words to that effect.

---

92. See Robert C. Casad & William B. Richman, Jurisdiction in Civil Actions §§ 4-7, 5-2[4][f] (3d ed. 1998) (discussing the reach of supplemental personal jurisdiction).

93. See Restatement (Second) of Judgments § 9 (1982) (specifying the effect of appearance).

The rendering court can permit claim splitting.[94] The court will do so when special circumstances justify a second action, such as when only at trial could the plaintiff's counsel perceive the breadth of the claim. The court in the second action will defer to a specification that the judgment is *without prejudice.*

Consider this twist on judicial permission. Sometimes an error by the court may cause or contribute to the splitting. For instance, the plaintiff may have sought in the same lawsuit to assert his claim for personal injury and property damage stemming from a single accident, and the trial court may have erroneously dismissed part of the claim because of misjoinder. The plaintiff, although winning on the other part, could appeal the erroneous ruling. If he fails to do so, will a later suit seeking recovery on the deleted part be precluded by the doctrine of merger? Whatever may be the theoretical explanation, the answer should be in the negative: the plaintiff's second suit should not be held precluded by the erroneous first judgment.[95] The plaintiff did not cause the splitting. Through no fault of his, two suits on the same claim will be required in any event, whether he is permitted to sue separately on the erroneously dismissed part of the claim or whether he is obliged to seek a reversal of the erroneous judgment and a second trial on remand. The public interest in economy of judicial effort would hardly be promoted by a rule requiring the intervention of an appellate court in such a case. The defendant can hardly argue disadvantage, because if she pushed the issue of misjoinder, she in effect consented to the splitting. Moreover, the erroneous ruling that the two harms were not parts of the same claim would probably be binding on the parties by direct estoppel. All those are good arguments. The easiest explanation of the negative answer, however, would simply envisage the first court as permitting the claim splitting.

Incidentally on this subject of res judicata specifications by the rendering court, if the court in the first action takes upon itself to specify that its judgment is *with prejudice*, the specification is not binding on the court in the second action, but in close cases that second court will ordinarily give that specification great weight in deciding whether claim preclusion applies. If, by contrast, the earlier judgment was a dismissal inherently off the mer-

94. See Restatement (Second) of Judgments §26(1)(b) (1982); 18 Charles Alan Wright, Arthur R. Miller & Edward H. Cooper, Federal Practice and Procedure §4413 (1981 & Supp. 1999).

95. See Restatement (Second) of Judgments §26 cmt. d (1982).

its—as for lack of jurisdiction, improper venue, or absence of an indispensable party—then the second court should disregard the specification of prejudice; the first court may actually lack the power to dispose finally of a case not rightly before it, and it likely lacks any good reason to try to do so.[96]

4. Party Agreement

The parties can agree that the plaintiff may split the claim, or the defendant might even inadvertently acquiesce in splitting.

The parties can agree to claim splitting.[97] Although the doctrine of res judicata in its various aspects—merger, bar, and issue preclusion—is predicated upon public interests including economy of judicial effort, as well as upon the parties' interests in being free of repetitious litigation of the same claims or issues, the public interests are not so strong as to prevent successive litigation of the same matters if the parties desire it.[98] Thus, a defendant may waive the right to avoid a second action on the same claim, that is, may consent to the splitting of the claim. Such consent may be express and rest on tactical reasons or, more likely, may consist of a failure to assert the defense of res judicata when the second action is brought.

When the plaintiff has commenced two different actions on the same claim, and both are pending at the same time, the defense of res judicata is not available to the defendant until one of the actions proceeds to a judgment. Many courts, nevertheless, hold that the defendant waives the right to object to the splitting of the claim unless the defendant somehow challenges the splitting in a timely fashion in one or the other of the concurrently pending suits. Under that approach, the defendant cannot remain silent until judgment has been entered in one action and then plead claim preclusion in the other.[99]

---

96. See Saylor v. Lindsley, 391 F.2d 965 (2d Cir. 1968); Restatement (Second) of Judgments § 20 cmt. d (1982); 9 Charles Alan Wright & Arthur R. Miller, Federal Practice and Procedure § 2373, at 408-12 (2d ed. 1995 & Supp. 2000).

97. See Restatement (Second) of Judgments § 26(1)(a) (1982).

98. See infra Chapter 11-A.

99. See Todd v. Central Petroleum Co., 124 P.2d 704 (Kan. 1942); 18 Charles Alan Wright, Arthur R. Miller & Edward H. Cooper, Federal Practice and Procedure § 4404, at 24-25, § 4415, at 124-25 (1981 & Supp. 1999); Joseph E. Edwards, Annotation, Waiver of, by Failing to Promptly Raise, Objection to Splitting Cause of Action, 40 A.L.R.3d 108 (1971).

For example, simultaneously in the same court, *P* brings an action for personal injury and another action for property damage resulting from the same accident. *D* defends both, without raising in either action the defense of other action pending.[100] One action goes to judgment, and *D* then raises claim preclusion in the other. The result generally is no claim preclusion because, at least in these extreme circumstances, failure to object to claim splitting is deemed acquiescence.[101]

5. Generalized Exception

In treating prior judgments, courts show a *limited* amount of flexibility in making case-by-case exceptions to claim preclusion, such as when reasons of constitutional, statutory, or other substantive policy counsel that the plaintiff should be allowed to split the claim.

In general, the law is reluctant to recognize exceptions to claim preclusion.[102] Thus, the law tends to limit the generalized exception to a few special situations, while often erecting special procedural hurdles for the plaintiff trying to escape claim preclusion by fitting within those situations.

a. Conflict with Substantive Policy

The policy of avoiding repetitious litigation is a strong one, but not so strong as to override all conflicting considerations. The normal consequences of claim preclusion might in some cases produce results so contrary to the objectives of specific constitutional or legislative provisions or to their fair and equal implementation that successive suits on the same claim must be permitted.[103]

A well-known illustration of specific policy concerns warranting the nonapplication of claim preclusion is the case of *White v. Adler*.[104] The superintendent of banks successfully sued a bank shareholder who owned 326 shares of stock in an insolvent bank to recover the statutory assessment on 1 share only. Later he sued to recover the assessment on the remaining 325

100. See supra Chapter 2-H.

101. See Restatement (Second) of Judgments § 26(1)(a) cmt. a, illus. 1 (1982).

102. See Federated Dept. Stores v. Moitie, 452 U.S. 394 (1981) (rejecting exceptions to claim preclusion); 18 Susan Bandes & Lawrence B. Solum, Moore's Federal Practice § 131.24[6] (3d ed. 1999); 18 Charles Alan Wright, Arthur R. Miller & Edward H. Cooper, Federal Practice and Procedure § 4415 (1981 & Supp. 1999); supra Chapter 4-B.

103. See Restatement (Second) of Judgments § 26(1)(d) cmt. e (1982).

104. 43 N.E.2d 798 (N.Y. 1942)

shares. Under normal principles of res judicata, the claim for the assessment on the 326 shares would have been considered a single claim, and merger would have precluded the second suit. That result, however, would have penalized the bank's creditors for the mistake of the bank superintendent and would have undermined the statute's policy of ratable assessment on all shareholders. In the actual case, the court found that the shareholder had contributed to the confusion leading to the splitting, and thus there were overtones of waiver or acquiescence as well as the overriding substantive concerns in a fair and equal regulatory scheme. The latter concerns should be sufficient in themselves.

b. Misrepresentation by Defendant

If the plaintiff has been misled by representations, concealment, or overreaching by the defendant, and the misleading caused the plaintiff to sue on less than the entire claim in the first action, the defendant will not be permitted to rely on the defense of claim preclusion when the plaintiff sues later for the part omitted from the first action.[105] For instance, if the defendant had committed several breaches of contract before the plaintiff first sued for damages, but the defendant concealed some of the breaches so that the plaintiff did not include them in the first suit, the first judgment would not merge the plaintiff's claim based on them.

A specific example here comes from *Hyyti v. Smith.*[106] The plaintiff was a young, uneducated Finlander who had lived with her parents and spoke only Finnish. She sued for the wrongful death of her parents in an automobile accident, recovering $872 for only out-of-pocket expenses. The defendant's attorney misrepresented to her that this was the extent of her rights, assuring her that his advice came from the goodness of his heart. When she later sued for loss of support, the court held against merger.

This exception apparently may apply even when the defendant was not aware of the falsity of the representations leading to the plaintiff's splitting. But some courts have gone beyond the case of innocent misrepresentation and have held that claim preclusion should not result when the plaintiff's own mistake or ignorance caused the splitting of the claim. The more widely accepted view, and the one seemingly more consistent with the policies of res judicata, however, is that the plaintiff's own mistake or ignorance of the extent of the claim at the time of the first action is not a sufficient

---

105. See Restatement (Second) of Judgments § 26(1)(f) cmt. j (1982).
106. 272 N.W. 747 (N.D. 1937).

reason to deny to the judgment its normal claim preclusion effect, unless the misstep was attributable to the defendant in some way.[107]

Some courts have tightened up this exception by holding that the defendant's misbehavior does not automatically negate the customary claim preclusion effect of the first judgment. To avoid the consequences of claim preclusion, under this view, some sort of direct attack on the judgment's conclusiveness must first be made.[108] This might take the form of a motion for relief from judgment, or it might follow the procedure by which a party seeks equitable relief from a judgment.[109]

c. *Other Extraordinary Situations*

Sometimes, applying the doctrine of claim preclusion in its normal fashion is absolutely unacceptable. For example, litigation might leave the relations between the parties in such an unsatisfactory state that subsequent litigation is necessary to produce an acceptably coherent end to the matter.[110]

A case often used to illustrate this exception is *Adams v. Pearson.*[111] Adams had contracted to sell land to Pearson, the conveyance to be by a warranty deed executed by Adams and his wife. Pearson made a down payment and took possession. The wife, however, was not a party to the contract and refused to sign the deed. Pearson then sued Adams for specific performance with abatement in the price, this being unprecedented relief that would have compelled Adams to convey his interest at the contract price reduced by the value of his wife's dower interest. Adams counterclaimed for rescission, asking for restoration of possession even though there really was no basis for rescission. Judgment was denied on both parties' claims. Later Adams sued for ejectment, and Pearson counterclaimed for specific performance by Adams alone without abatement in the price. Both parties' claims were held to be within the scope of the claims asserted in the earlier action. But to hold both parties precluded would mean that Pearson could never get title and Adams could never get possession. The court declined to bar Pearson's claim, viewing it as offering the more just way out of this intolerable situation, but thus rejecting the normal application of claim preclusion.

---

107. See Estate of Hunt v. United States, 309 F.2d 146 (5th Cir. 1962).
108. See Restatement (Second) of Judgments § 26(1)(2) (1982).
109. See infra Chapter 12-A.
110. See Restatement (Second) of Judgments § 26(1)(f) cmt. i (1982).
111. 104 N.E.2d 267 (Ill. 1952)

A party trying to get within this extraordinary-situation exception must not only show an extraordinary need for an exception, but also show it clearly and convincingly. And again, the party probably should have to make the showing on direct, rather than collateral, attack.[112]

C. Special Applications: Counterclaims

Claim preclusion also applies to claims asserted by the defendant against the plaintiff.

1. Interposition of Counterclaim

A defendant who asserts a counterclaim is ordinarily treated, with respect to that claim, as a plaintiff under the normal rules of claim preclusion. The rarely applicable exception centers on the proposition that if the defendant is unable to obtain an award for full recovery because of the court's jurisdictional or procedural limitations (e.g., a ceiling on damages in a court of limited jurisdiction from which the defendant could not transfer the case to a court of general jurisdiction in the same court system), claim preclusion does not operate to preclude a subsequent action for the unrecovered portion.

Statements of the rule of merger commonly describe it as applicable only to a judgment in favor of the plaintiff asserting the claim. Bar is the term used to refer to the res judicata effect of a judgment for the defendant. It must be understood, however, that the terms "plaintiff" and "defendant" here do not refer to the formal designation of the parties in the caption of the suit. Claims may be presented for adjudication by a party technically designated as a defendant in the form of a counterclaim, recoupment, or setoff or, sometimes, as a pure defense. Claims asserted by a defendant, and sometimes even claims not asserted, may be held precluded by a judgment. For this reason, it is probably less confusing to speak of claim preclusion as the effect of a judgment for or against the claimant rather than the plaintiff.

A defendant may have a claim against the plaintiff at the time the plaintiff's action is initiated. In such a situation, the defendant may have various options for asserting the claim, depending upon local procedural rules. Nearly everywhere today the defendant can assert such a claim as a coun-

112. See Restatement (Second) of Judgments § 26(1)(2) (1982).

terclaim in the plaintiff's action (at least if it is closely related to the plaintiff's claim) and, if successful in establishing the claim, get an affirmative judgment for whatever the defendant is entitled to, reduced by whatever the plaintiff recovers on the main claim. Assertion of a claim by a defendant under such circumstances should produce the same res judicata consequences as claims asserted by plaintiffs. Thus, a judgment rendered on a counterclaim in jurisdictions where affirmative recovery on such claims is permitted will have all the claim preclusion effect that would accompany a judgment on the claim if it had been asserted in an independent action. If the defendant interposes a counterclaim, whether required to do so or not, a successful judgment will have the normal effects of merger. If the defendant loses on the asserted counterclaim, later action on that claim will be barred.[113]

As suggested, affirmative recovery on a claim asserted by a defendant has not always been possible, and still is not in all jurisdictions in all cases. Before the code pleading reforms, the only procedures available for the assertion of claims by a defendant were the devices of recoupment (defensive assertion of a claim arising from the same transaction as the plaintiff's claim) and setoff (defensive assertion of a claim for a liquidated debt, even though the claim might have no factual relation to the plaintiff's claim). Defendants were not compelled to use claims defensively as recoupment or setoff, and no positive recovery was possible on them even if the defendant's claim was proved and the plaintiff's was not. Under such circumstances, the general view was that no claim-preclusive effect attached to recoupment or setoff. A later independent action thus could be brought by the former defendant on the same claim, except where the claim had been established and fully satisfied by way of reducing the plaintiff's successful claim. This apparently remains true today in situations where affirmative recovery is still not possible on the defendant's counterclaim.

To generalize, an exception to the rule of claim preclusion is recognized if the defendant cannot, because of institutional impediments in the legal system, obtain full recovery on the counterclaim. Although rare, there may be cases where full recovery is not possible, because of a monetary maximum on the jurisdiction of the court or some other reason. In such a case, if there is no means, such as transfer to a court of general jurisdiction, by which the defendant can use the counterclaim to get full recovery, judgment on the counterclaim will not preclude a later action for the balance

---

113. See Restatement (Second) of Judgments §§21(1), 23 (1982).

of the claim in a competent court—although issue preclusion likely will apply.[114]

2. Failure to Interpose Counterclaim

A defendant who does not formally assert a counterclaim is generally unaffected by claim preclusion with respect to that claim.

This complementary rule becomes difficult to justify when the facts forming the basis of the potential counterclaim also constitute the basis of a defense that the defendant does assert. After all, the same basic set of facts, besides constituting a basis for relief, may constitute a defense to an action. Thus, when the defendant had pledged a crop to secure a promissory note, and the promisee-pledgee-plaintiff had sold the crop for more than the amount of the note, the same facts would give the defendant a claim for recovery of the sale's balance and also a defense if sued upon the note. Or a patient, negligently treated and injured by a physician, would have a claim for malpractice and also a defense of failure of consideration if sued by the physician for services rendered.

If the claim for preclusion purposes is defined in transactional terms, it is arguable that the defense and the potential counterclaim should be considered parts of the same claim, and thus that a judgment in an action in which the facts are asserted as a defense should preclude a later action in which the facts are asserted as a basis for affirmative relief.[115] Indeed, a few decisions suggest that the later action seeking affirmative relief is precluded even if the defense resting on the same facts was not, but merely might have been, raised in the prior suit.[116] These decisions would further the policy of settling all related matters between the parties in a single action.

The majority approach, however, is that in the absence of a compulsory counterclaim rule, the assertion of facts as a defense (and, a fortiori, the failure to make such an assertion) does not preclude in a later action the

114. See Restatement (Second) of Judgments § 21(2) (1982).

115. See Musco v. Lupi, 164 N.Y.S.2d 84 (Sup. Ct. 1957); Mitchell v. Federal Intermediate Credit Bank, 164 S.E. 136 (S.C. 1932).

116. E.g., Boggiano v. Thielecke, 326 S.W.2d 386 (Mo. Ct. App. 1959); cf. Blair v. Bartlett, 75 N.Y. 150 (1878) (although the opinion spoke of issue preclusion, the issues involved were not actively litigated, and so issue preclusion would not seem appropriate under the usual rule).

defendant's assertion of a claim based on the same facts.[117] This simple approach is fairer to the defendant. The doctrinal explanation is that a defense and a claim are simply not the same claim in spite of factual identity between them, and thus that the res judicata doctrines of merger and bar are inapplicable. A later action on the claim would be subject to the application of issue preclusion, however. As a practical matter, then, a later action on a claim resting on facts that were asserted unsuccessfully as a defense will normally be precluded—not as matter of bar, but as a matter of issue preclusion. In sum, the thought is that the majority approach is relatively workable and less of a trap for the unwary, that the defendant's interest in selecting the forum for bringing the claim outweighs the undesirability of possibly duplicative litigation, and that here as elsewhere issue preclusion will apply to retrieve in part the policies behind res judicata.

In sum, the majority approach is that claim preclusion generally does not apply unless the defendant asserts a counterclaim. The defendant may indeed bring a later action on an unasserted permissive counterclaim after litigating the same facts in the form of a defense. Nevertheless, the defendant is not completely free of claim preclusion upon failure to interpose a counterclaim. There are two important areas where claim preclusion prevails, even under the majority approach:

a. Compulsory Counterclaim Statute or Rule

A statute or rule of court might effectively provide that under certain circumstances, failure to assert an available counterclaim precludes bringing a subsequent action thereon.

Under Federal Rule of Civil Procedure 13(a), the defendant is required to assert any claim against the plaintiff that "arises out of the same transaction or occurrence that is the subject matter of the opposing party's claim." Most states have adopted a similar compulsory counterclaim statute or rule. If the defendant's claim falls within the scope of such a compulsory counterclaim provision, the judgment in the action will preclude later assertion of that claim, whether or not the defendant actually pleads it as a counterclaim. If the defendant does plead the counterclaim, it requires no stretching of the principles of res judicata to conclude that a judgment on that claim should preclude a later action on the same claim. A claim actu-

---

117. See Schwabe v. Chantilly, Inc., 226 N.W.2d 452 (Wis. 1975); Restatement (Second) of Judgments § 22(1) (1982).

ally asserted by the defendant as a counterclaim, whether compulsory or not, is subject to the same res judicata rules of claim preclusion as would have applied if the claim had been asserted in an independent action. But even if the defendant fails to assert the compulsory counterclaim, later action on the claim is nevertheless precluded.[118] Here the explanation becomes trickier.

The effect of a judgment in barring an unasserted compulsory counterclaim is most often described in res judicata terms.[119] The claim adjudicated is said to include both the plaintiff's claim and the compulsory counterclaim. Certainly, the rationale underlying the compulsory counterclaim statute or rule is similar to that underlying res judicata in its claim preclusion aspect. Both are devices to compel the assertion in a single lawsuit of matters so closely related that no sufficient advantage would result from trying them separately as to warrant the harm that would be entailed. The resulting doctrines are similar too. The tests that have arisen to determine when a counterclaim is to be regarded as compulsory under compulsory counterclaim statutes and rules rest on the same considerations as the transactional test for the dimensions of a claim.

Other authorities view compulsory counterclaim preclusion solely in terms of equitable estoppel or waiver, rather than in terms of the more rigid doctrine of res judicata.[120] Accordingly, when appropriate, a court will later foreclose from seeking relief a party who has unfairly neglected to comply with the compulsory counterclaim statute or rule.

It is probably best, however, to ascribe the effect of compulsory counterclaim preclusion simply to the statute or rule itself without trying to invoke additional explanations.[121] Claim preclusion is simply the sanction that enforces the compulsoriness of the compulsory counterclaim provision. The counterclaim need not be called part of the plaintiff's claim. No resort to equitable estoppel or waiver need be made, as long as the situation falls within the words of the statute or rule.

---

118. See Restatement (Second) of Judgments § 22(2)(a) (1982).

119. See Austin Wakeman Scott, Collateral Estoppel by Judgment, 56 Harv. L. Rev. 1 (1942).

120. E.g., Dindo v. Whitney, 451 F.2d 1 (1st Cir. 1971); see 6 Charles Alan Wright, Arthur R. Miller & Mary Kay Kane, Federal Practice and Procedure § 1417, at 132-38 (2d ed. 1990); Charles Alan Wright, Estoppel by Rule: The Compulsory Counterclaim Under Modern Pleading, 38 Minn. L. Rev. 423 (1954); supra Chapter 2-E.

121. See Allan D. Vestal, Res Judicata/Preclusion 156 (1969).

As explained above, if facts that would constitute a counterclaim are also grounds of defense to the plaintiff's claim, and if the defendant asserts them only defensively without pleading them as a counterclaim seeking relief, a judgment theoretically will not preclude a later action by the defendant. However, a defendant's claim resting on facts that would also constitute a defense to the plaintiff's claim normally would arise out of the same transaction or occurrence as the plaintiff's claim, and so could very well be a compulsory counterclaim. In federal courts and in the courts of states that have adopted a compulsory counterclaim provision like Federal Rule 13(a), a defendant's claim that rests on facts that also constitute a defense will almost always bear such a relationship to the plaintiff's claim as to make it a compulsory counterclaim, and so an independent action will normally be precluded whether a counterclaim is asserted or not in the earlier action. Thus, the special proposition (that omitting a compulsory counterclaim produces claim preclusion) all but eats up the general proposition (that asserting a defense alone does not produce claim preclusion). Yet it does not completely eat up that general proposition, because in some places no compulsory counterclaim provision exists, and because sometimes the situation falls into the compulsory counterclaim statute or rule's exceptions.

b. Common-Law Compulsory Counterclaim

Even in the absence of an applicable statute or rule, failure to assert an available counterclaim precludes bringing a subsequent action thereon if granting relief would *nullify* the judgment in the initial action.

Claim preclusion simply must apply when the effect of the defendant's later-asserted claim would be to nullify the earlier judgment for the plaintiff. This "common-law compulsory counterclaim rule" applies whether or not a compulsory counterclaim statute or rule exists. That fact explains why its very name declares it to be a common-law doctrine. It also applies whether or not the prior judgment was by default. Thus, a defendant is precluded from bringing an action for a declaratory judgment of nonliability after the plaintiff has obtained a judgment on the same transaction, even if the plaintiff's judgment was obtained by default. So also, a judgment quieting title to real estate in the plaintiff precludes a later suit by the defendant to claim title based on facts existing at the time of the earlier judgment.

Note that this narrow rule applies only when the relief sought in the second action would inherently undo the first judgment. Thus, *D* may default in *P*'s personal-injury action and then bring a separate action against *P* for *D*'s injuries sustained in the same accident, the idea being that a judgment for *D* would not nullify *P*'s prior judgment. It might be logically and practically incompatible, but it does not undo the prior judgment. So also, although a defendant purchaser of goods should be precluded from suing for restitution in an action based on fraud in the inducement after the plaintiff seller had obtained and executed on a default judgment for the price,[122] an action by the defendant seeking damages from the fraud should not be precluded in the absence of an applicable compulsory counterclaim statute or rule.[123]

The common-law compulsory counterclaim rule is incredibly important, as it works to guarantee that even default judgments mean something and cannot be undone by later litigation. Still, it is obvious that the scope of the rule is tricky. What precisely does nullify mean? The rule's genesis implies its scope. It emerged as a specific aspect of a broad principle of claim preclusion: a valid and final judgment generally precludes the defendant from later asserting mere defenses to the claim. Therefore, the defendant cannot later pursue a claim that is *no more than* a mere defense to an already adjudicated claim.[124]

---

122. See Massari v. Einsiedler, 78 A.2d 572 (N.J. 1951); Restatement (Second) of Judgments § 22(2)(b) cmt. f, illus. 9 (1982).

123. See Linderman Mach. Co. v. Hillenbrand Co., 127 N.E. 813 (Ind. App. 1920).

124. See generally 18 Charles Alan Wright, Arthur R. Miller & Edward H. Cooper, Federal Practice and Procedure § 4414, at 110-14 (1981 & Supp. 1999).

CHAPTER 7

Issue Preclusion

A. Requirements of Rule

Claim preclusion—by its subdoctrines of merger and bar—aims at limiting the number of lawsuits that may be brought with respect to the same basic controversy. A second suit on a claim that has gone to judgment generally will meet claim preclusion, even if there was no actual contest of the issues in the case. If claim preclusion applies, the whole second lawsuit will terminate, regardless of what issues were or were not litigated in the first lawsuit.

Issue preclusion—by its subdoctrines of direct and collateral estoppel—instead concerns only repeated litigation of the same questions. Thus, issue preclusion, which merely avoids reconsideration of parts of the second lawsuit that were decided in the first lawsuit, would apply only if claim preclusion was inapplicable. If claim preclusion did not apply, either because an exception applied or because a different claim was in suit, then issue preclusion acts to prevent relitigation of essential issues.

The doctrine of issue preclusion rests on the premise that one court should be as capable as any other to resolve the issues in dispute. Once a judgment resolves the issues after the adversary system of adjudication has run its full and fair course, the issues should not again be open to dispute by the same parties in any court. Issue preclusion not only accords with the dictates of fairness but also serves the interests of economy of judicial effort, fosters the certainty and stability of repose, and tends to prevent the anomalous situation, so damaging to public faith in the judicial system, of two authoritative but conflicting answers being given to the very same question.

Granting the premise that one court is normally as capable as another, there are nevertheless some good reasons why issue preclusion should not apply to every question decided in every case. Some tribunals may not actually be as adequate as a court of general jurisdiction to deal with the issues. Also, the discovery and trial of evidence is often expensive and inconvenient, and so if the amount involved in the first action was not enough to warrant an all-out effort to prove the parties' positions, it might be unfair to hold the losing party forever bound by determinations made in that case. Sometimes all the implications of a particular issue are not known or even foreseeable at the time of the first action. A litigant should not be bound by a determination of an issue unless there was a full and fair opportunity, and incentive, to put forth an effective case on that issue in the first action. For these and other reasons, absolute prohibition of relitigation of all issues in all situations is not justified. The interest in avoiding repetitious litigation of the same issues must be weighed against contrary considerations of fairness and efficiency.

The conflict between these opposing policy aims is reflected in the rule and exceptions governing issue preclusion. Basically, the rule of issue preclusion is as follows:

> **A party may not relitigate the *same issue* that was *actually litigated and determined* and was *essential to the judgment* rendered.**[1]

Before getting to the exceptions, we should elaborate on the fact that this legal rule imposes three requirements for application of issue preclusion.

1. Same Issue

For the doctrine of claim preclusion, a primary problem is that of determining whether the same claim is presented in both actions. For the doctrine of issue preclusion, a comparable problem is determining whether the same issue is presented in both actions. Quite simply, prohibiting relitigation of the same issue requires definition of an "issue."

a. Dimensions of Issue

The problem of defining just what comes within an issue—the dimensions of an issue—has been called "perhaps the most difficult problem in

1. See generally Restatement (Second) of Judgments § 27 (1982).

the area of issue preclusion."[2] Its resolution certainly is critical to fixing the reach of issue preclusion. Broadly or narrowly defining issue means a widely applicable doctrine or an insignificant one.

The problem can be illustrated in one of its simpler aspects by the following case: *A* brings a negligence action against *B* for *A*'s injuries in an accident. *B* pleads *A*'s contributory negligence as a defense. The jurisdiction has no compulsory counterclaim rule. Judgment goes for *B* on the specific finding that *A* was contributorily negligent. Later *B* sues *A* for *B*'s own injuries caused by *A*'s negligence in the same accident. Does the judgment in the earlier action based on *A*'s contributory negligence preclude *A* on the issue of *A*'s negligence in the second suit? In other words, is the issue of *A*'s negligent behavior the same in both suits?

The determination of negligence, of course, entails a finding that the facts violate a given legal standard. There may be a dispute as to the standard, or as to the facts, or as to the application of the standard to the facts, but the determination would normally have collateral estoppel effect whether viewed as a question of law or of fact or as a mixed question. Issue preclusion can apply to any sort of issue, even one of pure law.

But is the same issue involved in the cases of *A* v. *B* and *B* v. *A*? Although the contributory-negligence duty to exercise care is owed to oneself, rather than to someone else, the kind of behavior constituting lack of due care is the same in both cases. Facts showing negligence in the one sense would seem also to establish negligence in the other. Nevertheless, it is up to the applicable substantive law to define the required level of care. Arguments exist for fixing the level for contributory negligence either above or below the level fixed for negligence. Given this ambivalence, the legal definitions of the defense of contributory negligence and of the claim for negligence are the same in most jurisdictions. Therefore, because of both the factual and the legal overlap, it is generally assumed, even though express holdings are hard to find, that the issues in our illustration are identical.[3]

Consider two more illustrations, to which we shall repeatedly return, and in which most courts take respectively a broad and a narrow view of an issue's dimensions: (1) In a litigated tort action that the defendant won because of the plaintiff's failure to prove negligence by speeding, an issue was the broad matter of defendant's negligence, thus precluding in a subsequent

---

2. Restatement (Second) of Judgments § 27 cmt. c, reporter's note (1982).

3. See, e.g., Little v. Blue Goose Motor Coach Co., 178 N.E. 496 (Ill. 1931); Restatement of Judgments § 68 cmt. n, illus. 8 (1942).

action between the same parties on a different claim arising from the same accident the plaintiff's assertion of a different manner in which the defendant may have been negligent, such as by drunkenness.[4] It was fair and efficient to require the plaintiff to air all negligence grounds in the first action. (2) In an installment contract action that the plaintiff won, the sole litigated and determined issue was the narrow defensive matter of the contract's illegality, thereby leaving open the defense of the contract's nonexecution or the statute of frauds as a different issue in a subsequent action on the different claim for a later installment.[5] It was not fair and efficient to require the defendant to air all defenses in the first action.

The modern view is that the dimensions of an issue should be measured in light of the efficiency/fairness rationale of res judicata. Whether a matter to be presented in a subsequent action constitutes the same issue as a matter presented in the initial action is a pragmatic question, turning on such factors as the degree of overlap between the factual evidence and legal argument advanced with respect to the matter in the initial action and that to be advanced with respect to the matter in the subsequent action.

The Second Restatement adopts this approach to the dimensions of an issue. It suggests a flexible approach:

> The problem involves a balancing of important interests: on the one hand, a desire not to deprive a litigant of an adequate day in court; on the other hand, a desire to prevent repetitious litigation of what is essentially the same dispute. When there is a lack of total identity between the particular matter presented in the second action and that presented in the first, ... several factors ... should be considered in deciding whether for purposes of the rule ... the "issue" in the two proceedings is the same, for example: Is there a substantial overlap between the evidence or argument to be advanced in the second proceeding and that advanced in the first? Does the new evidence or argument involve application of the same rule of law as that involved in the prior proceeding? Could pretrial preparation and discovery relating to the matter presented in the first action reasonably be expected to have embraced the

4. See Restatement (Second) of Judgments § 27 cmt. c, illus. 4 (1982).
5. See Jacobson v. Miller, 1 N.W. 1013 (Mich. 1879).

> matter sought to be presented in the second? How closely related are the claims involved in the two proceedings?[6]

The approach suggested thus is analogous to that endorsed by the Second Restatement's drafters in connection with determining the scope of a claim for claim preclusion purposes. The scope of the issue for issue preclusion purposes is likewise to be determined by analysis of pragmatic considerations relevant to the two "important interests" to be balanced retrospectively in each situation.

Implications of Modern View. This modern approach is not quite the jumble of airy and meaningless words that it seems at first impression. It has some unavoidable implications, which reveal issue preclusion's practical difficulty and profound significance. Here are a couple:

(1) This modern approach means that the parties' wording in the pleadings and even their actions in litigation do not unfailingly define the issue. The parties' words and actions are good guides, but not infallible guides. On the one hand, in some cases issue preclusion should not apply to some questions framed in the pleadings. That is, just as the actualities of trial can broaden the pleadings, trial can narrow them too: thus, an issue might be narrower than the pleadings suggest, as where the case appears by the pleadings to turn generally on contractual liability, but at trial actually turns on the contract's legality. On the other hand, issue preclusion should apply in some cases to matters that were not in fact contested through adversary presentations. That is, an issue might be broader than the parties' contest, such as where the broad issue of negligence forecloses new grounds of drunkenness and other carelessness even though the parties focused on speeding in the initial action. Thus, the definition of issue is not a mechanical one.

(2) This modern formulation implies that the identity of issue does not strictly depend on the litigation setting. An issue of negligence in a small suit for property damages is the same issue as contributory negligence in a later heart-rending personal-injury case arising from the same accident. An issue litigated by a criminal defendant in trying to exclude evidence as a consequence of a police misstep does not morph into a different issue when it arises in his claim for violation of civil rights. An issue litigated against the government or against a small and sympathetic party does not become a different issue because now the opponent is a huge and despicable cor-

6. Restatement (Second) of Judgments § 27 cmt. c (1982).

poration. That is to say, even though a specific determination of a specific dispute adjudicated in a specific setting will be affected by all those specifics, the law treats the issue as a dispute over a free-floating matter of determinate truth for all contexts. Thus, the definition of issue is not a soft-hearted one.

Different Levels of Abstraction. A major part of the difficulty in determining whether the issues raised in successive cases are identical arises because in any given case the matter in dispute can be viewed at different levels. For instance, in an automobile accident case, the plaintiff may allege, and the defendant deny, that the defendant was negligent in failing to keep a proper lookout. The plaintiff may adduce, in support of the claim, various evidence, controverted by the defendant, indicating that vision through the defendant's windshield was obscured by frost. If such a case is submitted to the jury for a general verdict with interrogatories, and the jury answers in the negative the question, "Was the defendant negligent," just what has been decided? The judgment against the plaintiff would bar a later suit on the same claim, but for suit on a different claim what issues would the judgment conclusively establish? That the defendant was not negligent at all in the matter? That the defendant did not fail to keep a proper lookout? That the defendant's windshield was not covered so as to obscure vision? That it was not obscured by frost?

First, if collateral estoppel is viewed as a device to prevent multiple litigation of the very same particulars, and nothing more, then preclusion should apply only to the issues narrowly framed by competing evidentiary contentions. In the example, this position would indicate that the issue was whether the windshield was obscured by frost or not. Broader claim preclusion could apply in a later action on the same claim by virtue of the doctrine of bar, but issue preclusion would apply only to this narrow issue in a later action on a different claim. The parties did not present evidence in support of competing contentions on the issue of whether the windshield was obscured by other matter, or whether the defendant otherwise failed to keep a proper lookout, or was speeding or otherwise negligent.

Second, the case framed in the pleadings was broad enough that the plaintiff could have produced any evidence of whatever kind tending to show that the defendant failed to keep a proper lookout. Should the plaintiff not have been expected, as a matter of fairness and efficiency, to produce any existing evidence on this more general question raised in the pleadings, namely, the issue of failure to keep a proper lookout? Should he not be held to have litigated that broader question once and for all as between himself and the defendant? In other words, should not the pleadings trump the evidence, so that the issue resolved by the judgment would include at least everything that might tend to show that the defendant failed to keep a proper lookout?

Almost all courts would answer "yes." That is, they would hold that the more proper level at which to view the issue, in this instance, is the level reflected in the terms of the pleadings. If the case is tried without supplanting the pleadings by a pretrial order and without amending them to conform to the trial evidence, the resulting judgment will often have preclusive effect on issues defined at least as broadly as the terms of the pleadings, even if evidence was introduced on only a narrow aspect of that broader issue.

Indeed, most courts would go farther in this particular instance, defining the issue as negligence. They would not limit the issue to whether the defendant failed to keep a proper lookout. In most jurisdictions, the plaintiff could have pleaded negligence generally, or could easily have managed to introduce evidence of any sort of negligence. Accordingly, this broadly defined issue of negligence would attract most courts.

To make the same point with the earlier example, assume that *A* brings a negligence action against *B* for personal injuries resulting from an automobile accident allegedly caused by *B*'s speeding. At trial, *A* tries to show *B* was negligent in driving at an excessive speed. After judgment for *B* on a general verdict, *B* sues *A* for *B*'s own injuries caused by *A*'s negligence in connection with the same accident (assume that no compulsory counterclaim rule was in force). *A* is precluded from setting up *B*'s negligence as a defense, whether the alleged contributory negligence is based on excessive speed or drunkenness, or otherwise. The issue to which preclusion applies is the issue of *B*'s negligence, not just the speeding issue toward which the complaint and the evidence were actually addressed. (However, this conclusion does not mean that the issue must be viewed at that level and no other. The more specific issue relating to driving at excessive speed was actively litigated and determined, and was essential to the judgment rendered. Issue preclusion could be applied to that narrower fact too.)

Thus, courts face quite a temptation to define issues very broadly. If an issue for issue preclusion purposes is to be defined as broadly as modern general pleading permits, is the result not tantamount to holding a party conclusively bound for purposes of later litigation on an issue that might have been litigated but was not? Is that consistent with issue preclusion's basic notion of preventing *re*litigation, the notion that distinguishes it from claim preclusion? Obviously, the principles and policies of issue preclusion and claim preclusion start to merge as the definition of issue expands. Yet the rules and exceptions of the two doctrines differ, so some sense of boundary is necessary. Maintaining that boundary requires adhering to a realistic view of the issue's dimensions that does not undermine issue preclusion's defining requirement of "actually litigated and determined." Even though the parties could have, or even have, pleaded what seems a broad question, they may have contested a narrower question. The latter should be deemed the issue for issue preclusion purposes unless the former question is evidentially and legally a unity, as is negligence.

Recall the other example of an installment contract action that the plaintiff won, where the sole litigated and determined issue was the narrow defensive matter of the contract's illegality, thereby leaving open the defense of the contract's nonexecution as a different issue in a subsequent action on a later installment. The courts' temptation is to expand preclusion by defining the issue as the obligation to pay under the contract, especially where the subsequent action was foreseeable by the defendant. Courts nevertheless must, and most do, resist that temptation and aim instead at the optimal dimensions of the issue as delineated by the relevant policies. As to fairness, defining the separate defenses as separate issues is not too unfair to the plaintiff, because the plaintiff will not have to go over the same legal or factual ground a second time when litigating against the different defense. The defendant might have had good reasons of cost and convenience in forwarding only one defense in the particular circumstances prevailing in the first case—"such as the smallness of the amount or the value of the property in controversy, the difficulty of obtaining the necessary evidence, the expense of the litigation, and his own situation at the time."[7] As to efficiency, allowing litigation of the different defense raises no risk of wasteful relitigation or of inconsistent adjudications, as the subsequent action is the first time the parties and the court face the matter of the contract's execution vel non. Efficiency, indeed, cuts quite the other way. A broad definition of issue might result in overlitigation in the first case, as the parties would fight over matters than might never have to be adjudicated. Therefore, most courts would fix the issue as the contract's illegality, not the broader question of the contractual obligation to pay.

In summary, it is always possible as a logical matter to state the issue in a variety of ways, in ascending levels of abstraction. Courts certainly do not

7. Cromwell v. County of Sac, 94 U.S. 351, 356 (1877).

fix the issue in the narrowest terms possible, nor do they readily resort to the broadest terms possible. Instead, guided primarily by what the parties actually contested, the courts fix the issue in between, in accordance with the particularistic dictates of fairness and efficiency.

b. Applications

Multiple Parties. In a case where a single act injures two persons, the issue of the actor's negligence to one injured party is generally regarded as identical to the issue of the actor's negligence to the other injured party. Although the doctrine of mutuality, which is discussed in the next chapter, may prevent an injured party from taking advantage of the determination of the actor's negligence established in a prior suit brought by another party injured by the same conduct, the issue of the actor's negligence is nevertheless normally regarded as identical in both cases.

The same principle would apply in a case where two defendants were found negligent in causing an accident that injured the plaintiff. In a later suit by one of the co-defendants against the other co-defendant for damages resulting from the same accident, the issues of negligence are generally regarded as identical to those previously adjudicated. Although again the parties in the second action may be prevented from invoking the issue preclusion effect of the prior determination of the negligence of each—this time because of the next chapter's principle that limits the use of collateral estoppel when the parties were not actual adversaries in the earlier action—the negligence issues are normally regarded as identical.

In short, the application of issue preclusion in such situations of multiple parties can proceed without automatically running into the impediment of different issues. Unlike claims, for which different parties normally mean different claims, issues do not become different issues because of multiple parties. Thus, issue preclusion stands ready to expand mightily in the direction of new parties.

Same Circumstances, but Different Law. When different legal standards are applicable to the conduct characterized as negligent in the first suit and the same conduct in the second suit, however, the issues are not identical. For instance, in *Capps v. Whitson,*[8] a bus passenger had recovered damages in a prior action against both the bus company and the driver of a car that had collided with the bus. When the bus company later sued the driver of the car for its own damages resulting from the same collision, the driver ar-

8. 160 S.E. 71 (Va. 1931).

gued that the judgment in the earlier action had established the company's contributory negligence. But the court held that, even if the parties were actual adversaries in the earlier action, the judgment had not determined the issue. The duty of care owed by the company to its passenger was higher than that owed the driver of the car or to itself. Moreover, the last-clear-chance doctrine might be applicable in the suit between the bus company and the driver.

Yet the principle of *Capps v. Whitson* was said to be one of very narrow application in *James Talcott, Inc. v. Allahabad Bank.*[9] That case involved a bank's claim against the drawee of commercial paper. The issue there was whether the bank was the alter ego of a third-party corporation, disqualifying it as a holder in due course of the paper transferred to it by that corporation. The alter ego question had been raised in an earlier action among the parties when it had been asserted that the bank by certain behavior and through its alter ego relation had waived the corporation's right to arbitration, but the waiver argument had failed because the court had rejected the alter ego contention. Although the legal standards were not, strictly speaking, identical in the two usages, the court in the second case nevertheless held that the alter ego issue was the same in both cases, and therefore collateral estoppel prevented the drawee from relitigating the issue.

This *James Talcott* case is not a total rejection of *Capps v. Whitson*, but it does suggest that the differences between the legal standards must be substantial to justify a conclusion that an issue should not be foreclosed when the same facts are involved. For example, the confusion of the consuming public as to the origin of goods is the same issue in a state claim of unfair competition and in a later federal trademark claim.[10] Nevertheless, if the legal standards really do differ, the issues are different. For example, the issue of public confusion in a company's successful federal action for cancellation of another firm's similar trademark differs from the issue of public confusion in the company's later federal suit for trademark infringement. The issue differed because the cancellation case turned legally on confusion between the names Beam's and Beamish in the abstract, while the infringement suit turned legally on confusion in the marketplace between the actual labels on the alcohol bottles.[11]

---

9. 444 F.2d 451, 459 (5th Cir. 1971).

10. See Berlitz Schools of Languages of Am. v. Everest House, 619 F.2d 211, 215 (2d Cir. 1980).

11. See Jim Beam Brands Co. v. Beamish & Crawford Ltd., 937 F.2d 729, 734 (2d Cir. 1991).

Same Law, but Different Circumstances. If the law is the same, but the facts have changed, it is easier to defeat issue preclusion. So, if the allegedly confusing goods are substantially different ones in the trademark case from the goods involved in the unfair competition case, the issues may very well differ.[12] Or if a court finds a contracting party to be insane, the finding likely will not carry over to invalidate a different contract executed after a considerable passage of time. Changed circumstances change the issue.

The best way to view changed circumstances is as an aspect the same-issue requirement of the rule of issue preclusion. If the invoker of issue preclusion makes a prima facie showing in support of the issue preclusion rule but the invokee raises the nonidentity of issues, the invoker must show that the two cases involve the same issue.

Same Issue by Inference. Sometimes a court will treat an issue in Action #2 as the same issue as that in Action #1, even though the two sound quite distinctive, because the first outcome implies a certain outcome for the second case. For example, if *A* v. *B* produces the finding that *B* was not negligent, and if a later case raises the issue of *B*'s willful and wanton misconduct in the accident, the first outcome will preclude the second case. The absence of simple negligence implies the absence of worse recklessness.[13]

Note, however, that such inference is not a two-way street. If *B* first overcame an allegation of willful and wanton misconduct, *B* could not later use that victory to preclude *A* on an issue of negligence. That should be obvious.

2. Actually Litigated and Determined

The defining requirement of issue preclusion is that it applies only to issues "actually litigated and determined"—in contrast to claim preclusion, which precludes later consideration of matters that might have been contested but were not. This issue preclusion requirement, however, needs refinement. What constitutes "litigation and determination" (with the "actually" just adding emphasis)?

For preclusive effect, the parties to be bound and benefited must have submitted the issue for decision, and the adjudicator must have decided

---

12. See Berlitz Schools of Languages of Am. v. Everest House, 619 F.2d 211, 216 (2d Cir. 1980).

13. See Little v. Blue Goose Motor Coach Co., 178 N.E. 496 (Ill. 1931); 18 Susan Bandes & Lawrence B. Solum, Moore's Federal Practice § 132.03[3][e], [4][c] (3d ed. 1999).

the issue. Thus, issue preclusion does not result from a default, admission, or stipulation. The rationale is that a rule of issue preclusion without the requirement of actually litigated and determined would unnecessarily and undesirably intensify litigation.

Issues Litigated and Determined. For issue preclusion, all that the parties must do is submit an issue for decision, and all that the court must do is decide such an issue. An issue can therefore be litigated and determined by motion, as well as by trial. Issues raised by motions to dismiss for failure to state a claim or for judgment on the pleadings, like issues raised by motions for summary judgment, are litigated and determined. A judgment dismissing a claim on a threshold issue such as improper venue does not bar a later suit on the same claim, but for issue preclusion purposes such a judgment is a litigation and determination of the issue that led to the dismissal.

One should not imagine that the actually litigated and determined requirement necessitates hair and teeth flying in open court. Nor must there have been a thorough airing of the arguments or presentation of the evidence. Indeed, the litigation can take place entirely on paper. Or the determination can rest on a total failure of proof leading to a certain decision through the medium of the burden of proof. All that is necessary is the reaching of a decision on an issue submitted by the pleadings or otherwise.[14]

Issues Not Litigated and Determined. An outcome arrived at through other means—by default, confession, admission, consent, or stipulation or by failure to prosecute or voluntary dismissal—would not be a litigation and determination of particular issues. Such an outcome may dispose conclusively of the claim, but not of particular issues.

Why should the law allow a defendant to default yet avoid issue preclusion? The defendant should be free to choose whether or not to contest the plaintiff's action without risking more than is demanded in the prayer for relief. If the defendant chooses not to contest the plaintiff's allegations at that time and in that court, preferring instead simply to default, or to consent to the plaintiff's demand, the defendant should not be held to have forfeited the right to contest the particular issues in another setting. As to fairness, the defendant may have had excellent reasons of cost and convenience to hold back in the circumstances of the first action. The plaintiff is not especially burdened by limiting the effect of a default. As to efficiency,

14. See Restatement (Second) of Judgments § 27 cmt. d (1982).

allowing the defendant later to litigate the point avoids the danger of discouraging compromise as well as the incentive to overlitigate the first action and, because the point was never litigated or determined in the first action, entails no waste of relitigation or risk of actually inconsistent decisions.

A similar situation may be presented if the defendant, instead of defaulting, answers by admitting some and denying others of the averments in the plaintiff's pleading. If the case is tried and a judgment is won by the plaintiff, will it have collateral estoppel effect as to all of the matters essential to plaintiff's claim? Or only as to those matters denied by the defendant? Again, the rule is that issue preclusion applies only to the matters actively disputed. Issue preclusion does not apply to facts admitted by the defendant, even though those facts were essential to the outcome of the case and even though the admissions themselves would normally be admissible in evidence.[15]

a. Applications

Pleaded but Uncontested Issues. The plaintiff's pleading must allege, in some form, the facts upon which recovery depends. As just explained, these facts are not in issue unless the defendant chooses to deny them. Those undenied facts have no issue preclusion effect even though they are necessary elements of the plaintiff's claim and even though the plaintiff won judgment.

Conversely, if an essential issue is formed in the pleadings by the defendant's denial of the plaintiff's averments, a judgment after trial of the case will be conclusive on all issues thus raised in the pleadings, and relitigation of those issues will be precluded, even if no evidence was offered by one or both sides on one or more of those issues.[16] Unless the issue joined in the pleadings is withdrawn—as by amendment, stipulation, or pretrial order—the resulting judgment will have issue preclusion effect as to any such issue that was essential to the judgment. If the party having the burden of production on the issue offers no evidence on it, and a judgment is consequently entered against that party, the point has been litigated and determined, and issue preclusion will apply to it.

If a fact is alleged in a pleading to which no responsive pleading is required—for example, an affirmative defense under the Federal Rules[17]—

---

15. See Restatement (Second) of Judgments § 27 cmt. e (1982).
16. See Slater v. Skirving, 70 N.W. 493 (Neb. 1897).
17. See Fed. R. Civ. P. 7(a), 8(d).

it is not deemed admitted by a failure of the party to deny it. It will be deemed denied. It will be in issue unless the party expressly admits it in some manner before evidence is offered on the issue at trial.

Unpleaded but Contested Issues. Issues not framed in the pleadings or pretrial order may nevertheless be submitted by the parties for determination by means of a motion raising issues of fact or law, or by the presentation of evidence or argument at trial on a point not pleaded.[18] Issues thus actually raised and contested will receive preclusive effect if actually submitted for a decision, as long as the decision on the issue is essential to the judgment rendered.

b. A Contrary View

Contrary views exist on all three requirements for issue preclusion. Those authorities who would relax the actually litigated and determined requirement are not only representative of the dissenters, but also the most important group in dissent.

Some cases have departed from this requirement in order to apply issue preclusion to default judgments.[19] Others have treated consent judgments similarly, in spite of the usual rule.[20] The basic theory of these cases is that the truth of all the facts alleged by the plaintiff and necessary to the recovery are raised by the plaintiff's pleading, and the defendant should not be able to escape the effect of judgment by waiving the right to contest them. However, this approach is not only unfair and inefficient, but also fictional in treating as established the facts that were never decided. Ordinarily, although a default or consent judgment has claim preclusion effect, it should not generate issue preclusion.[21]

More broadly, take again as an example the second action on an installment contract, after the first action in which the losing defendant litigated only the contract's illegality and did not raise or contest the contract's nonexecution. The majority rule holds that at most the defendant admitted execution, but did not litigate it. Professor Vestal questioned the soundness of this rule that denies issue preclusion effect under all circumstances to facts pleaded and necessary to a plaintiff's recovery if the defendant does

---

18. See Fed. R. Civ. P. 15(b).

19. See E.H. Schopler, Annotation, Doctrine of Res Judicata As Applied to Default Judgments, 77 A.L.R.2d 1410, 1425-30 (1961).

20. See Sheldon R. Shapiro, Annotation, Modern Views of State Courts as to Whether Consent Judgment Is Entitled to Res Judicata or Collateral Estoppel Effect, 91 A.L.R.3d 1170, 1183-91 (1979).

21. See Arizona v. California, 120 S. Ct. 2304, 2319 (2000).

not actively dispute them. Ordinarily, if the defendant does not attack the plaintiff's averments, it is a good indication that they are probably true, especially when future litigation is foreseeable. In his view, "a default judgment or a failure to defend on a particular matter would establish such issues and there would be preclusion on such matters unless the precluded party is able to explain his failure to defend in the earlier suit or is able to convince the court that he should be allowed to contest the issue in the instant suit."[22] Rejecting both the rule that would always deny issue preclusion and one that would always apply it, he thus suggested the compromise of a rebuttable presumption of preclusion as to all issues necessary to judgment. This compromise might sound sensible in theory: judicial economy would be served by generally applying preclusion, but the litigant's right to a day in court would be preserved in cases where good reasons other than the probable truth of the opponent's averments existed for the litigant's failure to contest them. However, the majority rule is preferable in practice: it plays safe as to fairness, while displaying a sound skepticism as to whether judicial economy would really be advanced by such a fuzzy approach that would substitute litigation over the invokee's right to avoid preclusion in lieu of relitigation of the issue for which preclusion is sought.

3. Essential to the Judgment

In the course of a lawsuit, several issues may be litigated. Some of the issues actually determined may have no bearing on the ultimate outcome of the case. Some of the issues may be determined against the party who ultimately obtains the judgment. Such determinations, even though the products of actual and vigorous litigation, are not "essential" and do not have issue-preclusive effect, according to the usual rule.[23]

Under the majority view, issue preclusion applies only to a determination that was essential to judgment. Thus, a determination not strictly necessary to reaching the court's ultimate result is not binding. The idea behind this requirement is that such a determination in the nature of dicta may not have been fully and fairly contested and considered, and appeal on it may have been unavailable or unmotivated. Moreover, society wants neither to stimulate the parties to fight further over such asides nor to encourage courts so to make unnecessary pronouncements.

---

22. Allan D. Vestal, Res Judicata/Preclusion 200-01 (1969).
23. See Restatement (Second) of Judgments § 27 cmt. h (1982).

For example, in a state following the common-law contributory negligence rule, if the court specifically finds in an accident case that both the plaintiff and the defendant were negligent, the determination of the latter issue would have no effect: that is, it was not essential to the judgment rendered, and issue preclusion would not apply to it.[24] The plaintiff loses the case, whether or not the defendant was negligent. The court's finding on the defendant's negligence should just vaporize. Note, in particular, that no argument that the finding of the defendant's negligence was factually, legally, or logically primary or prior to the finding of the plaintiff's contributory negligence would succeed in overcoming the rule of nonpreclusion.

The rule is explained on the ground that such a determination, being unnecessary or immaterial to the judgment rendered in the case, does not bear sufficient assurance of correctness to warrant giving it issue preclusion effect. Nothing ultimately turned on it, so the litigants may not have done their best. It might not have received the court's most careful consideration. An additional justification for not extending issue preclusion effect is that often the party against whom the finding or conclusion was made could not appeal or had no incentive to appeal; it would be unfair to bind by a ruling that was not open to review.

As to the precise meaning of essential, one must look to the policies of res judicata— and especially to whether the issue received active litigation and careful determination and to whether the loser on the issue had the opportunity to appeal—rather than to the literalism of essentiality. The second court does not parse the earlier judgment, seeing whether some ground logically narrower than the first court's ground of decision was possible, in order to get down to the bare essentials. Moreover, some litigated determinations not strictly or surely necessary, such as evidentiary decisions, have issue preclusion effect as long as they were links in the chain leading to judgment. Furthermore, inducing a voluntary dismissal with prejudice or suffering a default judgment after an unfavorable ruling, thereby making the ruling in some sense nonessential, does not prevent the judgment from having issue preclusion effect as to that ruling. However, the essential to judgment requirement retains a sharp bite. Even hotly fought and carefully weighed decisions against the eventual judgment winner should not be binding, because normally they are not essential. In sum,

24. See Cambria v. Jeffery, 29 N.E.2d 555 (Mass. 1940).

decisions that led toward the judgment are essential, but not those that standing alone would have led toward the opposite outcome.

Consider two problems right at the boundary: (1) Some courts accord issue preclusion effect to findings and conclusions on interlocutory issues announced before the parties short-circuited the trial-court process by reaching a settlement, yielding a consent judgment rather than an adjudicated judgment.[25] These cases appear incorrect, unless the parties intended by their settlement contract to retain issue preclusion effect.[26] The pre-settlement rulings were not truly essential to judgment—although they probably helped induce the settlement. The losing party on those issues could not appeal them— although admittedly that party did choose to waive appeal. These cases discourage settlement—although smart parties can contract out of (or into) issue preclusion effect by the terms of their settlement. (2) Once a case is litigated to judgment, settlement on appeal does not destroy the judgment's issue preclusion effect. The court cannot vacate the judgment in order to effectuate the parties' desire to undo issue preclusion.[27] The pre-settlement rulings were essential to the lower-court judgment.

B. Exceptions to Rule

In some situations coming within the rule of issue preclusion, the circumstances are such that it would seem improper to hold a party precluded from relitigating an issue. Fairness concerns might suggest exceptions, as where there has been no full and fair opportunity to litigate. Efficiency concerns also might counsel exceptions, especially the policy against encouraging parties to overlitigate the initial action by fighting every conceivable issue to the death. Finally, independent substantive policies might overwhelm the policies behind res judicata. After all, by issue preclusion, courts are just trying to pursue those policies that weigh against relitigation of some issue. Clearly, other policies will often point in the other direction. An iron-clad rule of issue preclusion hardly seems the appropriate resolution.

---

25. E.g., TM Patents, L.P. v. IBM, 72 F. Supp. 2d 370, 375-76, 378-79 (S.D.N.Y. 1999); Cities Serv. Co. v. Gulf Oil Corp., 980 P.2d 116, 128 (Okla. 1999).

26. See Avondale Shipyards v. Insured Lloyd's, 786 F.2d 1265, 1272-73 (5th Cir 1986).

27. See U.S. Bancorp Mortgage Co. v. Bonner Mall Partnership, 513 U.S. 18 (1994).

In actual practice, courts apply issue preclusion quite flexibly, invoking many exceptions in situations squarely within the rule's three requirements.[28] Some such situations have been recognized frequently enough to be considered general exceptions to the rule of issue preclusion.

1. Certain Issues of Law

Courts tend not to apply issue preclusion to a relatively *pure* issue of law arising in a claim substantially *unrelated* to the claim in which it was previously determined. Also, courts tend not to apply issue preclusion to any issue of law on which it would create *inequity*, such as where binding someone to a legal ruling outmoded by a later change in the decisional law would cause troublingly different legal treatment of similarly situated people. In cases such as these, society inclines to rely only on the more flexible doctrine of stare decisis to guide the courts' handling of past legal rulings.

a. Pure Questions of Law

The trial of a lawsuit may involve disputes over questions of law, over questions of fact, or over applications of law to fact. Rulings on questions of law may have some binding effect upon the parties in later litigation by virtue of the doctrine of stare decisis. Moreover, parties may be precluded from relitigating particular questions of law through the operation of direct or collateral estoppel.

Rulings on questions of law are seldom made in the abstract. Nearly always questions of law are decided with reference to particular facts. In this respect it is often difficult to separate questions of law from questions of law application. A ruling embodying the application of undisputed legal principles to established facts—as, for instance, on a motion for a directed verdict or a judgment as a matter of law—is technically a ruling on a question of law. Such a ruling may at the same time effectively decide one of the key factual disputes. In a breach of contract action, for illustration, a ruling that a given written communication constitutes an offer might apply an accepted legal standard to admitted facts, so ruling on a question of law and at the same time adjudicating a key fact. If the legal significance of the

28. See generally Restatement (Second) of Judgments §28 (1982).

same historical fact should again become a matter of dispute between the parties, the rule of issue preclusion should normally apply, at least if the claims involved in the separate suits are closely related.[29] All the usual policies against relitigation are in play. Thus, if the matter of whether a particular agreement constitutes a legally binding contract has been litigated and determined in a suit for breach, the judgment essentially based on that determination will preclude the parties from relitigating that matter in a subsequent suit for a later breach of the same contract. So also, if it has been litigated and determined in a suit to obtain payment of a bond that the issuance of the series of bonds that included the one in suit was induced by fraud, that essential determination will be binding on the parties in a later suit to collect on a different bond in the same series.

An actual dispute over the proper legal standard or rule to apply, or what it exactly provides, is also clearly an issue of law. But it is a much purer issue of law. And it can arise in a totally unrelated claim. If the second action is substantially unrelated to the first, collateral estoppel effect will not be accorded to fairly pure issues of law decided in the first action. It would be undesirable to hold litigants bound for all times and for all purposes by a questionable ruling of law. "Such preclusion might unduly delay needed changes in the law and might deprive a litigant of a right that the court was prepared to recognize for other litigants in the same position."[30]

The dividing line between appropriate and inappropriate collateral estoppel on issues of law is not a precise one. The First Restatement said that issue preclusion does not apply to true questions of law, unless the causes of action in the two suits "arose out of the same subject matter or transaction."[31] This would seem to limit the collateral estoppel effect of determinations on issues of law to successive actions on the same contract or based on the same tortious act, for instance. One of the leading cases, *Commissioner v. Sunnen*,[32] seemed to support this view as to the scope of collateral estoppel with respect to issues of law. That case distinguished between situations in which the legal significance of a single set of historical circumstances is involved in both cases and situations in which historically

29. See Restatement (Second) of Judgments §§ 27, 28(2) (1982); Restatement of Judgments § 70 (1942).

30. Restatement (Second) of Judgments § 28(2) cmt. b (1982).

31. Restatement of Judgments § 70 (1942).

32. 333 U.S. 591 (1948).

distinct but analytically identical facts are involved in both cases. The question involved was whether patent royalties payable under licensing agreements and assigned by the patentee to his wife were taxable income to him or to her. One agreement was made in 1928 and others at later times. A 1935 judgment involving payments to the wife in 1929-1931 under the 1928 agreement had determined, against the government's contention, that the royalties were taxable income to the wife, not the patentee. In a later action involving royalty payments in 1937 under the 1928 agreement and also under the other agreements, the Supreme Court declared that the government was not collaterally estopped by the 1935 judgment from relitigating whether the payments under the later agreements were taxable income to the patentee, even though those agreements were identical to the 1928 agreement. The Court did not justify the distinction it drew, except to say that collateral estoppel should be applied narrowly in tax cases.

The Second Restatement approaches the matter from the opposite direction, producing a rule that permits issue preclusion to be applied to true issues of law on a broader basis. It declares that preclusion does apply to pure issues of law, except if the claims in the two actions are "substantially unrelated."[33] This seems the better approach. On the one hand, it eliminates the need to distinguish issues of law from issues of ultimate fact in those ambiguous cases where the question disputed was the application of undisputed legal principles to established facts. All such cases would trigger issue preclusion because any cases in which the same historical facts were involved would be closely related. On the other hand, rulings resolving disputes over the applicable legal principles would have collateral estoppel effect only on a more limited basis, not reaching substantially unrelated claims. The interests served by the rule of issue preclusion hardly justify universally binding a party, while not binding other persons, to a possibly incorrect legal ruling—even one on the meaning of the Constitution—just because that party once litigated the legal issue in a different kind of case.

b. Inequitable Administration of Law

The *Sunnen* Court also announced another exception on the application of issue preclusion to legal issues, an exception that gives the sounder explanation for the case's result. When there has been a significant change in the "legal climate" between the time of the earlier ruling and the later suit,

---

33. Restatement (Second) of Judgments § 28(2) (1982); see Montana v. United States, 440 U.S. 147, 162-63 (1979) (dictum).

issue preclusion effect may be denied to the earlier ruling even though the same document or event is involved in the later suit. In the *Sunnen* case, a Supreme Court tax decision intervening between the 1935 ruling involving the royalties paid under the 1928 agreement and the suit involving the 1937 royalties so changed the legal climate as to make the application of issue preclusion improper, even as to the 1928 agreement. The change in legal climate did not undo the 1935 ruling, but it stopped future issue preclusion by that old decision.

The point of this exception to the issue preclusion effect of legal rulings is avoidance of the inequity that might result from perpetuating special treatment for one person when the law currently prescribes different treatment for others similarly situated. The law cannot justify such special treatment merely because the person once litigated the legal issue, if the legal climate has changed significantly in the interim. Cases invoking this exception have generally been contests between private parties and public authorities,[34] but the rationale is not necessarily so limited.[35] Any significant change in the decisions interpreting the law that causes inequity should result in the denial of issue preclusion effect to issues of law or application of law to fact decided in an earlier case.

Applying this exception necessitates some clarity of mind. It is an exception, so the burden of proof is on the invokee of issue preclusion, that is, the person seeking to avoid issue preclusion. It is distinguishable from the changed circumstances limitation on the rule of issue preclusion: when the facts or law involved in the second case have changed from those in the first, the issue involved becomes a different issue. But here the issue is exactly the same, although the legal environment has evolved so that a court would now decide the issue differently. If that is so, and if the potential difference among persons' legal treatment is serious enough to amount to inequitable administration of the laws, then the invokee will be able to make out this exception to issue preclusion.

Note also that it is only a person being stuck by the outmoded legal view who can raise the change in legal climate. Thus, in *United States v. Moser*,[36] a naval officer named Moser had won the right to a higher federal pension than had another officer named Jasper, to whom the court had later applied a different view of the relevant statute. Subsequently, the court indicated that it had read the statute unsoundly for Jasper. Then, when Moser had to

34. See Bishop v. City of Fall River, 191 N.E.2d 769 (Mass. 1963).

35. See Restatement (Second) of Judgments § 28(2) cmt. c, illus. 5 (1982).

36. 266 U.S. 236 (1924).

sue again for a later installment, the United States tried unsuccessfully to avoid issue preclusion by raising the different results for Moser and Jasper. As between Moser's earlier result against the United States and Moser's current position, there was no intervening change in the legal climate. So the Supreme Court affirmed that there should be no exception. (If instead Jasper had sued the United States again, it would have been Jasper who could have used this exception.[37])

2. Inferior Rendering Court

If a subsequent action is beyond the jurisdiction of the initial court, the subsequent court may apply an exception to issue preclusion. The court in the subsequent action will not carry over a determination by an inferior court having very much more informal procedures, such as a small-claims court. Also, a court of special competence will not carry over a determination by a regular court if the jurisdictional scheme indicates a legislative purpose against such issue preclusion.

a. Procedural Informality

The premise behind issue preclusion—that the judgment of one court having jurisdiction of the parties and subject matter and affording procedural due process is as likely to be correct as that of another—is of doubtful validity in cases where the court that rendered the first judgment is one of very limited jurisdiction. Often such courts as small-claims courts or justice of the peace courts are staffed by judges that lack legal training. The procedures of such courts are commonly designed for cases to be presented by the parties themselves, without the assistance of professional legal counsel. The rules of evidence used in superior courts may have no application. The amount in controversy is usually limited to a low figure. So even if the possibility of future litigation to which the issue would be relevant is foreseeable at the time of the first suit, it would seem unreasonable to expect a party to litigate the issue to the hilt in such a court. Similarly, there may be no practical motivation for appeal by the losing party, even if appeal would lead to a trial de novo in a higher court. Under such circumstances, holding the losing party bound on particular issues in later actions in other courts would seem unfair.

It has, accordingly, been urged by some that issue preclusion effect simply should not be given to the judgments of any court of limited jurisdic-

37. See United States v. Stone & Downer Co., 274 U.S. 225 (1927).

tion.[38] The First Restatement, in fact, endorsed this position.[39] However, most courts disagreed.[40] Indeed, in view of the weight of authority, the First Restatement withdrew its blanket position in its 1948 Supplement.

Although the authorities have not accepted an exception denying issue preclusion effect to the judgments of all courts of limited jurisdiction, it does not follow that all such judgments should receive the same issue preclusion effect as those of courts of general jurisdiction. If the procedures in the first action were not comparable to the better procedures available in the second action, in terms of quality and extensiveness, then the second court will not carry over the determinations of the first. On the one hand, a small-claims court is set up to render informal, quick, and cheap justice. No one intended its determinations to control a court of general jurisdiction handling a much more serious claim. On the other hand, this exception for informal procedure contemplates differences that cause mistrust of the earlier determinations. The mere absence of a jury right in the first action is not such a difference in procedure.[41]

The Second Restatement takes this position of recognizing an exception for procedural informality.[42] At its heart, the exception, like the Second Restatement as a whole, turns on the question of whether the invokee of issue preclusion had a full and fair opportunity to litigate the issue thoroughly in the first court.

b. Jurisdictional Specialization

Statutes purporting to confer exclusive jurisdiction over certain subjects on particular courts present the problem of whether issue preclusion effect will be given in such courts to judgments of other courts. A common situation putting the problem into play arises when certain issues essential to a case over which the federal courts have exclusive jurisdiction have previously been litigated and determined in a state court proceeding on a different claim.[43] For instance, original jurisdiction of civil actions "arising under" federal patent or copyright laws, such as infringement actions, is

---

38. E.g., Sanderson v. Niemann, 110 P.2d 1025, 1030-31 (Cal. 1941).

39. See Restatement of Judgments §71 cmt. d (1942).

40. E.g., Gollner v. Cram, 102 N.W.2d 521 (Minn. 1960); see E.H. Schopflocher, Annotation, Res Judicata As Affected by Limitation of Jurisdiction of Court Which Rendered Judgment, 147 A.L.R. 196, 226-32 (1943).

41. See Parklane Hosiery Co. v. Shore, 439 U.S. 322, 332 n.19 (1979).

42. See Restatement (Second) of Judgments §28(3) cmt. d (1982).

43. Cf. Loomis v. Loomis, 42 N.E.2d 495 (N.Y. 1942) (denying preclusive effect in state divorce action to prior state family court determination of marital status).

vested exclusively in the United States District Courts.[44] State courts, nevertheless, can entertain some kinds of cases, such as unfair competition claims or suits seeking enforcement of licenses, which require interpretation of the federal patent or copyright laws, require application of those laws to particular facts, or require finding those facts. If, in adjudicating such a case, the state court decides an issue in a way that would otherwise be appropriate for issue preclusion, will the federal court permit relitigation of that issue in a later action arising under those laws and, as such, within the exclusive jurisdiction of the federal court? To get more specific, assume that a manufacturer promises to pay for the licensing of a patent; that the patentee has to sue to enforce the agreement in a state court, but the manufacturer successfully defends by establishing that the patent was void; and that later the patentee sues the manufacturer in federal court to enjoin infringement of the patent. Will the state court's ruling preclude federal relitigation of the issue of the patent's validity?

The First Restatement took the negative position by generally providing in § 71: "Where a court has incidentally determined a matter which it would have had no jurisdiction to determine in an action brought directly to determine it, the judgment is not conclusive in a subsequent action brought to determine the matter directly." Thus, the First Restatement declared that the state judgment would not preclude relitigation of the patent issue in federal court.[45]

Certain federal cases, however, indicate that the answer may not be so simple. In *Becher v. Contoure Laboratories*,[46] the Supreme Court ruled that a federal court in a suit for patent infringement had to give collateral estoppel effect to a particular state court judgment, which had determined that the patentee had received the information on which the patent was based from the defendant's assignor, even though the inevitable consequence of that determination would be to invalidate the patent.

Judge Learned Hand, in *Lyons v. Westinghouse Electric Corp.*,[47] sought to reconcile the result in the *Becher* case with the quoted provision of the First

44. See 28 U.S.C. § 1338(a).

45. See Restatement of Judgments § 71 cmt. c (1942).

46. 279 U.S. 388 (1929).

47. 222 F.2d 184, 188-89 (2d Cir. 1955) (in this antitrust treble damage action, the federal court ruled against issue preclusion by a prior state judgment in an accounting suit that had found the challenged conduct did not violate the antitrust laws).

Restatement, saying there is a distinction "between the finding of one of the constituent facts that together make up a claim and the entire congeries of such facts, taken as a unit; an estoppel is good as to the first but not as to the second. It is possible to read § 71 of the Restatement of Judgments with such a limitation: that is to say if 'matter' be read as all the 'operative facts' that together make up a right." More helpful than this distinction between constituent facts and congeries of facts was Judge Hand's more general conclusion in the *Lyons* case: "Thus the inquiry comes down to whether, when Congress gave exclusive jurisdiction to the district court over wrongs committed under the Anti-Trust Acts, it only meant that the 'person who shall be injured' must sue in the district court to recover damages; or whether it also meant that the district court must have unfettered power to decide the claim, regardless of the findings of any other courts ...." He concluded that in the case of the antitrust laws, the grant of exclusive federal jurisdiction over treble damage actions implies "an immunity of their decisions from any prejudgment elsewhere," at least where the estoppel would include "the whole nexus of facts that makes up the wrong."

The grant of exclusive jurisdiction in patent cases, however, would not necessarily carry the same implication. The question, basically, goes to the legislative purpose underlying the grant of exclusive jurisdiction. The cases require any legislative purpose against issue preclusion to be clearly expressed.[48] Accordingly, most recent cases have indicated that state patent decisions will carry over to federal court.[49] In other types of suits, although in some circumstances state rulings will not carry over to exclusive federal jurisdiction,[50] most often they will.[51]

Because of cases like those patent cases, the Second Restatement is unwilling to subscribe to the categorical exception contained in the First Restatement, and it follows instead a narrower approach that looks essentially to the legislative purpose. "The question in each such case would be resolved in light of the legislative purpose in vesting exclusive jurisdiction in a particular court."[52]

---

48. See Kremer v. Chemical Constr. Corp., 456 U.S. 461, 468 (1982).

49. See, e.g., Syntex Ophthalmics, Inc. v. Novicky, 767 F.2d 901 (Fed. Cir. 1985); Vanderveer v. Erie Malleable Iron Co., 238 F.2d 510 (3d Cir. 1956).

50. See, e.g., Brown v. Felsen, 442 U.S. 127 (1979) (certain issues in bankruptcy case).

51. See generally 18 Charles Alan Wright, Arthur R. Miller & Edward H. Cooper, Federal Practice and Procedure § 4470 (1981 & Supp. 1999) (citing cases).

52. Restatement (Second) of Judgments § 28(3) cmt. e (1982).

3. Different Burden of Persuasion

Courts will not preclude an issue if the burden of persuasion in the subsequent action would be more favorable to the side that initially lost on the issue than it was in that initial action.

Generally, the failure to prove by the party having the burden of persuasion on the existence of a fact conclusively establishes the nonexistence of that fact for issue preclusion purposes. However, if the party who failed to carry the burden of persuasion on the issue in the first action would not have to bear it in the second, that party should not be precluded from relitigating it in the second suit. For an example from the old days, assume that in a state where the plaintiff had the burden of proving freedom from contributory negligence, *A* was unable to recover from *B* because *A* failed to bear that particular burden regarding *A*'s own negligence. The state had no compulsory counterclaim rule. In a later suit by *B* against *A* for negligence in connection with the same accident, *B* would then have the burden of proof on the issue of *A*'s negligence, and therefore *A* would not be precluded by the earlier judgment.[53] This result is not to say that the issue of *A*'s negligence is not the same in both cases. Instead, the burden of persuasion difference operates as an exception to the rule of issue preclusion, according to the usual analysis.

Similarly, even though the burden may be upon the same party in both actions, issue preclusion should not apply if the invokee of issue preclusion had a significantly heavier burden in the first action, or if the invoker has a significantly heavier burden in the second action. Thus, acquittal of the defendant in a criminal prosecution for theft of public property would not preclude the government in its later civil damage action against the defendant.[54]

4. Inability to Appeal

Courts generally will not bind a party on an issue if as a matter of law that party could not in the initial action have obtained appellate review on that issue.

Occasionally a party is unable as a matter of law to get appellate review of what may be an erroneous ruling. This can happen if the case becomes

53. See Restatement (Second) of Judgments § 28(4) cmt. f, illus. 10 (1982).

54. See generally 18 Charles Alan Wright, Arthur R. Miller & Edward H. Cooper, Federal Practice and Procedure § 4422 (1981 & Supp. 1999).

moot while the appeal is pending. The general rule is that there should be no issue preclusion in this situation.[55] In some jurisdictions, when a case becomes moot while on appeal, the appellate court is empowered both to dismiss the appeal and to vacate the lower court's judgment, and then it may be necessary for the party whose appeal is dismissed because of mootness to request that the appellate court also vacate the lower court's judgment in order to avoid its issue preclusion effect.[56]

If appeal is impossible for other reasons, such as an insufficient amount in controversy, the rationale of the exception recognized in the mootness cases would seem equally applicable. But this exception would not apply when appeal is legally possible, but the party decides to forgo it because of the small economic value involved or because the parties are settling. Nor does the exception apply when appeal is legally possible, but the appellate court in its discretion denies review.[57]

What if the party who was *unsuccessful* on an issue nevertheless won the judgment? In this situation, normally the issue was not essential to the judgment rendered, so there would be no issue preclusion anyway. But what if the winning party was *successful* on an essential issue, but in a later case that issue's prior determination has become unfavorable to the party's position? Because one can appeal only rulings adverse to one's interests, usually this party could not have appealed. Therefore, the inability-to-appeal exception means that issue preclusion usually does not work to bind the party who prevailed on an issue.

5. Unforeseeability

In compelling circumstances, a court will not apply issue preclusion if such application was unforeseeable at the time of the initial action and such unforeseeability may have affected the effort therein by the party now sought to be precluded.

The most famous case to have struggled with the problem of unforeseeability was *Evergreens v. Nunan.*[58] To deal with the problem, Judge Learned Hand again drew a rarefied distinction, this time between "ultimate facts" and "mediate data," the latter being premises from which the

55. See Restatement (Second) of Judgments §28(1) (1982).

56. See United States v. Munsingwear, 340 U.S. 36 (1950).

57. See generally 18 Susan Bandes & Lawrence B. Solum, Moore's Federal Practice §132.03[4][k] (3d ed. 1999).

58. 141 F.2d 927, 929 (2d Cir. 1944).

ultimate facts could be inferred. To place a reasonable restriction on the overreach of issue preclusion, he focused on the role played by the facts in the second action and ruled that only ultimate facts therein were subject to preclusion. This difficult approach had some impact on res judicata law for a time, but it has since faded from view.

Much more influential in the long run was an approach that Judge Hand passed up. In the course of explaining the court's position, he expressed some significant considerations that had not been so well stated before:

> The stake in the first suit may have been too small to justify great trouble and expense in its prosecution or defense; and the chance that a fact decided in it, even though necessary to its result, may later become important between the parties may have been extremely remote.... What jural relevance facts may acquire in the future it is often impossible even remotely to anticipate. Were the law to be recast, it would... be a pertinent inquiry whether the conclusiveness... of facts decided in the first might not properly be limited to future controversies which could be thought reasonably in prospect when the first suit was tried.... Logical relevance is of infinite possibility; there is no conceivable limit which can be put to it. Defeat in one suit might entail results beyond all calculation by either party; a trivial controversy might bring utter disaster in its train.

But if unforeseeability of the possible future significance of the fact is the important matter, why not phrase the doctrine so as to reflect that directly? Judge Hand apparently felt he could not stray so far from prior precedent.

Some later courts did not feel so limited. In *Hyman v. Regenstein*,[59] for instance, the Fifth Circuit purported to build upon the *Evergreens* policy and "restated" the principle as being that "collateral estoppel by judgment is applicable only when it is evident from the pleadings and record that determination of the fact in question was necessary to the final judgment and it was foreseeable that the fact would be of importance in possible future litigation."

The Second Restatement expresses general disapproval of any rule that would limit issue preclusion to Judge Hand's ultimate facts. Its approach establishes instead an exception, so that "preclusion should not operate to foreclose redetermination of an issue if it was unforeseeable when the first

59. 258 F.2d 502, 511 (5th Cir. 1958) (dictum).

action was litigated that the issue would arise" again; it further required that the lack of foreseeability "may have contributed to the losing party's failure to litigate the issue fully."[60]

In fact, the drafters of the Second Restatement warned that such exceptional cases should be rare and that relitigation should follow only a clear and convincing showing of need. Their examples of where their constrained exception for unforeseeability would apply included a determination as to a taxpayer's specific property that acquires tremendously greater financial significance in a second action after an intervening amendment to the tax code.

6. Generalized Exception

In compelling circumstances, a court will neither bind on an issue someone who for some reason lacked a full and fair opportunity to litigate it, nor apply issue preclusion when substantive policies overwhelm res judicata.

Relative to claim preclusion, issue preclusion has numerous and flexible exceptions.[61] But this free-wheeling approach represented by the generalized exception has its dangers. "If relitigation were permitted whenever it might result in a more accurate determination, in the name of 'justice,' the very values served by preclusion would be quickly destroyed. The risks of imposing a wrong decision on later litigation, moreover, are accounted for in many ways by a wide array of limitations already explored.... Truly exceptional cases may justify recognition of an additional general power to make exceptions in the name of justice. Any such exceptional principle, however, must be confined within narrow limits if it is to do more good than harm."[62] Accordingly, this generalized exception has crystallized around two ideas:

a. Lack of Full and Fair Opportunity

The Second Restatement ends its treatment of issue preclusion by generalizing that the doctrine should not apply when the invokee lacked a full and fair opportunity, or incentive, to litigate the issue. Here the risk that the exception will consume the rule is glaringly obvious. Therefore the

---

60. Restatement (Second) of Judgments § 28 cmt. i (1982).

61. See supra Chapter 4-B.

62. 18 Charles Alan Wright, Arthur R. Miller & Edward H. Cooper, Federal Practice and Procedure § 4426, at 265-66 (1981).

drafters again warned that such exceptional cases should be rare and that relitigation should follow only a clear and convincing showing of need. Their examples made the point:

> In an action in which an issue is litigated and determined, one party may conceal from the other information that would materially affect the outcome of the case. Such concealment may be of particular concern if there is a fiduciary relationship between the parties.[[63]] Or one of the parties may have been laboring under a mental or physical disability that impeded effective litigation and that has since been removed. Or it may be evident from the jury's verdict that the verdict was the result of compromise.[[64]] Or the amount in controversy in the first action may have been so small in relation to the amount in controversy in the second that preclusion would be plainly unfair.
>
> ...Such a refusal to give the first judgment preclusive effect should not occur without a compelling showing of unfairness, nor should it be based simply on a conclusion that the first determination was patently erroneous. But confined within proper limits, discretion to deny preclusive effect to a determination under the circumstances stated is central to the fair administration of preclusion doctrine.[65]

b. Conflicting Substantive Policy

Within constitutional bounds, the legislature is free to prescribe the circumstances in which res judicata will and will not be applicable. Statutes expressly doing that are rare, nonetheless.

Courts also can effectuate substantive policies by creating exceptions from issue preclusion.[66] Out of respect for courts' limited lawmaking role, however, they should do so only in compelling circumstances of substantive need.[67]

---

63. See Spilker v. Hankin, 188 F.2d 35 (D.C. Cir. 1951).

64. See Taylor v. Hawkinson, 306 P.2d 797 (Cal. 1957).

65. Restatement (Second) of Judgments § 28(5)(c) cmt. j (1982).

66. See, e.g., United States v. LaFatch, 565 F.2d 81 (6th Cir. 1977) (bribery and extortion).

67. See Restatement (Second) of Judgments § 28(5)(a) (1982).

C. Special Applications: Multiple Determinations

Some special applications of issue preclusion illuminate how it works.

1. Cumulative Determinations

If several issues in a case were litigated and determined, each is precluded provided that its determination was essential to judgment.

Consider as an example that *P* sues *D* for extensive property damage resulting from an automobile accident. *D* defends by denying both her own negligence and *P*'s ownership of the car. After trial, there is a valid and final judgment for *P*. Pursuant to an agreement between *P* and *D* permitting claim-splitting, *P* then sues *D* for personal injury in the same accident and invokes issue preclusion on *D*'s negligence, with ownership not being in issue as to personal injury. The result is that issue preclusion or, more precisely, direct estoppel applies.

The example in fact describes the very common situation where a court makes a series of rulings on issues to reach a judgment, and each of them is a necessary step toward that judgment. In such a situation, each ruling supports issue preclusion. The norm is that issue preclusion could lie on a multitude of issues in a case.

Contrariwise, if the adjudicator in the initial action ruled that *D* had been negligent but that *P*'s nonownership prevented recovery, there would be no issue preclusion in the subsequent action because the finding of *D*'s negligence was not essential to judgment.

2. Ambiguous Determinations

If one cannot tell which of several possible issues was determined in a case, then none is precluded.

Whenever a party seeks to invoke the doctrine of issue preclusion to foreclose an issue, it is necessary for that party to prove that the issue in fact was determined in the prior action. If the invoker fails, issue preclusion will not apply.

Often the invoker can make the required showing from the formal record of the prior proceeding. Sometimes the judgment itself will reflect the fact that certain issues were contested and decided. More commonly, however, the invoker will have to present other elements of the record as well. If the case was tried to a jury and decided on a special verdict or a general verdict accompanied by answers to interrogatories, the jury instructions will show what was litigated, the verdict will normally show what was decided, and the judgment will reveal which issues were essential to the judgment rendered. If the case was tried to the judge, the judge's findings of fact and conclusions of law will show what was decided and essential, although it may not accurately reveal whether the issues were actually litigated. If the case was decided on a motion to dismiss or for summary judgment, the motion will usually reveal the issues litigated, and the judgment will show what was decided and essential. If such a motion is denied, it does not generate a judgment, but the ruling on it nevertheless should reflect a litigated and determined issue that may have preclusive effect when a final judgment in the action is rendered. For example, if the defendant moves to dismiss for failure to state a claim on the ground that the complaint showed on its face that the statute of limitations had run and if the defendant fails thereon, the court's order should show its determination of a litigated issue; if the case later proceeds to judgment for the plaintiff, the judgment will reveal that the determination was essential, thus bringing the rule of issue preclusion to bear on it.

In other situations, it may not be possible to show from the materials in the official record just what was determined in the prior action. The plaintiff's pleading may be in the form of a common count, and the defendant may have pleaded a general denial. The case may have been submitted to a jury and decided on a general verdict. Resort may then have to be had to a transcript of the trial, or other evidence extrinsic to the judgment record itself, to prove what issues were actually litigated and determined in such a case. Extrinsic evidence may show that issues apparently framed by materials in the record in fact were abandoned, as by admission or stipulation. Such extrinsic evidence is broadly admissible today under the rules of evidence in most jurisdictions, and the extrinsic evidence can even contradict the formal record in order to show the true prior situation.[68]

Unless the party seeking to invoke issue preclusion can prove, either by the record or by extrinsic evidence, that the issue was actually litigated and determined and was essential to the judgment, there will be no preclusion and the issues may be relitigated. This is true even though it is clear that *some* issues were actually litigated, determined, and essential.[69]

Reconsider the preceding example, except that in the initial action *D* won by a jury's general verdict, and in the subsequent action it was *D* who

68. See infra Chapter 11-B-2.
69. See Russell v. Place, 94 U.S. 606 (1877).

pleaded issue preclusion to refute her negligence. That is, *P* sued *D* for extensive property damage resulting from an automobile accident. *D* defended by denying both her own negligence and *P*'s ownership of the car. After trial, there was a valid and final judgment for *D* on a general verdict. Pursuant to an agreement between *P* and *D* permitting claim-splitting, *P* then sued *D* for personal injury in the same accident, and *D* invoked issue preclusion on *D*'s negligence, with ownership not being in issue as to personal injury. The result is that issue preclusion does not apply, because one cannot tell if the jury found nonnegligence or nonownership.

For a similar example, in an action in which both the defendant's negligence and the plaintiff's contributory negligence were in issue, a judgment for the defendant on a general verdict would have to be based on a finding either that the defendant was not negligent or that the plaintiff was contributorily negligent, or both. But unless it can be shown by extrinsic evidence which of the possibilities is correct, there will be no collateral estoppel effect if the defendant needs to carry over just one of them. (Contrariwise, if the defendant is happy to carry over either one of them, as where the plaintiff sues the defendant for the same accident, then ambiguity would no longer present itself. Either nonnegligence or contributory negligence would suffice to defeat the new lawsuit, and the jury found at least one of them in the prior action.)

So runs the usual approach: ambiguity defeats issue preclusion. A few cases hold that an ambiguous judgment will be preclusive on either issue (say, nonnegligence or contributory negligence), whichever is needed.[70] But most cases do not. If the decisive issue cannot be identified as having been determined, the interest in judicial economy that would be promoted by preclusion is too weak to outweigh the party's interest in a chance to prove the party's case.

3. Alternative Determinations

Here is a special rule on a very close question: if the adjudicator determined several issues in a case and each of those determinations without the others sufficed to support the judgment, then none by itself is precluded under the view of the Second Restatement. Older authority held each to be precluded, and this might still be the preferable view and seems to be regaining favor in the courts.

70. See, e.g., Kelley v. Curtiss, 108 A.2d 431 (N.J. 1954).

Consider again the continuing example of *P* v. *D*, except that in the initial action *D* won by a jury's special verdict finding both nonnegligence and nonownership. That is, *P* sued *D* for extensive property damage resulting from an automobile accident. *D* defended by denying both her own negligence and *P*'s ownership of the car. After trial, there was a valid and final judgment for *D* on a special verdict finding both nonnegligence and nonownership. Pursuant to an agreement between *P* and *D* permitting claim-splitting, *P* then sued *D* for personal injury in the same accident, and *D* invoked issue preclusion on *D*'s negligence, with ownership not being in issue as to personal injury. Now what result?

This variant of the example reveals that a case may involve litigation and determination of two or more alternative issues, any of which would be sufficient to support the judgment rendered. In such a case, one of the alternatives is essential to the judgment, but no particular one. At the same time, it is true that the other alternative rulings are nonessential, and accordingly should have no issue preclusion effect. The trouble is that there is no way to say which of the alternative determinations is essential and which nonessential. If there is no way to say which is the essential one, preclusion should apply to all or to none. Cases have taken both positions.[71]

The Second Restatement takes the position that the judgment is not preclusive on any of the alternative issues.[72] Its position is based on cases like *Halpern v. Schwartz*.[73] Evelyn Halpern had been involuntarily adjudicated a bankrupt on each of three different grounds, only one of which had involved a finding of actual intent to hinder, delay, or defraud creditors. In a later proceeding Halpern sought a discharge in bankruptcy, although the Bankruptcy Act provided that a discharge shall not be granted if the court finds the bankrupt acted with such an intent. The trial court denied Halpern her discharge, holding that the prior determination of intent was preclusive. The United States Court of Appeals for the Second Circuit reversed, holding that a judgment resting on alternative grounds is not preclusive as to any of the grounds.

The Second Restatement's rationale is that any one of the alternative issues may not have been fully contested. It may not have been so carefully or rigorously considered as it would have been if it had been presented alone, and so it has some of the characteristics of dicta. Moreover, the loser

---

71. See generally 18 Susan Bandes & Lawrence B. Solum, Moore's Federal Practice § 132.03[4][b] (3d ed. 1999).

72. See Restatement (Second) of Judgments § 27 cmt. i (1982).

73. 426 F.2d 102 (2d Cir. 1970).

may have been rightly discouraged from appealing by the strength of another alternative determination, thinking that this latter ground would be upheld and others not even reached; society indeed has no interest in creating incentives to take such doomed appeals.

The drafters of the Second Restatement were not blind to the arguments against wasteful relitigation: the issue was litigated and determined; the determination supported the judgment; and, unlike nonessential rulings, the party was able to appeal the alternative losses. The drafters felt, however, that the arguments for nonpreclusion are slightly more persuasive on balance. But they also recognized that the balance can swing. If there was an appeal, then any alternative determination that was affirmed becomes binding. The idea is that the exercise of appellate review swings the balance of conflicting policies toward preclusion. So, all authorities agree that if the losing party does appeal the judgment, and the appellate court upholds the judgment as to one alternative but not the other, the issue upheld on appeal, and only it, will support preclusion. Likewise, if the appellate court upholds the lower court on both issues, the judgment will have preclusive effect as to both.[74]

Moreover, even without an appeal, if all the alternative issues arise in the subsequent action, issue preclusion will apply. This situation in fact is much more common than the *Halpern* situation. An example would be where the defendant wins by specific findings of both nonnegligence and contributory negligence, the plaintiff sues the defendant again for the same accident, and the defendant then pleads issue preclusion. Here all authorities agree that *D* will succeed, because all the policy arguments for nonpreclusion have fallen away. But to get to that result, the Second Restatement must resort to the awkward analysis that the alternative rulings of nonnegligence and contributory negligence are merely alternative bases for an essential determination of a single "issue" more broadly defined as nonliability.[75]

However, let us return to the initial example of two unappealed alternative determinations of nonnegligence and nonownership, where someone is trying to carry over just one of them. Is the Second Restatement right in singling out this situation for a rule of nonpreclusion? Admittedly, the judgment is not based on one issue more than on the other, so it must be said that it is conclusive as to neither issue or as to both. The Second Restatement opted for neither being preclusive. But the First Restatement endorsed

74. See Restatement (Second) of Judgments § 27 cmt. o (1982).

75. See Restatement (Second) of Judgments § 27 cmt. i, illus. 16 (1982).

the view that the judgment is preclusive on both issues, explaining: "It seems obvious that it should not be held that neither is material, and hence both should be held to be material."[76]

Unfortunately, the First Restatement's explanation failed to convince. The question is anything but "obvious." Its resolution turns on rather subtle concerns. It is a close and difficult balance of many considerations. The final consideration that seems to us to swing the balance against the Second Restatement's rule is that under it *D* is in a worse position after winning on two issues than if she had won just on nonnegligence. That is bizarre. What could her attorney have done to avoid this quandary? Not much, in the usual case. If *D*'s attorney abdicates on the ownership issue and litigates just negligence, this strategy avoids the rule for alternative determinations but risks losing the whole case. Imagine trying to explain that losing strategy to the client! *D*'s attorney might instead attempt to get the judge to cooperate in subverting the rule by reaching the nonownership issue only if necessary, but such cooperation is unlikely to be forthcoming or be efficacious. Thus, the Second Restatement's rule can put a party in a serious fix for no great reason.

Noteworthily, this Second Restatement rule has not received wide acceptance in the courts,[77] and even the Second Circuit has since backed away from its *Halpern* decision.[78] After consideration of all these arguments pro and con, and the implications of and reactions to the "modern" rule regarding alternative determinations, it does appear on balance that the law would be better off returning to the First Restatement rule. Preclusion should be the rule for alternative issues. In the relatively few cases of inappropriate collateral estoppel on alternative issues, such as in the situation of unforeseeability, the law can avoid issue preclusion by means of one of the varied exceptions to issue preclusion.

---

76. See Restatement of Judgments §68 cmt. n (1942).

77. See Adam Siegler, Note, Alternative Grounds in Collateral Estoppel, 17 Loy. L.A. L. Rev. 1085, 1100 n.106 (1984).

78. See Winters v. Lavine, 574 F.2d 46, 66-68 (2d Cir. 1978).

CHAPTER 8

EFFECTS ON NONPARTIES

A. Privies

The conclusory label of "privies" is used to describe people who were nonparties to an action but who in certain circumstances are nevertheless subject to generally the same rules of res judicata as are the former parties, the basis for this treatment being some sort of representational relationship between a former party and the nonparty. Normally, a privy is *bound* by and entitled to the *benefits* of claim and issue preclusion as though the privy stood in the shoes of the related party.

As a general proposition, a judgment can bind only persons who were before the court. Being bound by a judgment includes being bound by the preclusive effects of the judgment, as well as being bound in other ways. From this it would seem to follow that only named parties to the action can be bound by res judicata—and only those named parties who have been reached by the court's process or have submitted to jurisdiction. This proposition would seem implicit in the concept of due process. But this proposition is not strictly true. The law of res judicata has historically recognized that some persons not parties in any sense may be bound in some ways by a judgment. And this result does not contravene due process notions.

Due process is concerned with the substance of fundamental fairness: the full and fair day in court. That hearing, however, may be supplied by devices other than the formal joinder of every party to be affected by the judgment, now or forever. For instance, once an issue relating to an interest in real property has been fully litigated between the title owner and another party, the issue is settled against later purchasers or devisees as well.

A beneficiary may be bound on issues litigated by the trustee. Due process, then, is not violated merely because a nonparty is held bound. In fact, all that due process guarantees is a full and fair day in court enjoyed in person *or through a representative.* Without that qualification, the right to a "day in court" is but a misleading slogan.[1]

Due process allows binding many more nonparties than most persons assume. After all, the loose demands of due process explain how the legislature and administrators can bind people and their property, when those people have received representation only in the loosest sense. Analogously, a court's judgment could bind, among others, all similarly situated persons whose interests received adequate representation, binding them not only through the flexible doctrine of stare decisis as it does but also through the strictures of res judicata as it could.

Society, however, has chosen, as expressed in its res judicata law, to go much less far in binding nonparties by judgment than it constitutionally could. It is this restraint that helps sharply to distinguish adjudication from the rest of governmental decisionmaking. Res judicata will bind only those nonparties closely related to the representative party or, as the law phrases it, those in privity with a party.[2]

Which nonparties, then, are closely related enough to a party to be bound under the law of res judicata? As suggested, they are labeled privies. But privity is a term that is not self-explanatory. It is a term of art used in many fields of law, with very different meanings. On the one hand, privity for res judicata purposes is not to be narrowly defined as some sort of quasi-party, because persons may sometimes be bound by judgments who do not fall close to any vernacular sense of parties. Privies include more persons than that. On the other hand, privity for res judicata purposes does not go so far as to bind all persons in some sense represented in the action, or those represented to the degree required by due process. Privies include far fewer persons than that. So, res judicata law binds many nonparties, but it chooses to bind fewer nonparties than it could.

Okay, so whom does the law in fact choose to place into this group of privies? Unfortunately, the term is not used with consistent meaning by all writers. Indeed, only certain of the writers maintain that the term ultimately

1. See Robert G. Bone, Rethinking the "Day in Court" Ideal and Nonparty Preclusion, 67 N.Y.U. L. Rev. 193 (1992).

2. See Tice v. American Airlines, 162 F.3d 966 (7th Cir. 1998).

has meaning—that privity is an independently meaningful concept, one that serves to identify at least some, although maybe not all, cases in which nonparties may be bound by a judgment's preclusive effects.

Henry Campbell Black, for instance, adopted for res judicata purposes the classic definition of privity as a "mutual or successive relationship to the same rights of property"; noting that some authorities had recognized other forms of privity for other purposes—privies in law, in blood, or in representation—Black insisted that "we have to do only with privies in estate."[3] To square his limited definition of privity with what he characterized as the "universal rule" and "canon of general jurisprudence" that "all who are neither parties to a judgment nor privies to such parties are wholly free from the estoppel of the judgment," Black found it necessary to recognize as exceptions the cases of warrantors, indemnitors, and certain other "especial cases" where nonparties were bound.[4]

Professor James William Moore also saw privity as a term that is independently meaningful in this context, although his view of its scope was considerably broader than Black's. He held that privity is present in the following three relationships: successive relationship to the same right of property (e.g., that of transferor and transferee); concurrent relationship to the same right of property (e.g., that of trustee and beneficiary); and representation of the interests of the same person.[5]

In view of the diversity and looseness of views concerning the meaning of privity in this context, the term's utility is rather limited. To the extent that the term connotes successive or concurrent interests in property, it is helpful as a test of inclusion. That is, it does suggest certain kinds of cases in which nonparties may be bound. But the term does not help at all as a test of exclusion. There is nothing inherent in the concept of privity that explains why in some situations nonparties are bound and in others they are not.

Accordingly, some authorities, including the First Restatement,[6] have used the term to describe any relationship that is sufficient to warrant applying a judgment's preclusive effects against a nonparty. Under that view, privity "is merely a word used to say that the relationship between the one

3. 2 Henry Campbell Black, A Treatise on the Law of Judgments 830 (2d ed. 1902).

4. 2 Henry Campbell Black, A Treatise on the Law of Judgments 908 (2d ed. 1902).

5. See 1B James Wm. Moore, Moore's Federal Practice ¶ 0.411[1], at III-215 (2d ed. 1996).

6. See Restatement of Judgments § 83 cmt. a (1942).

who is a party on the record and another is close enough to include that other within the res judicata."[7]

Under such a conclusory definition, the term privity is of little, if any, help in identifying the situations in which a nonparty may be bound by res judicata. Therefore, the Second Restatement eliminated the use of the term privity in connection with the preclusive effects of judgments. Instead, it treats in more than twenty separate sections the specific classes of nonparties falling to some degree within the reach of the binding rules of res judicata.[8]

However, if the word privity is clearly recognized as being conclusory, it remains useful as a general descriptive term. It facilitates a statement of the doctrine of res judicata in all of its phases: res judicata is generally applicable in later actions between the same parties or those in privity with them. Thus, persons in privity with a party—some subset of those persons whose interests are represented by a party to the action—may be bound. Of course, if privies are bound by a judgment, they would also be entitled to the benefits of res judicata. In sum, the First Restatement's usage is a good one.

Still, whichever approach is taken—defining privity, using it as a conclusory label, or discarding the term—some stab at identifying the nonparties who are bound remains necessary. The premise is that res judicata law goes much less far than it constitutionally could. There must be some substantial reasons in policy to bind a nonparty, outweighing the social costs of binding a nonparty. The law then draws a clear, simple, and rigid rule that approximates that policy balance. For example, nonparties whose claims are extinguished by judgments obtained by others include future holders of interests in property involved in litigation and beneficiaries of a trust involved in litigation to which the trustee is a party. Contrariwise, nonparties who have interests adverse to all parties suffer no issue preclusion effect. The doctrine of privity then makes sense, even if it will appear somewhat arbitrary at the boundary.

Incidentally, the problem of identifying privies often is not so acute in the case of merger and bar, because those subdoctrines apply only to later suits on the same claim, and the question of who may be bound normally turns on the same considerations that determine identity of claim. Issue preclusion can apply to many different claims, however, and the question

---

7. Bruszewski v. United States, 181 F.2d 419, 423 (3d Cir. 1950) (Goodrich, J., concurring).

8. Restatement (Second) of Judgments §§ 39-63 (1982).

of which persons are bound is one of the most important questions associated with it.

Moreover, once some categories of privies are identified, it becomes obvious that they differ widely in nature, and especially in the nature of the relationship of privy to party. As the intensity of the privity relationship tails off, qualifications and exceptions to the binding effects of the judgment start sprouting up. This subject thus becomes even more complicated. Indeed, the only general thing safe to say is that this subject is dominated by many complicated specific formulations.

Let us nevertheless look, after all this buildup, at various common situations in which nonparties may be bound. There are two basic categories of privies for purposes of res judicata according to the Second Restatement. It classifies them either as persons having substantive legal relationships with a party or as persons represented by a party. But its classification is a little misleading, because in fact the first class comprises only substantive relationships that involve some degree of representation and the second class requires more of a relationship than mere representation.

1. Substantive Privity

Privies include persons who have or had any one of a wide variety of substantive legal relationships with a party, when that relationship in a sense created a representative role. For example, a successor in interest to property is a privy with respect to a judgment determining his predecessor's interest in that property.[9] For a different example, a member of a partnership is to a more limited extent deemed a privy with respect to a judgment to which her partner was a party.[10]

a. Successive Interests

As noted, all users of the term privity use it to include one basic situation in which nonparties may be bound by judgments: that in which the nonparty has an interest in the property that was the subject of the former proceeding. A transferee of an interest in property, who received the interest after the commencement of an action concerning the property between the transferor and a third party, is in privity with the transferor and so is bound or benefited by the adjudication relating to that property interest.

9. See generally Restatement (Second) of Judgments §§ 43-44 (1982).
10. See generally Restatement (Second) of Judgments § 60 (1982).

The rule is a broad one. First, the form of transfer is irrelevant, so long as it was a valid one; purchasers, mortgagees, donees, heirs, trustees, and receivers may be bound by judgments relating to property entered against their predecessors in title.[11] Second, although this rule does not apply when the transferee acquired the interest before the commencement of the action involving the transferor, it does apply if the interest was acquired after the judgment against the transferor, and also when the interest was acquired pendente lite. Third, the rule applies even if the transferee was unaware of the action involving the transferor, unless the subject of the action was like a negotiable instrument and the transferee was like a holder in due course, or unless the third party knew that the transferee was unaware of the action.[12]

Although transferees of a property interest thus may be bound by a judgment affecting that interest, the judgment may not have strictly the same effects on the transferee—the bound privy—as it does on the transferor—the actual party. The transferor will be precluded from relitigating the same issues in any later suit against the third party, whether or not the later action concerns the property affected by the earlier judgment. The transferee, contrariwise, will be bound only insofar as the issues are relevant to the interest in the transferred property. Thus, assume both *A* and *B* own bonds of the same series issued by *C* Corporation, and *A* brings action on one of the bonds against *C*. In that action it is held that the bond issue was ultra vires. *A* next sells her bonds to *B*, who later sues *C* on the bonds received by transfer from *A* and also on those previously owned by *B*. Then *B* is bound on the ultra vires issue insofar as the bonds acquired from *A* are concerned, indeed all of them, but not with respect to the bonds *B* previously owned.[13]

In its other usages, the term privity of estate describes a relationship that runs both ways, so that the predecessor in interest is in privity with the successor, and vice versa. In the context of preclusion, however, the term marks a one-way street. A successor in interest may be bound by a judgment to which the predecessor was a party, but the converse is not true. That is, a judgment in an action to which the successor was a party will not have preclusive effect on the predecessor.[14]

11. See Restatement (Second) of Judgments §43 cmt. f (1982).
12. See Restatement (Second) of Judgments §44 (1982).
13. See Restatement of Judgments §89 cmt. f, illus. 7 (1942).
14. See Restatement (Second) of Judgments §43 cmt. e (1982).

In summary, if the term privity is understood as relating to the relationship of successive ownership of the same interest, it does serve to identify some kinds of cases in which nonparties may be bound by the preclusive effects of judgments. If the term were used only in that limited sense, however, the traditional statement that "res judicata binds only parties or their privies" would not be accurate, because many other nonparties may be bound in certain situations. To begin with, privity includes other substantive relationships of lesser intensity than successive ownership. But the lesser relationship implies that fewer of the party preclusion rules will carry over to the privy.

b. *Other Substantive Relationships of Decreasing Closeness*

The Second Restatement treats a whole series of privies, including bailors and bailees, assignors and assignees, family members, co-obligors, co-obligees, partnerships, and associations. Each has its own special res judicata rules and exceptions.[15] For our purposes of explanation, however, the focus needs to be narrower.

Partners. Generally, if an injured person sues a partner upon a liability incurred in the course of partnership business and wins, the judgment renders the property of the partnership subject to execution. If instead a partner sues an outsider upon a claim in favor of the partnership, judgment extinguishes the claim, and also gives rise to issue preclusion in any subsequent action concerning obligations of the partnership. Otherwise, the other partners are not bound merely by virtue of their partnership.[16]

That sounds somewhat complicated. But that is the point. As the substantive relationship tails off, the res judicata rules and exceptions for privies become less preclusive, and hence more complicated. And as always, each jurisdiction's res judicata law could differ on this subject.

Indemnitors. The third-party impleader authorized by Federal Rule of Civil Procedure 14 is a device that makes a nonparty into a party. In the case of indemnity, warranty, contribution, or subrogation, a defendant may make a person into a third-party defendant under Rule 14, and thus into a party to the action who will be bound in a way similar to an original party. The third party to be impleaded must be susceptible to personal jurisdiction, however. And even when jurisdiction exists, the trial court still may

---

15. See Restatement (Second) of Judgments §§45-61 (1982).
16. See Restatement (Second) of Judgments §60 (1982).

deny impleader in the exercise of its discretion. In *Goodhart v. United States Lines,*[17] a defendant employer, who had been sued for damages stemming from the negligence of its employee, was denied the right to implead the employee on the ground that the effect might be unfairly to prejudice the plaintiff by encouraging in the jury the false supposition that the employee would actually pay the judgment. Although the employee was legally bound to indemnify the employer in such a case, this employee in fact was essentially judgment-proof.

What to do when impleader is thus unavailable? At early common law, a special writ, called a writ of voucher, was available in connection with certain real actions to compel a warrantor of title to defend an action brought against the warrantee. Later a similar procedure became available in cases involving other types of warrantors and, more generally, indemnitors. The defendant, if entitled to indemnification for liability that might result from the action, could notify the one liable over to the defendant to appear and defend the action. This notice did not make the indemnitor a party, as in the title warranty situation, but it did have the effect of making the indemnitor a privy, so permitting issue preclusion to be asserted by the indemnitee against the indemnitor in the event that the defendant was found liable to the plaintiff.[18] As with any other application of privity, the vouched-in indemnitor could be so bound even though not subject to personal jurisdiction in that first action.[19] This practice has persisted in modern procedure.[20]

How does this preclusion work? In a later action by the indemnitee against the indemnitor for indemnification, the indemnitor who received such simple notice, and who thus had an opportunity to defend the earlier action, would be precluded from relitigating the issues relating to the fact and amount of the indemnitee's liability. If the vouched-in indemnitor did respond to the notice by defending the earlier action, he would be bound by the issue preclusion effect of the judgment in that action as one who

17. 26 F.R.D. 163 (S.D.N.Y. 1960).

18. See State Bank v. American Sur. Co., 288 N.W. 7 (Minn. 1939); Restatement of Judgments § 107(a) cmts. c-i, § 108 (1942).

19. See First Nat'l Bank v. City Nat'l Bank, 65 N.E. 24 (Mass. 1902); Ronan E. Degnan & Alan J. Barton, Vouching to Quality Warranty: Case Law and Commercial Code, 51 Cal. L. Rev. 471, 477-80 (1963); Paul Stephen Ware, Note, Vouching: In or Out?, 42 Wash. & Lee L. Rev. 121 (1985). But see Peter A. Gross, Comment, Constitutional Limits on Vouching, 118 U. Pa. L. Rev. 237 (1969).

20. See Restatement (Second) of Judgments §§ 57-58 (1982).

controlled the litigation, even if he was not made a formal party to it. But even if he failed to exercise his right to defend the earlier action, he would nevertheless be bound by issue preclusion in the later action brought by the indemnitee. The indemnitor could litigate in that later action the existence of the indemnitor-indemnitee relation or the sufficiency of the notice to defend. He could not, however, relitigate the issues determined in the earlier suit.[21]

If the indemnitee neither impleads nor vouches in the indemnitor, the indemnitee does not thereby lose the right to indemnity. The indemnitee must, however, establish the right without reference to the prior judgment, unless a contract provides otherwise. That is, in a new action, the indemnitee would have to offer practically the same proof used by the injured person to establish the case against the indemnitee. This may leave the indemnitee the loser because of differing views of the evidence by the two factfinders, and in any event it is a needless expense.

Nonparties Affected by Injunctions. An injunction sometimes can apply to certain persons who are not parties to the action, if they know of the injunction's existence. In such case, the court can enforce the injunction directly against the nonparty by contempt proceedings. In the contempt proceedings, the nonparty cannot relitigate the propriety of the injunction and so, in that restricted sense, is bound on the issues adjudicated in the action that led to the injunction. The nonparty thus has an obligation to obey or at least not to obstruct the injunction, although this binding effect is distinguishable from res judicata.[22]

An injunction may expressly address not only the named defendant but also its agents, including its officers, servants, employees, and attorneys. Binding these nonparties could perhaps be described as cases in which the nonparty's interest was represented by a party to the prior action. The agent's interest in acting as agent is essentially identical with the interest of the principal. The principal was a party to the prior action and represented that interest of the agent. Correspondingly, a nonparty agent is bound by the decree only insofar as it applies to acts of the agent done within the scope of the agency.[23]

More substantive justifications for an injunction's binding effect exist. Injunctions issued against public officers normally bind successors to that

21. See Benjamin Hinman, Note, Development of the Common Law Rule Making a Judgment Conclusive Against Warrantors and Indemnitors, 34 Va. L. Rev. 321 (1948).

22. See Restatement (Second) of Judgments § 63 (1982).

23. See Nickerson v. Dowd, 174 N.E.2d 346 (Mass. 1961).

particular office.[24] In some states nonparty successors to property may be bound by an injunction relating to the use of the property, but in other states mere privity in the form of successive ownership is not in itself enough to bind a nonparty by an injunction. A distinction is made by some courts between in rem injunctions and other injunctions, the former binding the property and therefore binding successors in title, while the latter acts only in personam.[25]

Another category of nonparties who may be bound by injunctions is that of aiders and abettors—or "persons in active concert or participation with" the parties, to use the language of Federal Rule of Civil Procedure 65(d). The court can forbid only the act of a party. But other persons are in jeopardy if they act to bring about the forbidden act in the party's interest and with the party's express or implied authorization.[26]

Some courts go further, reaching nonparties who act independently but act to obstruct enforcement of the decree. This extension builds on the idea that the government could adopt a criminal obstruction-of-justice statute against deliberately interfering with parties' compliance with a decree.[27]

Indeed, older cases issued injunctions purporting to bind everyone to whom knowledge of the order may come. Yet this exceeds the limit. The idea that injunctions could apply so widely was effectively repudiated by Judge Learned Hand in the classic *Alemite* case,[28] but the use of such sweeping language in injunctions has not entirely disappeared.[29]

The exact location of the outer limit on an injunction's binding effect is a bit arbitrary. Due process would evidently allow greater binding effect, but the law has drawn a series of rules that limit the effect to the above-described categories of nonparties. That limit approximates the optimal compromise between society's interest in efficacious judgments and its interest in the nonparties' day in court.

---

24. See Fed. R. Civ. P. 25(d); Lucy v. Adams, 224 F. Supp. 79 (N.D. Ala. 1963), aff'd mem. sub nom. McCorvey v. Lucy, 328 F.2d 892 (5th Cir. 1964).

25. See United States v. Dean Rubber Mfg. Co., 71 F. Supp. 96 (W.D. Mo. 1946); Note, Binding Nonparties to Injunction Decrees, 49 Minn. L. Rev. 719, 727-31 (1965).

26. See Alemite Mfg. Corp. v. Staff, 42 F.2d 832 (2d Cir. 1930).

27. See United States v. Hall, 472 F.2d 261 (5th Cir. 1972); 11A Charles Alan Wright, Arthur R. Miller & Mary Kay Kane, Federal Practice and Procedure § 2956 (2d ed. 1995).

28. Alemite Mfg. Corp. v. Staff, 42 F.2d 832, 832 (2d Cir. 1930) ("If it assumes to do so, the decree is pro tanto brutum fulmen, and the persons enjoined are free to ignore it.").

29. See Note, Binding Nonparties to Injunction Decrees, 49 Minn. L. Rev. 719, 735 (1965).

2. Procedural Privity

Privies also include persons who were actually represented in the litigation by a party, thus including beneficiaries represented by a trustee.[30] A similar idea makes privies of persons who assumed control of the prosecution or defense of an action, as well as persons who agreed to abide by an action between others.[31]

a. Actual Representation

The principal justification for applying preclusion to nonparties who occupy a relationship of privity with a party in relation to the rights involved in litigation is the expectation that the nonparty's interest will be adequately protected by the party, so that the nonparty will have no substantial need for an independent day in court. This rationale obviously can apply to situations other than those in which the party and nonparty share interests in the same property. It can apply to any situation in which the interest of the party is very similar to that of the nonparty, and where there is adequate assurance that all relevant evidence and arguments in support of that interest will be adduced by the party.

Yet res judicata does not bind all persons represented by parties. That is, it does not extend, as the phrase goes, to the limits of *virtual representation.*[32] Instead, the relationship must be closer. It must be representation plus something else. The something might be a relatively weak substantive relationship or some sort of conduct signifying consent. Still, the unifying notion here is representation. Indeed, if in the circumstances the applicable law requires actually adequate representation for privity to attach, the subsequent court will inquire into the adequacy of representation before binding the nonparty.

Representation by a Fiduciary. A sufficiently representational situation could exist whenever one person is expressly empowered to represent another in litigation. Trustees, executors, administrators, guardians, conservators, next friends, receivers, and other such fiduciaries are examples. Some actions brought by persons so described could bind nonparties by virtue of substantive privity, but here it is the party's representation of the same basic interest as the nonparty's interest that is the significant point, rather

---

30. See generally Restatement (Second) of Judgments §§ 41-42 (1982).

31. See generally Restatement (Second) of Judgments §§ 39-40 (1982).

32. See 18 Charles Alan Wright, Arthur R. Miller & Edward H. Cooper, Federal Practice and Procedure § 4457 (1981 & Supp. 1999).

than any peculiarities of property law. In such cases, the beneficiary's interest is actually represented by the fiduciary, and the special duties imposed by the law upon the fiduciary tend to ensure that the beneficiary's interest will be represented well even if the beneficiary is not a formal party.[33]

This principle of representation also applies to situations where successive fiduciaries representing the same beneficial interest are involved in different actions. That is, the judgment in the earlier action involving the predecessor fiduciary will bind the successor fiduciary.[34]

When the parties hold concurrent interests, as in the case of trustee and beneficiary, preclusion can run both ways. That is, a judgment in a suit concerning the trust property in which the beneficiary was a party would have preclusive effect in a later suit concerning the property in which the trustee is a party. The same result would obtain if the trustee were the party in the first suit and the beneficiary in the second.[35]

If the position taken by the trustee in the first action was potentially in conflict with the role of trustee, however, the resulting judgment may not preclude the beneficiary from relitigating the same matter, even if the litigation concerned the trust property and even if there was no fraud or collusion between the trustee and the third party.[36] Thus, if the third party sues the trustee in its fiduciary capacity to recover from the trust estate a claim that is really the personal obligation of the trustee, the judgment against the trustee will not preclude the beneficiaries unless they knowingly and specifically consented to the trustee's representation of their interests in that action.[37] This problem is avoided in most jurisdictions by rules that characterize both trustee and beneficiaries as indispensable parties to such an action, so that both would have to be parties.

Representation by a Public Official. Apart from the fiduciary relation, there are some other situations in which nonparties may become bound by judgments because their interests were represented by parties. Public officials are sometimes empowered on a nonexclusive basis to bring action to protect the interests of the public. A judgment against the public official

33. See Restatement (Second) of Judgments §41 (1982).

34. See Restatement (Second) of Judgments §36 cmt. g (1982).

35. See 1B James Wm. Moore, Moore's Federal Practice ¶0.411[1], at III-215 to -216 (2d ed. 1996).

36. See Restatement (Second) of Judgments §42(d) cmt. e (1982).

37. See Snelling v. American Freehold Land Mortgage Co., 33 S.E. 634 (Ga. 1899).

may sometimes preclude a private individual who later sues to remedy the same misconduct.[38]

Assume that a zoning ordinance restricts the use of real property in the zone to single-family dwellings. The city attorney sues to enjoin the occupancy of a house in the zone by a group of five individuals. The court denies the injunction based on a finding that the five individuals are members of the same family within the meaning of the ordinance. Later an adjoining owner sues to enjoin the same condition as a nuisance. The adjoining owner would be precluded by the earlier judgment from relitigating the issue of whether the five are members of the same family. The private interest involved in the second action was encompassed by the public interest asserted in the earlier one, so the adjoining owner's interest was represented. The city attorney was not representing only an interest separate from the private interest.[39]

Contrariwise, if the adjoining owner had sued first, the judgment would probably not have preclusive effect in a later suit by the city attorney. The public interest would probably not be deemed to have been represented in the earlier private suit, unless it was prosecuted as a class action.

Representation in a Class Action. An action may be brought by or against named parties as representatives of a class of absent persons similarly situated. The judgment in such a class action binds all persons included within the class, not just those named as parties.[40] Matters litigated by the class representatives cannot be relitigated by class members. This does not constitute a violation of due process so long as the representatives provided the other class members with adequate representation, which means in this context that the absentees truly agreed with a named party as to general objectives on the merits, that the party vigorously and competently pursued those objectives, and that the absentees had some ties to the party, whether through their substantive interests or their procedural conduct.[41]

Class actions are permitted by procedural rules like Federal Rule of Civil Procedure 23 on a fairly broad basis. But such rules establish a pragmatic screening device to let through only those cases clearly appropriate for class-

38. See Restatement (Second) of Judgments §41(d) cmt. d (1982).

39. See Rynsburger v. Dairymen's Fertilizer Coop., 72 Cal. Rptr. 102 (Ct. App. 1968).

40. See Restatement (Second) of Judgments §41 cmt. e (1982).

41. See Richards v. Jefferson County, Ala., 517 U.S. 793 (1996); Hansberry v. Lee, 311 U.S. 32 (1940).

action treatment. Rule 23(a) imposes four initial requirements that must all be met: (1) the class must be "so numerous that joinder of all members is impracticable"; (2) there must be "questions of law or fact common to the class"; (3) the claims or defenses of the representatives must be "typical" of the class; and (4) "the representative parties will fairly and adequately protect the interests of the class." Rule 23(b) requires the proposed class action also to fall into one of three situations: (1) the situation where bringing separate actions would create a risk of establishing incompatible standards of conduct for the class opponent; (2) the situation where the defendant has allegedly based conduct on the characteristics of the plaintiff class, thereby making appropriate class-wide final injunctive relief or equivalent declaratory relief, as opposed to relief consisting predominantly of money damages; or (3) the situation where the potential class action does not fall into either of the two preceding situations, but where "the questions of law or fact common to the members of the class predominate over any questions affecting only individual members" and also "a class action is superior to other available methods for the fair and efficient adjudication of the controversy," with this latter issue of the desirability of class-action treatment entailing such factors as manageability. Rule 23(c)(2) contains special provisions applicable only to actions under Rule 23(b)(3), not to the naturally more cohesive or desirable classes falling within Rule 23(b)(1) or (2); the (b)(3) class member has a right to notice of the action, a right to enter an appearance through counsel, and a right to withdraw from the class—and thus escape the burdens, and lose the benefits, of the eventual judgment. Rule 23(c)(4) expressly authorizes actions to be maintained as class actions as to particular issues only. Rule 23(d)(2) authorizes the court in any class action discretionarily to order notice to class members advising them of any step in the action or any right they may have.[42]

To ensure the adequacy of the representation and thereby to obviate the nonjoined class members' need for an independent day in court, class-action rules commonly require, as does Rule 23(a), that the court prospectively test commonality, typicality, and representativeness by deciding at the outset whether to certify the case as a class action. Appropriate notice to class members may be required, although it is usually not necessary that a class member has received notice in order to be bound by the judgment. On collateral attack, an absent class member can attack a class-action judg-

42. See generally Charles Alan Wright, Law of Federal Courts 507-25 (5th ed. 1994).

ment's binding effect by raising the due process question of inadequate representation of the class member's interests.[43]

b. Other Procedural Relationships Based on Nonparty's Conduct

Another justification for precluding a nonparty lies where the nonparty has conducted itself in a way that calls for preclusion. So, the focus shifts from the party's representational behavior to the nonparty's conduct.

All of the foregoing categories of privies are susceptible to significant stretching, as is this one. Illustrative here is the possibility of treating a nonparty as a privy for *failure to intervene* in a case about which the person knows and is concerned. But before reaching that point, the law of res judicata has drawn a line. In other words, there is no general duty to intervene.[44] In the absence of the nonparty's inequitable conduct in inducing reliance on the judgment, a nonparty does not become a privy by the conduct of failing to intervene.[45] To become a privy merely by conduct, the nonparty's conduct must be a good deal more affirmative.

Persons Who Control Litigation. Sometimes the litigation of one side of a case will in fact be controlled by a nonparty. Control in this sense refers to the power to participate substantially in the decisions with respect to what issues will be litigated, what theories will be advanced, what evidence will be adduced, and whether an unfavorable judgment in the case will be appealed. A judgment against the controlled party in such a case would have issue preclusion effect on both the controlled party and the controlling nonparty.

A common instance of control of litigation by a nonparty may be seen in negligence cases when the defendant has liability insurance. The actual defense of the case will commonly be conducted by the insurance company through its agents, investigators, and attorneys. But the application of this principle that permits binding nonparties who control litigation is not limited to liability insurers, of course. The purpose of issue preclusion is to prevent a person from relitigating the same issues after one full and fair day in court. We have just seen many different instances in which that day-in-court requirement has been satisfied in spite of the fact that the precluded person was not a formal party. If one whose interests were represented by

---

43. See Note, Collateral Attack on the Binding Effect of Class Action Judgments, 87 Harv. L. Rev. 589 (1974).

44. See Martin v. Wilks, 490 U.S. 755 (1989).

45. See Restatement (Second) of Judgments § 62 (1982).

a party can be bound, it would seem even clearer that one who, although not a party, actually controlled the litigation should be bound. In every real sense, the nonparty has had a day in court.

Not all courts apply this principle to every nonparty who exercises control, however. It is often said that a nonparty should not be subject to issue preclusion, even though he actually controlled the presentation of the case, unless he had a proprietary or financial interest in the proceeding.[46] The First Restatement agreed.[47] For example, when a husband had controlled his wife's unsuccessful personal-injury action, the court in his own later suit for medical expenses and loss of consortium held that he was not precluded by the judgment against the wife, because he lacked the requisite stake in the first action.[48] A mere academic interest in establishing a judicial precedent has also been said to be insufficient.[49]

Nonetheless, although a nonparty who intrudes into litigation will usually have some sort of tangible stake in the issues litigated, it is not clear why such a stake should be a requisite to issue preclusion. Therefore, the Second Restatement rejects the notion that a controlling nonparty cannot be bound unless he had a proprietary or financial stake in the litigation, and it instead makes control itself the critical question.[50] Whether the nonparty did exert such control is a question of fact. A stake in the case might be evidence tending to support an inference of the requisite control, but "the essential question would appear to be whether, rather than why, control of the litigation was assumed."[51] Presumably the Second Restatement, contrary to the view of its predecessor, would permit issue preclusion against a controlling nonparty even if the motive for participation in it were intellectual curiosity.

By contrast, one who participates as an amicus curiae is neither a party nor a controlling nonparty, and is not thereby bound by any res judicata effects of the judgment.

Persons Who Agree to Abide. A person may explicitly, or with fair clarity implicitly, agree to abide by the outcome of some case to which the person is a nonparty. For example, an indemnitor might agree by contract in

---

46. See, e.g., Bigelow v. Old Dominion Copper Mining & Smelting Co., 225 U.S. 111, 126 (1912).

47. See Restatement of Judgments § 84 (1942).

48. Palmer v. Clarksdale Hosp., 57 So. 2d 476 (Miss. 1952).

49. See White v. Croker, 13 F.2d 321, 324 (5th Cir. 1926).

50. See Restatement (Second) of Judgments § 39 (1982).

51. Restatement (Second) of Judgments § 39 cmt. a, reporter's note (1982).

advance to accept the determination of common issues in an action brought by an injured person against the indemnitee. The agreement makes the nonparty into a privy. As the Second Restatement puts it:

> A person who agrees to be bound by the determination of issues in an action between others is bound in accordance with the terms of his agreement.[52]

B. Strangers

A person who had little or nothing to do with a judgment might benefit from its res judicata effects, but the judgment cannot bind such a person who is neither party nor privy. Good policy entitles such a person to a day in court, in person or through a representative, before a judgment has any legally binding effect on that person.

1. Parties Treated as Strangers: No Binding Effect

Persons who are named parties in the action and over whom the court has jurisdiction are normally bound by the judgment, and may not relitigate the matters that are subject to preclusion. Persons who, although not originally before the court, subsequently became parties by intervention, impleader, or other means are likewise bound with respect to those determinations made while they were parties.[53]

A party does not always come within the reach of the rules of claim and issue preclusion, however. A party may be in a particular posture in the litigation that prevents a full and fair opportunity to litigate certain aspects of the case, and therefore to a certain extent the application of res judicata would be inappropriate. It could be said that, to such extent, the party will be deemed a stranger.[54]

a. Nominal Parties

Procedural rules sometimes require actions to be brought by or against persons who have no real stake in the litigation. Such situations were not uncommon in the old days, because the common law recognized only the

---

52. Restatement (Second) of Judgments §40 (1982).
53. See generally Restatement (Second) of Judgments §34 (1982).
54. See generally Restatement (Second) of Judgments §§35-38 (1982).

titular holder of the legal interest as a proper party, even if that party had no beneficial stake in the action. Assignments of choses in action were not recognized at law, for instance, and so an action to enforce an assigned right had to be brought in the name of the assignor. Modern rules requiring actions to be brought in the name of the real party in interest, and similar rules relating to defending parties, have generally eliminated that problem.[55] Vestiges of it remain, however.

Examples are now seen mainly in connection with claims involving a casualty insurer. When negligence has caused damage to property that was insured against such a loss, and the casualty insurer has fully indemnified the owner and has thereby become subrogated to the owner's rights, the law in some states permits or even requires any negligence action against the tortfeasor to be brought in the name of the owner, even though the owner has no further interest in the matter. If the owner's only role in the action is the use of the owner's name, and the tortfeasor knows that, the owner will not be bound by preclusion resulting from the judgment.

To generalize, a nominal party is not bound by res judicata, as long as the opposing party has knowledge of the nominal party's lack of a stake in the litigation.[56]

b. Parties Under Incapacity

Actions by or against persons lacking juridical capacity, such as infants or incompetents, normally are brought by or against them in the name of a guardian ad litem or next friend. A different sort of example could be constructed involving an organization not recognized as a jural entity. If any such case is maintained by the proper representative, the resulting judgment will bind the incapacitated party, as previously explained.

If, however, the action is improperly brought by or against an incapacitated party in its own right, any judgment obtained would be regarded as void in some jurisdictions. The incapacitated party would not be subject to preclusion as a result of such a judgment.[57] But in most jurisdictions, such a judgment would not automatically be denied preclusive effect. The judg-

55. See, e.g., Fed. R. Civ. P. 17(a).

56. See Restatement (Second) of Judgments § 37 (1982).

57. Cf. Valdimer v. Mount Vernon Hebrew Camps, Inc., 172 N.E.2d 283 (N.Y. 1961) (effect of settlement).

ment's effectiveness would depend on whether the incapacitated party's interests were or were not adequately protected.[58]

c. Parties Litigating in Different Capacities

A party who litigated in one capacity is not treated like a former party when in a subsequent action the party appears in another capacity. The two capacities are deemed two different persons. For example, someone who sued as a representative for others is not precluded in a later action that she brings as an individual. This rule supposedly ensures a full and fair opportunity to litigate, while it avoids potential conflicts of interest.[59]

Assume a two-car collision between drivers *A* and *B*. Sadly, *B* was killed in the accident, and so *A*'s claim is against *B*'s estate. *A* sues *C*, the administratrix of the estate of *B*. Then *A* wins the judgment. Thereafter *C*, who was also injured in the collision, sues *A* for negligence in connection with the same accident. *C* is not precluded from relitigating. Even if *C* was also administratrix of the estate of *D*, who had also been killed in the accident, the judgment against her as administratrix of the estate of *B* would not preclude any claims or issues in her later suit against *A* in her capacity as administratrix of the estate of *D*.[60]

d. Nonadverse Parties

Issue preclusion, as noted previously, rests in part on the assumption that the determination by one court on a disputed issue is as likely correct as would be that of another court. This rationale in turn assumes that the adversary system will be operating normally in the prior action. If, however, the party did not have the opportunity, or incentive, to litigate an issue fully and fairly in the prior action, it would be unfair to deny the right to relitigate the issue.

One situation in which a party may actively participate in the litigation, but in which it might be unfair to apply issue preclusion, is where the opposing parties in the second action were co-parties in the first. Of course, co-parties will litigate as true adversaries with respect to issues involved in cross-claims. Interpleaded parties normally are true adversaries. But in many other situations co-parties are not adversaries, throwing into doubt

---

58. See Restatement (Second) of Judgments § 35 (1982).

59. See Restatement (Second) of Judgments § 36 (1982).

60. See Restatement (Second) of Judgments § 36 cmt. b, illus. 3, 5 (1982).

whether they should be precluded from relitigating issues that become matters of contention between them in a later action.

For instance, assume *A* was a passenger in a car driven by *B*, which collided with a car driven by *C*. *A* sues both *B* and *C* for damages, alleging that both were negligent. Will a judgment for *A* based on findings that both *B* and *C* were negligent have issue preclusion effect in a later suit by *B* against *C* for damages resulting from the same accident?

No, according to the traditional approach, which the First Restatement endorsed.[61] *B*'s and *C*'s positions with respect to the negligence issues were not sufficiently adverse to warrant precluding litigation of those issues in a later suit between them. To be adversaries for issue preclusion purposes, under this approach, some sort of claim must be pleaded by one of the coparties against the other. In the first suit they both were litigating the question in opposition to *A*, not in opposition to each other. Indeed, in the first suit by a faultless but injured *A* against two insured drivers in a judicial setting selected by *A*, both *B* and *C* may have been doomed to lose. Between former allies, it would be unfair to let *C* later use *B*'s loss when *B* chooses to sue *C* for *B*'s own damages.

In a practical sense, however, *B* and *C* often are active adversaries in the hypothetical situation. To disprove any negligence on their parts, both *B* and *C* may attempt to show that the accident was solely caused by the other's negligence. If this in fact was their position in the first suit, and if they had every opportunity and incentive to litigate the negligence issues fully and fairly, should not the determination of the first court on those issues have preclusive effect? Courts have increasingly so held,[62] and the Second Restatement agrees.[63] Under this approach, parties may be adversaries, for issue preclusion purposes, even if no claim is pleaded by one against the other. The two approaches are alike in that they deny issue preclusion as between parties who were not adversaries in the prior action, but this modern approach defines adversary not only in terms of the pleadings but also in terms of the actual positions taken on the issue in the prior action.

---

61. See Restatement of Judgments § 82 (1942).

62. See A.B.C. Fireproof Warehouse Co. v. Atchison, T. & S.F. Ry., 122 F.2d 657 (8th Cir. 1941); Schwartz v. Public Adm'r, 246 N.E.2d 725 (N.Y. 1969); V. Woerner, Annotation, Judgment in Action Against Codefendants for Injury or Death of Person, or for Damage to Property, as Res Judicata in Subsequent Action Between Codefendants as to Their Liability Inter Se, 24 A.L.R.3d 318 (1969).

63. See Restatement (Second) of Judgments § 38 (1982).

In sum, under the Second Restatement, the rules of res judicata do not normally apply between parties who were not on opposite sides of the relevant claim and who in actuality did not litigate the issue fully and fairly as adversaries to each other. No general approach is perfect on this problem, but the Second Restatement's approach appears to be the superior one.

However, with the widespread abandonment of mutuality, to be discussed in the next section, the realm for issue preclusion between nonadverse parties has expanded even beyond the Second Restatement's approach.[64] If a stranger could use *B*'s loss against *B*, an argument exists that *C* should be able to use the loss similarly, as long as *B* had a full and fair opportunity to litigate the issue against *A*—whether or not *B* and *C* were formally or actually adversaries. The persuasive counterargument is that *B* and *C* would thereby lose their right to present a united front against *A*, as well as the right to sue each other for their own damages in a setting of their own choosing; *B* and *C* would have to litigate fiercely against all, and forward all their claims to put themselves in the most sympathetic light, because this first suit will determine all future litigation over the accident. Consequently, the wide application of nonmutual estoppel should, although it likely will not, be tempered by excepting preclusion between former coparties who were neither formal nor actual adversaries in the prior action.

2. Strangers Treated as Parties: A Benefiting Effect

A stranger to a prior judgment cannot be *bound* by it. However, the stranger can *benefit* from it. The most important version of such benefit is a stranger using the prior judgment for collateral estoppel against a former party.

a. Mutuality of Estoppel

The old doctrine of mutuality held that a person may not benefit from a prior judgment if the person would not have been bound by any outcome of that initial action. Because strangers were never bound, the simple result was that they could never benefit. There came to exist, however, substantial extensions of res judicata under the mutuality doctrine, allowing strangers in some special circumstances to benefit.

64. See 18 Charles Alan Wright, Arthur R. Miller & Edward H. Cooper, Federal Practice and Procedure § 4450 (1981).

Normally, anyone who would have been bound by the res judicata effects of a judgment, if it were unfavorable, can claim the benefits of the judgment's effects, when it is favorable. That is, one who would have been bound can claim the benefits. For a long time, it was generally accepted that the converse was also true, that is, one who would not have been bound cannot claim the benefits. Thus, the estoppels of a judgment were mutual. Unless both persons could be bound, neither was bound as to the other, according to this doctrine of mutuality.

Because by definition one who was not a party or in privity with a party—a "stranger" to the prior judgment—could not be bound by issue preclusion, such a nonparty could not claim the benefit of issue preclusion either. "Relitigation of an issue with a new adversary is permitted because of the assumed unfairness of binding one party to a proceeding by the rules of res judicata while the other party is not bound . . . ."[65] Unfortunately, the unfairness was assumed rather than explained.

Secondary-Liability Situations. Certain extensions to the mutuality principle had long been recognized. The most important extension allowed a person whose liability was derivative and secondary to claim the benefit of issues adjudicated successfully by the one primarily liable.

To use a common illustration, an employer's vicarious liability for the tort of an employee is derivative and secondary. If the employee is not liable for a tort, the employer is not vicariously liable. So if the injured person sues the employee and loses—the employee being found not negligent—then the employer ideally should not be liable either.

If the rule of mutuality were to apply, however, the injured person would be permitted to relitigate the issue of the employee's negligence in a later action against the employer. In that later action, the injured person could not have precluded the employer if the judgment had been against the employee, because the employer was not a party or in privity with a party. It would be entitled to a day in court before being held liable. The employer thus being not bound, the injured person should not be bound either, according to the rule of mutuality.

The refusal to bind the injured person could lead to an anomalous result, however. The plaintiff who lost in the earlier suit against the employee might be successful against the employer. But if the employer is held liable to the plaintiff, it has a right to indemnification from the employee. The employee has already been held not liable for the tort in the earlier action.

---

65. Restatement of Judgments § 96 cmt. a (1942).

If the employee must now indemnify the employer, the employee's prior judgment of nonliability has been effectively nullified in an action to which the employee was a stranger. Yet if the employee does not have to indemnify, the employer has lost the right of indemnification without a day in court on indemnification.

The best resolution of that dilemma was to allow the employer to claim the benefit of the employee's judgment, even though he would not have been bound had the employee lost. This solution was accepted by the courts as an extension of preclusion under the mutuality regime.[66] The same rationale permitted the employer to assert issue preclusion as a ceiling on damages, even if the employee had lost in the first action. The employer, while defending the second suit on the merits, could claim the benefit of issue preclusion on the amount of damages, so that no judgment could be obtained against the employer for an amount greater than the amount for which the employee had been held liable.[67]

The extension was not limited to master-servant vicarious-liability cases. It could be invoked in any secondary-liability situation where a right like indemnification existed between two parties successively sued by the same injured party for the same injury. Moreover, perhaps with more imagination than rigor, it could extend to permit issue preclusion in nonindemnity situations where one person's liability was dependent on that of another. For instance, if *A* sues *B* for breach of contract and loses because no breach was shown to have been committed, *A* would be precluded from relitigating the same issue in a suit against *C* for inducing *B*'s breach.[68]

Because the heart of the rationale for this extension was the avoidance of the dilemma of either depriving the indemnitor of the benefit of a successful defense or else depriving the indemnitee of the right of indemnification, it was theoretically applicable only when asserted defensively by the indemnitee. Thus, in the typical vicarious-liability situation, if the plaintiff first sues the employer (indemnitee) and loses for failing to prove negligence, the rationale would not extend so far as to permit the employee (indemnitor) to preclude the issue of the employee's negligence in a later action by the plaintiff against the employee. Denying the employee the benefit

66. See Good Health Dairy Prods. Corp. v. Emery, 9 N.E.2d 758 (N.Y. 1937); Restatement of Judgments § 96(1)(a) (1942).

67. See Pinnix v. Griffin, 20 S.E.2d 366 (N.C. 1942); Restatement of Judgments § 96(1)(b) (1942).

68. See Israel v. Wood Dolson Co., 134 N.E.2d 97 (N.Y. 1956) (broad rationale for this result); Restatement of Judgments § 99 (1942) (narrow rationale).

of the employer's judgment means that the same issue might be decided in a contradictory fashion in the two actions, but that is an inevitable risk of the mutuality rule. There is simply no dilemma faced in allowing recovery against the one primarily liable after the one secondarily liable has been exonerated.[69]

Expansion of the Secondary-Liability Extension. Most courts, however, refused to limit the secondary-liability extension so strictly, and therefore allowed the indemnitor to rely upon a prior judgment in favor of the indemnitee to establish nonliability in a later suit by the same plaintiff. In *Giedrewicz v. Donovan*,[70] the court said: "As a matter of public policy and in the interest of accomplishing justice, the better rule would seem to be that, if it is clearly established, in the trial of an action either against the employee or against the principal for damages caused by the employee's negligent conduct, that the employee is not negligent, the judgment in the case first tried is a bar to a subsequent action by the same plaintiff for the same negligent act of the same employee."

Thus, the broader extension would permit issue preclusion to be asserted by the indemnitor as well as by the indemnitee—by the employee as well as by the employer. This "better rule" must have rested on a different foundation than the strict secondary-liability extension previously described. The cases were not very clear in articulating just what that foundation was. The broader extension seemed to rest on the theory that, if the alleged liability of *B* and *C* depends on the same factual situation and if the liability of one of them derives from the liability of the other because of some legal relationship between them, a judgment adverse to claimant *A* in a suit against *B* necessarily adjudicated that no primary liability arose from that factual situation, and therefore it ought to preclude *A* from retrying the same issues in a suit against *C*. This theory, which includes the secondary-liability situations contemplated by the narrower extension but much more as well, also explained the broader result in terms of the lack of any good reason to permit *A*, who complains of what is essentially a single wrong, to relitigate the issues after once failing to prove a wrong was done.

Some courts held that any extension to the mutuality rule applied only when the prior judgment was sought to be used defensively, because only in that situation did the logic of secondary liability apply.[71] Other courts,

69. See Bomar v. Keyes, 162 F.2d 136 (2d Cir. 1947); Restatement of Judgments §96(2) (1942).

70. 179 N.E. 246, 248 (Mass. 1932).

71. See, e.g., Elder v. New York & Pa. Motor Express, Inc., 31 N.E.2d 188 (N.Y. 1940).

however, allowed the assertion of issue preclusion without regard to whether it was invoked by a defendant or by a plaintiff in the second action. For instance, a master suing for damages was allowed to use a judgment previously obtained against the injured person by the servant.[72] And a plaintiff was allowed to establish his own lack of contributory negligence by collateral estoppel based on a judgment in an earlier action by which his opponent had unsuccessfully sought recovery against the plaintiff's insurer for the plaintiff's negligence.[73]

Consistent with this expansive attitude, courts occasionally suggested that absolutely any litigant should be able to claim the benefit of issue preclusion resulting from a judgment against one who was a plaintiff in the former action, with no limitation to secondary-liability situations. For example, "a plaintiff who deliberately selects his forum and there unsuccessfully presents his proofs, is bound by such adverse judgment in a second suit involving all the identical issues already decided. The requirement of mutuality must yield to public policy."[74] To recognize such a huge extension would almost destroy the rule of mutuality, however.

First Restatement Approach. The First Restatement recognized the propriety of defensive preclusion in the situation of secondary liability, but only if the allegedly primary tortfeasor or contract-breaker was a party to the first action, either plaintiff or defendant.[75] The First Restatement refused to depart from mutuality if the first action involved instead the one secondarily liable, even in the indemnitor-indemnitee situation.[76] That is, it rejected the idea that a servant could claim the benefit of a judgment in favor of the master. The First Restatement also refused to depart from the requirement of defensive use in the second action.[77] That is, it rejected the idea that the master could use the judgment in an action by the master for damages. In other words, the First Restatement insisted on sticking to the logic, such as the indemnity dilemma, that generated the extension initially. It thereby ignored a growing body of decisions taking a broader view.

Just as in binding privies, the law could constitutionally go much farther in benefiting strangers. The law must decide how far it should go, settling

---

72. See United Mut. Fire Ins. Co. v. Saeli, 71 N.Y.S.2d 696 (App. Div.), aff'd mem., 75 N.E.2d 626 (N.Y. 1947).

73. McCourt v. Algiers, 91 N.W.2d 194 (Wis. 1956).

74. Coca-Cola Co. v. Pepsi-Cola Co., 172 A. 260, 263 (Del. Super. Ct. 1934).

75. See Restatement of Judgments § 96 cmt. e (1942).

76. See Restatement of Judgments §§ 96, 97, 99 (1942).

77. See Restatement of Judgments § 96 cmt. f (1942).

on the point that optimizes the relevant policies. The First Restatement, then, decided that the optimum lay at the mutuality rule with a few defined extensions of res judicata.

b. Nonmutual Estoppel

Mutuality of estoppel was rejected wholesale by the California Supreme Court in *Bernhard v. Bank of America National Trust & Savings Association*.[78] Most jurisdictions have since come to agree in some significant part. The modern approach is that a stranger may invoke collateral estoppel against a former party, unless the former party lacked a full and fair opportunity to litigate the issue in the initial action or unless other special circumstances justify relitigation.[79]

Bernhard *Case.* Cook withdrew money from a woman's bank account before she died. He then became executor of the decedent's estate. Bernhard and other beneficiaries of the estate filed objections to his final accounting, citing his failure to list the withdrawn money as an estate asset. In that contested accounting action, the probate court held that the decedent had made an inter vivos gift of the money to Cook. Later Bernhard was appointed administratrix. She sued the bank to obtain the money, alleging it to have been withdrawn without authorization. The bank refused to pay the money on the ground that it had previously paid it to Cook upon authorization. Although the bank had not been a party to the probate accounting, it invoked issue preclusion. Bernhard argued that the issue was not foreclosed, invoking the rule of mutuality of estoppel.

The California Supreme Court held for the bank. Bernhard and the other beneficiaries had fully and fairly litigated that issue previously, and they were bound. Bernhard now represented them, and so she was bound. The fact that the bank was not a party or in privity with a party was of no importance. In a much-quoted opinion, Justice Traynor said: "The requirements of due process of law forbid the assertion of a plea of res judicata against a party unless he was . . . a party thereto or in privity with a party thereto. . . . There is no compelling reason, however, for requiring that the party asserting the plea of res judicata must have been a party, or in privity with a party, to the earlier litigation. No satisfactory rationalization has been advanced for the requirement of mutuality."[80]

---

78. 122 P.2d 892 (Cal. 1942).
79. See generally Restatement (Second) of Judgments § 29 (1982).
80. 122 P.2d at 894-95.

If the bank were liable to Bernhard, it would have had a right to indemnification from Cook, and so the case might have been decided with the same outcome on the basis of the recognized indemnitor-indemnitee extension to mutuality. "Justice Traynor chose instead to extirpate the mutuality requirement and put it to the torch."[81] The opinion thus constituted dicta, which perhaps explains Justice Traynor's failure to qualify carefully all the wide implications of his influential opinion.

New Rule. The immediate impact of the *Bernhard* case was slight. But eventually many state and federal courts came to follow its approach. Decisions in a few states have bucked the trend at least temporarily.[82] Nevertheless, the powerful and widespread trend has been toward the abandonment, to some degree, of the doctrine of mutuality—both in the easy situations and also in the situations where nonmutuality looks most questionable.

A defendant in the subsequent action can invoke collateral estoppel against a former party, say, a former plaintiff. Such "defensive use" by a stranger was authorized as part of the federal common law of res judicata by *Blonder-Tongue Laboratories v. University of Illinois Foundation*,[83] in which the U.S. Supreme Court held that an alleged infringer as defendant can preclude the patentee as plaintiff on the issue of patent invalidity, using the judgment suffered in an unsuccessful prior suit brought by the patentee against another alleged infringer.

The modern approach also permits a plaintiff in the subsequent action to invoke collateral estoppel against a former party, even a former defendant. Such "offensive use" by a stranger was authorized as part of the federal common law of res judicata by the U.S. Supreme Court in *Parklane Hosiery Co. v. Shore*.[84] This was an astounding case. In the first action, the SEC successfully sued Parklane for equitable relief, alleging that the company had issued a false proxy statement in connection with a merger. In the second action, a stockholder brought a class action for damages, based on that proxy statement. The stockholder moved for partial summary judgment on liability, invoking collateral estoppel. The Supreme Court approved

81. Brainerd Currie, Civil Procedure: The Tempest Brews, 53 Cal. L. Rev. 25, 26 (1965).

82. See, e.g., Armstrong v. Miller, 200 N.W.2d 282 (N.D. 1972); Keith v. Schiefen-Stockham Ins. Agency, 498 P.2d 265 (Kan. 1972). Also, Alabama, Florida, Georgia, Mississippi, and Virginia seem still to be in the mutuality camp.

83. 402 U.S. 313 (1971).

84. 439 U.S. 322 (1979).

collateral estoppel—despite the nonmutuality involved; despite the offensive use; despite the use against a former defendant; despite the fact that the former plaintiff was a powerful enforcement agency of the federal government; and despite the fact that Parklane had no jury right in the first action but would have had a jury right in the second action.

Some jurisdictions balked at going as far as *Parklane*, however, because the efficiency arguments for nonmutuality weaken there while the fairness worries mount. Therefore, these jurisdictions began a search for appropriate exceptions.

General Exception. Not all courts that accepted the *Bernhard* reasoning have been willing to permit the assertion of issue preclusion by a nonparty in all of the cases that fall literally within Justice Traynor's broad dicta. The strongest inhibiting factor has probably been the specter of the mass accident: the train, bus, or airline wreck in which one defendant is exposed to claims by multiple claimants. In such a case, plaintiffs could sue seriatim to recover for the defendant's negligence. Failure of one plaintiff to prove negligence would not preclude others from relitigating the same questions, because the unjoined plaintiffs would not be bound by the adverse judgment. Success of one plaintiff, however, would result in success for all subsequent plaintiffs, insofar as the issue of the defendant's negligence goes. The requirements of nonmutual issue preclusion would be met, so that the defendant would be bound by this adverse judgment.

This mass accident result has been challenged as tending to foster, rather than to curtail, repetitious litigation. Plaintiffs who might otherwise join together, or intervene, in a single lawsuit under modern permissive joinder rules would have incentive to sue separately and to hang back awaiting another plaintiff's favorable result. Moreover, the defendant could not afford to spare any effort in defending and appealing each claim, lest one failure result in liability to all plaintiffs who had not previously pursued their claims to judgment. The abandonment of mutuality in such cases—instead of reducing the amount of judicial effort required to resolve disputes turning on common issues, in accordance with nonmutuality's simplistic justification—might have the opposite effect.[85]

Nonmutuality has also been seen as grossly unfair in the mass accident situation. The defendant does not get to choose the setting for litigating the issue. The first plaintiff might very well be selected for being the most sympathetic of all potential plaintiffs. The subsequent plaintiffs have not earned

85. See James Wm. Moore & Thomas S. Currier, Mutuality and Conclusiveness of Judgments, 35 Tul. L. Rev. 301, 308-11 (1961).

their estoppel, in the sense that they are not trying to avoid relitigation but instead are trying to avoid having to litigate the issue at all. But most fundamentally, nonmutuality destroys the equivalence of litigating risk, weights the scale against the common party, and changes the most basic of the rules of the procedural system: the first plaintiff risks losing only the one case, which is all the defendant can win; in return, the defendant risks losing all the cases at once, so that over the series of cases the odds overwhelmingly favor the plaintiffs; and the first plaintiff thereby acquires tremendous settlement leverage, but in the absence of settlement will face an opponent willing to litigate down to the scorched earth. This fundamental departure from procedural neutrality will inevitably have many unintended substantive effects.[86]

Various modifications to the complete abandonment of mutuality have therefore been proposed. Of these, the most severe is one that would allow only the stranger's defensive use of issue preclusion.[87] The *Bernhard* case itself actually involved the defensive use of issue preclusion, and although the court's opinion did not suggest that issue preclusion could not be used offensively, that fact may have contributed to the reluctance of some courts to extend the abandonment of mutuality beyond instances of defensive use. This limitation would avoid, at any rate, the inefficiencies of the multiple-claimant situation. However, other courts have extended the abandonment of mutuality to permit offensive use of issue preclusion by nonparties, even in mass accident cases.[88]

Another theory for limiting the scope of *Bernhard*'s abandonment of mutuality would permit a nonparty to assert issue preclusion only against one who was the plaintiff in the prior action, or against one who had the opportunity to choose the occasion, the forum, and the adversary for litigating the issue.[89] Nonmutual issue preclusion against a former defendant can raise a real concern of unfairness in some circumstances. This limita-

86. See Note, A Probabilistic Analysis of the Doctrine of Mutuality of Collateral Estoppel, 76 Mich. L. Rev. 612 (1978); Note, Exposing the Extortion Gap: An Economic Analysis of the Rules of Collateral Estoppel, 105 Harv. L. Rev. 1940 (1992).

87. See Albernaz v. City of Fall River, 191 N.E.2d 771 (Mass. 1963); Michael Kimmel, Note, The Impacts of Defensive and Offensive Assertion of Collateral Estoppel by a Nonparty, 35 Geo. Wash. L. Rev. 1010 (1967).

88. See, e.g., Parklane Hosiery Co. v. Shore, 439 U.S. 322 (1979); United States v. United Air Lines, 216 F. Supp. 709 (E.D. Wash., D. Nev. 1962), aff'd sub nom. United Air Lines v. Weiner, 335 F.2d 379, 404-05 (9th Cir. 1964).

89. See Brainerd Currie, Mutuality of Collateral Estoppel: Limits of the Bernhard Doctrine, 9 Stan. L. Rev. 281, 309 (1957).

tion, proposed by Professor Brainerd Currie, was thoroughly considered, however, and rejected as a general limiting principle in the Second Circuit's *Zdanok* case.[90] So persuasive was Judge Henry Friendly's analysis in that case that even Professor Currie was convinced.[91]

The problem with these two limiting principles is that each tries to reconcile competing policies—such as the policy of avoiding repetitious litigation and the policy of ensuring practical fairness—through a rigid exception defined in terms that do not necessarily bear upon either policy. In *United States v. United Air Lines*,[92] where the offensive use of issue preclusion was permitted against one that had been defendant in the prior action, the court carefully examined the features of the case that bore upon the propriety of holding the defendant precluded on the issue of its liability for the airplane crash. Noting that claims of 24 of the 42 passengers had been combined in first suit, the court said: "The issue of liability of United Air Lines to the passengers on the plane was litigated to the hilt, by lawyers of the highest competence in their field .... The defendant has had its day in court on the issue of liability before a jury."[93] This particular result seems sensible.[94] Yet if either of those two limiting principles had been applied, the issues would have been relitigated.

Perhaps the best solution is to add to *Bernhard* a general exception, one that is highly flexible and so can be specially sensitive to the dangers of nonmutuality: the party against whom issue preclusion is asserted can defeat it by showing a lack of a full and fair opportunity, or incentive, to litigate the issue in the prior action. The more recent cases that have rejected mutuality have, for the most part, also adopted this full-and-fair-opportunity reservation.[95] It has been argued that engrafting the sensitive full-and-fair-opportunity reservation onto the *Bernhard* rule essentially nullifies the ben-

---

90. Zdanok v. Glidden Co., Durkee Famous Foods Division, 327 F.2d 944 (2d Cir. 1964).

91. See Brainerd Currie, Civil Procedure: The Tempest Brews, 53 Cal. L. Rev. 25, 29-31 (1965).

92. 216 F. Supp. 709 (E.D. Wash., D. Nev. 1962), aff'd sub nom. United Air Lines v. Weiner, 335 F.2d 379, 404-05 (9th Cir. 1964).

93. 216 F. Supp. at 728-29.

94. See Comment, Res Judicata: The Shield Becomes a Sword, 1964 Duke L.J. 402.

95. See, e.g., Parklane Hosiery Co. v. Shore, 439 U.S. 322 (1979); Blonder-Tongue Lab. v. University of Illinois Found., 402 U.S. 313 (1971); B.R. DeWitt, Inc. v. Hall, 225 N.E.2d 195 (N.Y. 1967).

efits of the rejection of mutuality. In the later action, instead of relitigating the issue previously decided, the parties now litigate the question of the fullness and fairness of the opportunity to litigate the issue in the first suit. In most cases, however, that question should be fairly easy to resolve. Moreover, that question should be triable to the court rather than to a jury.

Still, it is difficult to avoid the temptation to seek a rigid exception covering at least some of the most questionable cases. For example, another proposed limiting principle would deny the use of issue preclusion by a stranger in situations where inconsistent judgments had been rendered on the issue.[96] That approach would at least reduce the problem that the multiple-claimant mass-accident situation presents.

Class-Action Exception. Another situation in which the *Bernhard* doctrine and its derivatives probably will not be applied, even in jurisdictions that have generally abandoned the mutuality rule, is that involving opters-out of a class action brought under Federal Rule of Civil Procedure 23(b)(3) or its state-law counterparts.

Prior to the 1966 amendments to Rule 23, members of a plaintiff class in a so-called spurious class action were not bound by the judgment unless they were formal parties, either by initial designation or by intervention; but nonparty class members were permitted by some courts to intervene in the action after a successful judgment, and thereby claim all the benefits while having avoided the risk of any undesirable consequences of a judgment unfavorable to the class.[97] The 1966 amendments sought to abolish the possibility of "one-way intervention" in such cases by providing that the judgment would bind all the class members.[98]

It has been argued by some commentators that members of a Rule 23(b)(3) class action today can, in effect, still get the advantages of the former one-way intervention.[99] The member can opt out from the class, and thereby avoid the consequences of a judgment unfavorable to the class. If the class representatives are successful, however, the excluded class mem-

---

96. See Alan N. Polasky, Collateral Estoppel—Effects of Prior Litigation, 39 Iowa L. Rev. 217, 248 (1954); cf. Restatement (Second) of Judgments § 29(4) cmt. f (1982) (making inconsistent results a factor to consider).

97. See, e.g., Union Carbide & Carbon Corp. v. Nisley, 300 F.2d 561 (10th Cir. 1961).

98. See Fed. R. Civ. P. 23(c)(3).

99. E.g., Roger Furman, Note, Offensive Assertion of Collateral Estoppel by Persons Opting Out of a Class Action, 31 Hastings L.J. 1189 (1980) (collateral estoppel for absentees with strong individual interests in controlling their own litigation).

ber can invoke the *Bernhard* doctrine, and thereby claim the benefits of issue preclusion based on the judgment against the party who opposed the class.

The courts have blocked this stratagem.[100] They argue that to apply the *Bernhard* doctrine in such a way would undermine the purposes of the 1966 amendments. Even though the party opposing the class may have had a full and fair opportunity to litigate the matter to the utmost, "it would be anomalous to give one who opts out collateral estoppel benefits of the action from which he deliberately removed himself."[101] Thus, in class actions brought in the federal courts under Rule 23(b)(3), or in states that have copied its provisions, a class member who chooses to opt out from the class will not be bound, but also should not be permitted to claim the issue preclusion benefits of the class-action judgment.

Government-Litigation Exception. The U.S. Supreme Court in *United States v. Mendoza*[102] simply declared offensive nonmutual collateral estoppel to be unavailable against the federal government. This relatively rigid exception probably now extends to defensive use and to state governments.[103] Because of the scope of governmental litigation, this exception has enormous numerical importance.

The rationale is that substantive policies regarding governmental litigation supposedly overcome the usual efficiency and fairness arguments. The government frequently litigates important legal questions with many different parties. Society would be better off with a slow and strategic development of these issues by the government litigators, rather than by freezing the government to the first final court decision. The Supreme Court should not routinely feel obligated to grant certiorari to avoid such a freeze. Although all these policies could be accommodated by the usual case-by-case full-and-fair-opportunity exception to nonmutuality, *Mendoza* held a flexible exception too subjective to inform the government during the first action whether that first judgment will later be binding.

---

100. See, e.g., Premier Elec. Constr. Co. v. National Elec. Contractors Ass'n, 814 F.2d 358 (7th Cir. 1987)

101. Benjamin Kaplan, Continuing Work of the Civil Committee: 1966 Amendments of the Federal Rules of Civil Procedure (I), 81 Harv. L. Rev. 356, 391 n.136 (1967).

102. 464 U.S. 154 (1984).

103. See 18 Charles Alan Wright, Arthur R. Miller & Edward H. Cooper, Federal Practice and Procedure § 4465 (Supp. 1999); Note, Nonmutual Issue Preclusion Against States, 109 Harv. L. Rev. 792 (1996).

Depending on whether one accepts that rationale or not, the arbitrarily defined *Mendoza* exception is either underinclusive, in that the same or similar policies apply to nongovernmental litigants, or overinclusive, in that the exception permits the government abusively to force relitigation of fact-based issues in situations where no justification exists for such permissiveness.[104]

Second Restatement Approach. The Second Restatement has endorsed the general abandonment of mutuality, subject to the full-and-fair-opportunity reservation and subject to a further reservation relating to circumstances that might justify relitigation of the issue:

> **A party precluded from relitigating an issue with an opposing party... is also precluded from doing so with another person unless he lacked full and fair opportunity to litigate the issue in the first action or other circumstances justify affording him an opportunity to relitigate the issue.**[105]

This acceptance of nonmutuality is one of the major differences between the First and the Second Restatements. The reporter's note to the Second Restatement points out that there has been general acceptance of the *Bernhard* rule with the sensitive full-and-fair-opportunity proviso. It declares that "the distinct trend if not the clear weight of recent authority is to the effect that there is no intrinsic difference between 'offensive' and 'defensive' issue preclusion, although a stronger showing that the prior opportunity to litigate was adequate may be required in the former situation than the latter."[106] It also notes that when that adequate opportunity has been found to have existed in the first action, preclusion has been permitted in the second action against those who in the first action were defendants as well as against those who were plaintiffs.

Nevertheless, the Second Restatement demonstrates an awareness of the dangers of nonmutuality. Not only do all the usual exceptions to ordinary issue preclusion apply to meet those dangers, but also the circumstances of nonmutuality call into play a much heightened sensitivity. To aid in recognizing exceptions to its rule, the above-quoted section of the Second Re-

---

104. See Laura Emily Frossard, Collateral Estoppel of the Government: Striking the Necessary Balance Between the Interests of the Government, the Private Litigant, and Those Similarly Situated, 29 S. Tex. L. Rev. 385 (1987).

105. Restatement (Second) of Judgments § 29 (1982).

106. Restatement (Second) of Judgments § 29 reporter's note (1982).

statement goes on to list several "circumstances to which considerations should be given," namely, whether:

> (1) **Treating the issue as conclusively determined would be incompatible with an applicable scheme of administering the remedies in the actions involved** [this consideration of the Second Restatement would recognize that a statutory scheme such as antitrust might provide against nonmutuality];
>
> (2) **The forum in the second action affords the party against whom preclusion is asserted procedural opportunities in the presentation and determination of the issue that were not available in the first action and could likely result in the issue being differently determined** [this consideration would take into account the possibility of broader discovery, plenary as distinct from summary hearing, and other features of the second action, as well as matters relating to the convenience of the forum in the first action— but note that the absence of a jury right in the first action is not such a factor, according to the U.S. Supreme Court in *Parklane*];
>
> (3) **The person seeking to invoke favorable preclusion, or to avoid unfavorable preclusion, could have effected joinder in the first action between himself and his present adversary** [this consideration has tended to reach only blatant refusal to join, such as in the class-action exception];
>
> (4) **The determination relied on as preclusive was itself inconsistent with another determination of the same issue** [this consideration could be useful in checking the abusive possibilities of seriatim individual actions in multiple-claimant mass-accident situations];
>
> (5) **The prior determination may have been affected by relationships among the parties to the first action that are not present in the subsequent action, or apparently was based on a compromise verdict or finding** [this consideration would take account, for example, of the fact that the adjudicator in the first action may have been especially influenced by sympathy or other emotional response that ought not to influence the outcome in other cases];
>
> (6) **Treating the issue as conclusively determined may complicate determination of issues in the subsequent action or prejudice the interests of another party thereto** [this consideration would take account, for example, of the fact that precluding one party might prejudice a co-party];

(7) **The issue is one of law and treating it as conclusively determined would inappropriately foreclose opportunity for obtaining reconsideration of the legal rule upon which it was based** [this consideration would recognize that sometimes the more flexible doctrine of stare decisis suffices];

(8) **Other compelling circumstances make it appropriate that the party be permitted to relitigate the issue** [so, obviously, this listing is merely illustrative—indeed, the Second Restatement's final word on the subject is this: "The ultimate question is whether there is good reason, all things considered, to allow the party to relitigate the issue."[107]].

It seems likely that courts struggling with this problem, given that they have already abandoned mutuality, will find this approach a helpful one. If it does not offer simple answers, it at least provides a framework for analysis that should serve better than any rigid exception to reconcile the desire to avoid pointless relitigation with the need to preserve basic fairness for litigants.

Summary. Unlike in the old days, strangers today can benefit from a judgment by invoking collateral estoppel against a former party, other than a federal or state governmental party. But attempting to avoid real threats to efficiency and fairness, courts apply modern nonmutuality with great flexibility. They apply all the usual exceptions to issue preclusion. Additionally, courts exercise discretion to deny preclusion when the former party lacked a full and fair opportunity to litigate in the initial action or when all the circumstances otherwise justify allowing the former party to relitigate the issue. Factors affecting that discretion include among many others:

- whether there is some reason to suspect the accuracy of the prior determination, such as where it is inconsistent with some other adjudication of the same issue (a factor that partially solves the "multiple-plaintiff anomaly," where a string of potential plaintiffs sue an alleged tortfeasor seriatim, until one wins and theoretically so triggers collateral estoppel for the future plaintiffs);
- whether the stranger could reasonably have been expected to join or intervene in the initial action (a factor that explains the class-action exception); and

107. Restatement (Second) of Judgments § 29 cmt. j, reporter's note (1982).

- whether the former party did not choose the setting for the initial action (perhaps the most telling of all the general unfairness factors).

c. *Nonmutual Claim Preclusion*

Can the stranger benefit from res judicata other than through nonmutual collateral estoppel? Usually only parties and their privies can benefit from the other rules of res judicata, because for a stranger a different claim is necessarily involved. But sometimes a stranger can use a former party's victory on a claim to bar a new assertion of the opposing party's claim against the stranger.

A ready example lies in the old indemnitor-indemnitee situation. If the injured person litigates with the employee and loses—the employee being found not negligent—everyone agrees that the employer can invoke nonmutual collateral estoppel in the injured person's later action against the employer. But what if the injured party lost the prior action by failure to prosecute? The same indemnity dilemma argues for allowing the employer to use the prior judgment, even though this use would be an instance of nonmutual claim preclusion.

How far should the law go with this idea? Obviously, nonmutual claim preclusion cannot extend beyond the transaction or occurrence. The First Restatement applied nonmutual bar to its few secondary-liability extensions to mutuality.[108] The Second Restatement arbitrarily expanded nonmutual bar to the situation where the prior action was against the indemnitee, although it refused to go further with the idea.[109] The cases accord more with the Second Restatement's approach, but better arguments exist in favor of a more conservative approach limited to the few secondary-liability extensions.[110]

d. *Criticism of Modern Approach*

The rationale of the modern approach, then, is that the former party is entitled to only one opportunity to litigate an issue, regardless of any change in adversaries. But perhaps this view elevates simplistic notions of efficiency over real concerns of fairness and substantive policy.

---

108. See Restatement of Judgments §§96, 97, 99 (1942).

109. See Restatement (Second) of Judgments §51(1) (1982).

110. See 18 Charles Alan Wright, Arthur R. Miller & Edward H. Cooper, Federal Practice and Procedure §4463, at 567-70, §4464, at 586-89 (1981).

A basic choice exists between the rule of mutuality, with a few defined extensions, and the rule of nonmutuality, with lots of fuzzy exceptions. These two are not alternative formulations that end up at the same place in the middle. On the one hand, the extensions to mutuality were rare and limited, playing it safe and simple in extending res judicata to situations of real need such as secondary liability. The extensions certainly did not aim at reaching every case in which, on balance, preclusion would be desirable. On the other hand, the exceptions to nonmutuality are many, but they surely do not reach all situations beyond the coverage of mutuality's extensions. The prevailing exceptions do not even recognize all the reasons that preclusion might be undesirable.

Most jurisdictions have made the choice in favor of nonmutuality. But that choice is not necessarily stable. A sense is growing that the choice was more complicated than *Bernhard* represented. Moreover, the courts' ability and inclination to multiply exceptions gives them a ready route to undermine the rule of nonmutuality. In brief, the law remains in flux. So perhaps some jurisdictions will reopen the choice. If so, they should reconsider that choice on the basis of the usual grid of relevant policies (see grid, page 186).

The grid of policies appears to favor mutuality. If society is more risk averse as to intrusions on fairness by its courts than as to losses of efficiency, then that conclusion against nonmutuality becomes stronger.

Still, *Bernhard* undeniably struck a responsive chord. Society does not want, in this day and age, an adjudication to stand for as little as mutuality provides. But there are other ways, besides nonmutuality, to augment the efficacy of adjudication. If one considers the following three alternatives to nonmutuality, the conclusion against nonmutuality becomes even stronger:

Mandatory Joinder. The most mainstream alternative would be to expand mandatory joinder. This route would efficiently dispose of common matters in one shot, but in a fair shot. The joined parties would be bound, but only after being heard. Their opponent would be bound if it lost, but if it won it would win against all the joined parties. This procedural technique, which restores procedural neutrality by equating the parties' litigating risk, nicely demonstrates by contrast the most serious defect of nonmutuality, the destruction of procedural neutrality.[111]

111. See Elinor P. Schroeder, Relitigation of Common Issues: The Failure of Nonparty Preclusion and an Alternative Proposal, 67 Iowa L. Rev. 917 (1982).

Policies from Chapter 3	Arguments for Mutuality First Restatement's rule	Arguments for Nonmutuality Second Restatement's rule
Direct Expenditures	mutuality avoids overlitigation in the initial action; it avoids litigation in the subsequent action over the application of nonmutuality and all the exceptions	nonmutuality avoids relitigation; it encourages joinder of defendants, although it seriously discourages joinder of plaintiffs
Other Efficiency Concerns: inconsistency, decreased repose, and error costs	mutuality's rigidity fosters certainty and stability; it lowers error costs by not precluding in doubtful circumstances; it avoids nonmutuality's inherent and serious defect of stacking the odds heavily against invokee, causing erroneous outcomes and onerous settlements	nonmutuality avoids inconsistent adjudications
Fairness to Invokee of Res Judicata	preclusion frequently would be patently unfair, necessitating many exceptions, which would nevertheless fail to catch all cases of unfairness; a decision between specific litigants is a contextual truth that should have limited effect, rather than a determinate truth that should become free-floating	invokee should not be allowed to relitigate, especially when invokee is trying to abuse or could have joined invoker in the initial action; exceptions to nonmutuality can protect against most unfair preclusion
Fairness to Invoker of Res Judicata	under mutuality, invoker suffers no unfairness, as this new party faces no relitigation; invoker already derives benefits from invokee's initial loss, through improved settlement terms and stare decisis	under nonmutuality, invoker avoids burdens of litigation; sometimes fairness to invoker requires preclusion, as in the indemnitor-indemnitee situation
Fairness to Other Party	without mutuality, other party in the initial action faces an opponent willing to fight to the death, although other party does enjoy increased settlement leverage	
Other Fairness Concerns: fair doctrine and fair outcome	mutuality favors searching for the truth and deciding on the merits; it remains a clear and simple doctrine with need for only a few extensions; its rigidity fosters reliance interests and similar treatment	nonmutuality's one-day-in-court notion has intuitive appeal, although it does require a complicated set of exceptions
Substantive Policies	mutuality avoids nonmutuality's inherent and serious defect of stacking the odds heavily against invokee, causing unintended substantive effects; mutuality avoids the need for *Mendoza*-like provisos	

However, society has chosen, by balancing costs and benefits, to follow this mandatory joinder route no farther than such provisions as Federal Rule of Civil Procedure 19 on compulsory joinder. There is no provision for compulsory class actions, for instance.

Collateral Class Actions. A radical alternative would be for the courts to extend *Bernhard*, rather than to contract it. The argument would run that nonmutuality does relieve court congestion, but it introduces a lot of problems by operating as a one-way street. The cure would be to reintroduce mutuality, but to do so by binding as well as benefiting strangers. If *A* sues *B*, then *C*'s similar dispute with *B* would be precluded whether *A* won or lost. *A*'s representation of *C*'s interests would satisfy due process, and exceptions to res judicata could handle apparent excesses. The result would be broad collateral estoppel giving almost every case potential effects similar to those of a class action.[112]

Upon first impression, this collateral-class-action proposal sounds like a frightening abandonment of an essential tenet of adjudication, but a moment's thought produces the realization that stare decisis works along similar lines. The better counterargument to the proposal is that class-action provisions, such as Federal Rule of Civil Procedure 23, represent society's decision about how far to follow this route. In fact, this perspective illuminates the workings of the class action. The requirements of Federal Rule 23(a)-(b) are trying to ensure that the class members are similarly situated to and adequately represented by a party, while limiting the class device to certain situations where its benefits clearly outweigh its costs. The collateral-class-action proposal would create in effect a compulsory class action without the careful limitations and protections of Federal Rule 23.

Former Adjudication as Evidence. The above allusion to stare decisis should not hide that it is a flexible doctrine treating the former legal decision almost like mere evidence or a presumption. Perhaps a middle road like this, between no preclusion under mutuality and full preclusion under nonmutuality, offers promise. Strangers could get the benefits and burdens of former adjudications, even as to matters of fact. But the effects would be more evidential than preclusive.[113]

---

112. See Michael A. Berch, A Proposal to Permit Collateral Estoppel of Nonparties Seeking Affirmative Relief, 1979 Ariz. St. L.J. 511; Lawrence C. George, Sweet Uses of Adversity: *Parklane Hoisery* and the Collateral Class Action, 32 Stan. L. Rev. 655 (1980).

113. See Hiroshi Motomura, Using Judgments as Evidence, 70 Minn. L. Rev. 979 (1986).

Again, this evidential proposal at first sounds outlandish to American ears. But civil-law countries heavily employ this evidential use instead of expanding their doctrine of res judicata. Indeed, the United States does likewise in certain circumstances, such as by making felony convictions admissible.[114] One could therefore argue that the United States should do more of the same. However, the counterarguments against extending evidential weight to factual findings include that combining a past decision with new evidence is a bit like combining apples and oranges, especially when records of judgment do not convey the former evidence as a civil-law dossier does—how does one weigh a bare former finding of negligence against new evidence of weather conditions? Also, our jury system might especially have trouble in weighing a past decision— do one-shot adjudicators know how to handle a prior decision? Finally, the evidential approach lacks preclusion's advantage of avoiding trial altogether—is not the significance of trial vel non a driving force in the American procedural system? In brief, the limitation of stare decisis to legal decisions, as opposed to factual findings, is no happenstance. Our society has chosen how far to follow the evidential route as an alternative to preclusion. Although a few special types of adjudication are admissible, most former adjudications that fall outside of res judicata are of value mainly through stare decisis and, of course, in settlement talks by altering the apparent probability of the expected outcome.

Conclusion. As society has chosen not to pursue any of these three superior alternatives, the choice by the courts to work on their own the inferior reform of nonmutuality looks ever more questionable. Indeed, given the grid of policies, that so-called reform appears to have been a step backward. This is one area where the First Restatement seems to have gotten it right and the Second Restatement wrong. If the optimal doctrine lies between mutuality and nonmutuality, the law should seek it by extending res judicata cautiously from the pole of mutuality, rather than by pledging allegiance to nonmutuality while creating ever more exceptions.

---

114. See, e.g., Fed. R. Evid. 803(22).

CHAPTER 9

NONORDINARY JUDGMENTS

Up to this point, this book has been considering the subsequent effects of a judgment rendered in a prior action seeking *coercive* and *personal* relief in a *civil* tribunal called a *court*. But now we need to relax those assumptions. What if the plaintiff had sought declaratory relief? What if the plaintiff had relied on jurisdiction in rem or quasi in rem? What if the prior action had been a criminal case? Or what if the prior "action" had been an administrative or arbitration proceeding, rather than a court proceeding? These four questions are sequentially the subject of this chapter.

A. Noncoercive Judgments

The question here is what effects of claim and issue preclusion a declaratory judgment has in a subsequent civil action, assuming it was a valid and final judgment. But first some background on declaratory judgments is in order.

Parties bringing actions usually seek coercive relief, such as an award of money damages or an injunction. The traditional, restrictive view of the judicial process actually limited courts to such coercive, or active, relief. Formerly, at common law and in equity, any judicial declarations of the rights and duties of parties were merely incidental to judgments ordering or denying some form of active relief. Some judgments, most obviously any judgment for defendant, may have had consequences like those of a declaratory judgment, but these consequences were not the original object of the action. Indeed, the U.S. Supreme Court implied that a solid barrier to declaratory relief lay in the Constitution's limiting the federal judicial power to cases and controversies in Article III.[1]

Nevertheless, a practical need for declaratory relief could readily arise when a dispute has not progressed far enough to authorize active relief or when an aggrieved opponent does not yet choose to seek active relief. For example, a party to a contract might justifiably want to determine whether certain behavior would be or is a breach. In the 1930s, the Supreme Court reversed its previous direction, encouraging and then upholding congressional enactment of the Federal Declaratory Judgment Act of 1934.[2]

Federal courts, therefore, can today give declaratory judgments consisting of passive relief that does no more than define legal relations. A potential plaintiff or defendant may anticipatorily bring a federal action for a declaration of the rights, duties, and other legal relations of the parties. Federal subject-matter jurisdiction for the action must otherwise exist, and as always, the dispute must be advanced enough to constitute an actual controversy that falls within the constitutional limits of Article III. The declaratory remedy is then authorized and governed by the Federal Declaratory Judgment Act and Federal Rule of Civil Procedure 57. In sum, a federal court may in its discretion give a declaratory remedy in a case that has ripened beyond an abstract question into an actual controversy and that is otherwise within its jurisdiction.

A state court might be more restrictive or more permissive regarding declaratory relief than are federal courts. Nearly every state has adopted a procedure to permit a declaration of legal relations of parties on specific facts unconnected with any coercive remedy. Indeed, in some states, a declaratory judgment may be obtained before any events that might constitute a breach of duty have taken place. But in fact most states follow the federal approach regarding declaratory relief.

So, the declaratory remedy is a modern one. How has the old doctrine of res judicata adjusted to handle declaratory judgments?

A valid and final judgment in a suit solely for declaratory relief has two sorts of res judicata effects in a subsequent civil action. First, it is conclusive between opposing parties as to the matters declared, but it has no further claim preclusion effect and so does not preclude a later action for damages or other coercive relief. Second, a litigant is subject to issue preclusion, under the normal rules of that doctrine.[3]

---

1. Willing v. Chicago Auditorium Ass'n, 277 U.S. 274 (1928).
2. 28 U.S.C. §§ 2201-2202.
3. See generally Restatement (Second) of Judgments § 33 (1982).

A declaratory judgment is a personal judgment. It is conclusive between the parties on all the matters it declares, even if it was obtained by default. Moreover, under the rules of issue preclusion, in a case of nondefault, it is conclusive on all issues actually litigated and determined that were essential to the judgment rendered. It is usually held, however, that a declaratory judgment, even though it is a valid and final personal judgment, does not have claim-preclusive effect.[4]

Thus, a judgment for the plaintiff will not merge the claim in the judgment. If, at the time the plaintiff sought the declaratory judgment, no actual grounds for coercive relief had yet matured, it would seem reasonable not to preclude the plaintiff from later seeking damages or other relief if, in spite of the declaratory judgment, the defendant violates the rights the plaintiff was declared to have.

However, if the successful plaintiff could have joined a request for coercive relief with the declaratory request, the reasons for not according merger effect to the declaratory judgment are not so obvious. A plaintiff who has alternative theories for recovery might thereby be encouraged to split the claim. If the declaratory judgment is successful on one theory, the plaintiff can rely on the judgment as conclusively determining the issues in a later action for coercive relief. If the declaratory judgment is unsuccessful, the plaintiff can try the other theory in a later action for declaratory or coercive relief. This seems contrary to the policies of res judicata.[5]

A possible protection against such abuse of the declaratory judgment procedure is the principle, generally recognized, that a declaratory judgment is subject to the sort of judicial discretion normally associated with equitable remedies. A court may refuse to entertain the action if it appears the plaintiff is improperly refusing to present the whole case. This direct approach of nipping the problem of abuse in the bud seems preferable to the clumsier solution of applying the merger doctrine.

Thus, although a few courts have attributed merger effect to declaratory judgments where the plaintiff could have obtained in the first action the relief sought in the later action,[6] most courts persist in holding merger inapplicable.[7] Some cases in the majority reach their result by reasoning sim-

---

4. See E.H. Schopler, Annotation, Extent to Which Principles of Res Judicata Are Applicable to Judgments in Actions for Declaratory Relief, 10 A.L.R.2d 782 (1950).

5. See 18 Charles Alan Wright, Arthur R. Miller & Edward H. Cooper, Federal Practice and Procedure § 4446 (1981).

6. See, e.g., Mastercraft Lamp Co. v. Mortek, 183 N.E.2d 12 (Ill. App. Ct. 1962).

7. See Restatement (Second) of Judgments § 33 cmt. c, reporter's note (1982).

ilar to that outlined above in connection with the discussion of suits for injunction following judgments for damages for temporary nuisance or trespass.[8] The idea there is that policy favors the plaintiff's seeking a lesser remedy first. Just so, declaratory proceedings should permit initial treatment of a single potentially dispositive aspect of a bigger case. Other cases in the majority base their result on the policy, and even the text, of the declaratory judgment statute. Both the Federal Declaratory Judgment Act[9] and the Uniform Declaratory Judgments Act[10] provide for "further relief" based on a declaratory judgment. To apply the rule of merger, it is said, would be contrary to the statute's specific provision.

B. Nonpersonal Judgments

The question here is what effects of res judicata a nonpersonal judgment has in a subsequent civil action, assuming it was a valid and final judgment.

A nonpersonal judgment results from nonpersonal proceedings that seek a nonpersonal remedy, that is, a remedy that acts directly on a specific thing. Of course, proceedings that determine interests in a specific thing may be either personal proceedings producing a personal judgment or nonpersonal proceedings producing a nonpersonal judgment. Lots of issues and claims involving things arise in both personal and nonpersonal proceedings. It is not the nature of the dispute, then, that distinguishes personal from nonpersonal. The essential difference between personal and nonpersonal, instead, lies in the nature of the remedy sought—it is the remedy that is inherently either personal or nonpersonal. An action for a nonpersonal remedy, which acts directly on a specific thing, yields a nonpersonal judgment.

For nonpersonal remedies, such as partition of real estate that parties own jointly, the court must have nonpersonal jurisdiction over the thing.[11] For personal remedies, the court must have jurisdiction over the person. Often, however, in a court without jurisdiction over the thing, the plaintiff can accomplish the equivalent of a nonpersonal remedy by casting the action to seek instead a certain personal remedy addressed to the defendant

8. See supra Chapter 6-A-1-b.

9. 28 U.S.C. § 2202.

10. § 8, 12A U.L.A. 395 (1996).

11. See generally Kevin M. Clermont, Civil Procedure: Territorial Jurisdiction and Venue (1999).

and based on personal jurisdiction, such as seeking an order that commands the defendant to convey title. Again, both actions would determine interests in the land, but only the former action for partition would yield a nonpersonal judgment.

The traditional statements of the doctrines of res judicata have limited their application to personal judgments.[12] Similarly, this book to this point has treated only personal judgments. Why put off nonpersonal judgments, as nonpersonal judgments surely must settle some matters conclusively? They do, but the rules are special. The next part of this chapter, then, finally treats the res judicata effects of nonpersonal judgments.

1. In Rem

The term "in rem" is often used imprecisely in reference to any proceeding that is brought on jurisdiction over the thing, or "res," rather than on jurisdiction over the person of the defendant. More precise usage, however, recognizes that actions generally of this type include both those traditionally characterized as strictly in rem (i.e., actions to adjudicate the interests of all the world in the subject property) as well as those traditionally called quasi in rem (i.e., actions to adjudicate the interests of designated parties in the subject property). A proceeding predicated on jurisdiction over the res is properly called an in rem proceeding only if its object is to affect the interests of any and all persons, whoever and wherever they may be. It is properly called a quasi in rem proceeding if it seeks to determine the interests of designated persons in the thing. A judgment rendered in such a proceeding is referred to as a judgment in rem or quasi in rem, as the case may be.

Actions seeking in rem judgments may be entertained by a court whose territory includes the thing's location, or "situs," even though jurisdiction over the person of the defendants is lacking. Courts having jurisdiction over the thing can issue judgments acting directly on it, even if jurisdiction over the persons whose interests would be affected by such judgments is lacking. The situs court can exercise jurisdiction over the thing, and on that basis adjudicate the interests of anyone in that thing.

a. Pure In Rem

A judgment in rem has only two sorts of res judicata effects. It determines, conclusively with regard to all persons, the interests of all persons

12. See, e.g., Restatement (Second) of Judgments § 17 (1982).

in the thing. Also, any actual litigant is subject to issue preclusion, under the normal rules of that doctrine.[13]

Jurisdiction. Jurisdiction in rem can result in a judgment affecting the interests of *all* persons in a designated thing. Theoretically and formally, the action is against the thing. No personal liability or obligation results. Frequent examples of proceedings in rem include actions to register title to land, forfeiture actions, admiralty proceedings to enforce a maritime lien upon a vessel, and probate proceedings to settle an estate.

Jurisdiction in rem normally exists where the thing is, because that court has power and litigating there would not be unreasonable.

Preclusion. An in rem judgment can conclusively determine interests in the res. A judgment in rem for the plaintiff conclusively establishes the plaintiff's asserted interest in the property, even if the defendant defaults. A judgment in rem against the plaintiff conclusively establishes the nonexistence of the plaintiff's asserted interest in the property.

A judgment in a proceeding in rem does not purport to be a complete adjudication of the rights and duties of persons with respect to a certain transaction. It purports only to determine the ultimate issue of interests in specific property. Thus, it does not merge or bar the original claim. The application of merger and bar remains limited to personal judgments. Rather than merging or barring a claim, the in rem effect is simply one of determining everyone's interests in the thing conclusively in any later action.[14]

An in rem judgment may also conclusively establish issues that were actually litigated and determined against a litigant and were essential to the judgment rendered. Therefore, a judgment rendered in such an action has no issue preclusion effect unless a person appeared in some manner to defend.[15]

b. Jurisdiction over Status

Such a judgment determines, conclusively with regard to the parties and usually with regard to all other persons as well, the status in question. Also, any actual litigant is subject to issue preclusion.[16]

---

13. See generally Restatement (Second) of Judgments § 30 (1982).

14. See 18 Charles Alan Wright, Arthur R. Miller & Edward H. Cooper, Federal Practice and Procedure § 4412, at 100-01 (1981).

15. See 18 Charles Alan Wright, Arthur R. Miller & Edward H. Cooper, Federal Practice and Procedure § 4431, at 294-96 (1981).

16. See generally Restatement (Second) of Judgments § 31 (1982).

Jurisdiction. A related type of in rem jurisdiction is "jurisdiction over status." It can result in a judgment establishing, changing, or terminating a status, such as a family relationship, citizenship, or mental incapacity. By treating the status like a thing, the court may determine the status. For example, the state where the plaintiff spouse lives may grant a divorce; however, the state cannot adjudicate monetary support obligations without personal jurisdiction over the defendant spouse.

Jurisdiction over status, to satisfy the Due Process Clause's power test, normally must be exercised where the status is located. The exercise of jurisdiction must not be unreasonable, in accordance with the Due Process Clause's other jurisdictional test of fair play and substantial justice. All this means that a status can be sited in any place to which one party involved in the status has a significant connection. So, for example, imagine an unhappy husband who left his home in New York and went to Idaho, which had more permissive grounds for divorce. Having truly established his domicile in Idaho, he sued there for divorce. The wife defaulted. The jurisdiction in Idaho for that divorce was constitutional.

Preclusion. A valid and final judgment based on jurisdiction over status, and sought for the purpose of determining the status, has res judicata effects analogous to those of a pure in rem judgment. However, beyond that statement, it is difficult to generalize.

Obviously, to justify entertaining the proceeding at all, the determination itself of any status must have some conclusive effect, on which the parties and other persons can act in reliance. Also, issue preclusion against actual litigants presents no problems. These general propositions of res judicata resemble those for a pure in rem judgment. But the various statuses differ deeply in nature. Determinations of status can have vastly different impacts on persons' and the public's interests. Therefore, the peculiarities of status judgments lead to some differences of detail.

On the one hand, some cases go further in applying res judicata by allowing claim preclusion, although this extension is spotty and can be troublesome. For example, one court held that a husband's successful separation action based on the spouse's abandonment precluded the spouse's later annulment action based on the invalidity of the husband's divorce from a previous wife.[17] More commonly, a successful action for divorce precludes a later action for alimony, if personal jurisdiction was available in the first action.

---

17. Statter v. Statter, 143 N.E.2d 10 (N.Y. 1957).

On the other hand, many courts shy from applying res judicata that would conclusively establish a status against a particular stranger to the status proceeding who would suffer an unjust impact. For example, if a husband had to pay alimony until his former wife remarries, and if she remarries but then obtains an annulment of the remarriage, the annulment does not revive the husband's alimony obligation.[18]

In short, the res judicata law on jurisdiction over status tends to be rather messy and highly particularized in practice.

2. Quasi In Rem

There are two distinct varieties of proceedings quasi in rem: proceedings that seek as their object a judgment fixing the title to a thing, and proceedings aimed primarily at the satisfaction of a personal claim but operating under the guise of an action to apply property or other assets to the satisfaction of that claim.

In "subtype one," the plaintiff seeks to establish a *preexisting interest* in the thing as against the defendant's interest. Examples include suits to partition land, to quiet title, and to foreclose a mortgage, as well as suits to foreclose other liens on property or to remove a cloud on title to property. These kinds of actions are by no means rare in occurrence.

In "subtype two," the plaintiff seeks to apply the defendant's assets to the satisfaction of a claim against the defendant that is *unrelated* to the property. For example, New York plaintiffs could obtain jurisdiction in a New York state court for a tort claim arising from a plane crash in Turkey by garnishing a New York bank account belonging to the defendant, Turkish Airlines.[19] If successful, the plaintiff would apply the specific assets to awarded court costs and then to the satisfaction of the tort claim. Any extra funds would go back to the defendant. However, on such attachment jurisdiction, the plaintiff's recovery is limited to the assets. The defendant is not liable for any deficiency.

a. Subtype One

Such a judgment determines, conclusively with regard to the named parties, the interests of the named parties in the thing. Also, any party who actually litigated any issue is subject to issue preclusion.[20]

18. Gaines v. Jacobsen, 124 N.E.2d 290 (N.Y. 1954).
19. Feder v. Turkish Airlines, 441 F. Supp. 1273 (S.D.N.Y. 1977).
20. See generally Restatement (Second) of Judgments § 30 (1982).

Jurisdiction. Jurisdiction quasi in rem can result in a judgment affecting the interests of only *particular* persons in a designated thing. The difference between in rem and quasi in rem is that in the latter, the forum's law does not authorize a judgment affecting the interests of all persons in the world. Although a proceeding quasi in rem is formally brought against the named defendants, at stake are only their interests in the thing.

As in other nonpersonal actions, jurisdiction quasi in rem normally exists where the thing is.

Preclusion. For the purposes of preclusion, a subtype-one judgment receives basically the same treatment as a pure in rem judgment, except for the number of persons affected by the judgment. So, such a judgment can conclusively determine interests in the res, even if the judgment was obtained by default. Also, the judgment may conclusively establish issues in accordance with the doctrine of issue preclusion.

Recall that a claim targeting the thing (e.g., a claim seeking to foreclose a mortgage) and any associated claim against the person (e.g., a claim seeking to recover the underlying debt) are treated as different claims.[21]

Note that the defendant may choose to make a general appearance, which permits on any asserted personal claim a personal judgment with full res judicata effects. That is, if a named defendant does appear generally, and actually litigates questions upon which the determination of title to the thing depends, the appearance is normally treated as conferring personal jurisdiction on the associated personal claim, and the resulting judgment will have the same issue preclusion effect as any other in personam judgment.

Normally, the defendant cannot choose to make a limited appearance, a device whereby the defendant limits the appearance to defending a nonpersonal proceeding on the merits without submitting to personal jurisdiction. The reason is that a limited appearance should be available only if it is constitutionally unreasonable for the forum to exercise personal jurisdiction with respect to the additional claim concurrently with hearing the nonpersonal action. As proper subtype-one jurisdiction would be reasonable at the situs, then likely the desired personal jurisdiction for the associated personal claim would be reasonable too, making a limited appearance unavailable.

Yet even if the court permits a limited appearance in a subtype-one proceeding, so that the defendant can litigate the merits of the nonpersonal

21. See supra Chapter 6-A-1-b.

claim without submitting to personal jurisdiction on some personal claim, issue preclusion should apply. After all, when the defendant has fully and fairly litigated the essential issues that were actually entailed in the non-personal claim, preclusion should apply to any of those issues.

b. Subtype Two

Such a judgment determines, conclusively between the parties, the plaintiff's right to apply the particular thing to the satisfaction of the particular unrelated claim against defendant, but no more than that. Thus, the plaintiff may freely sue again for the unsatisfied portion of that claim, suing either in personam or on attachment of other property belonging to the defendant.[22]

Jurisdiction. This subtype of quasi in rem jurisdiction fundamentally differs from in rem jurisdiction and subtype one of quasi in rem jurisdiction. It comprises cases where the plaintiff has a personal claim against the defendant and seeks to satisfy it through attachment of particular property of the defendant—or by garnishment of an obligation owed the defendant by a third party—without obtaining personal jurisdiction over the defendant. Despite their uniqueness, actions of this second subtype are traditionally referred to as actions quasi in rem, because they technically concern the interests of particular persons in a designated thing. Actions of this second subtype are also referred to as proceedings on foreign attachment, and the jurisdiction is often termed attachment jurisdiction.

Subtype two of quasi in rem jurisdiction was formerly quite useful in facilitating recovery of claims owed by defendants who were not subject to personal jurisdiction. If the plaintiff had any claim against the defendant but failed to acquire personal jurisdiction, the plaintiff could proceed against any of the defendant's property within the territory, such as a bank account. The defendant usually defaulted, and the resulting judgment allowed the plaintiff to apply the property to satisfy the claim. The plaintiff could later bring a separate suit on any unsatisfied portion of the claim, either in personam or again by this subtype of quasi in rem against other property.

The validity of subtype two of quasi in rem jurisdiction in today's world, with the greatly expanded scope of personal jurisdiction, has been seriously questioned.[23] But this distinctive kind of jurisdiction persists. Of course, to

---

22. See generally Restatement (Second) of Judgments §32 (1982).

23. See Paul D. Carrington, The Modern Utility of Quasi In Rem Jurisdiction, 76 Harv. L. Rev. 303 (1962).

satisfy the power test, it normally must be exercised where the thing is. In the leading case of *Shaffer v. Heitner*,[24] the Supreme Court made clear that nonpersonal jurisdiction must also pass the unreasonableness test. Unreasonableness will then be the key test for attachment jurisdiction. Mere presence of some bit of the defendant's property is not enough to render reasonable entertaining a totally unrelated claim, even if the defendant's liability were limited to the value of that property. Something more—an adequate relation of the forum, the parties, and the litigation—has to exist before a court will, in its subjective opinion, deem jurisdiction to be fundamentally fair.

The result of *Shaffer v. Heitner*'s unreasonableness test is that this subtype of quasi in rem jurisdiction is now available only in four, rather special situations: (1) to secure a judgment being sought by the plaintiff elsewhere; (2) to enforce a judgment already rendered for the plaintiff elsewhere; (3) to recover where personal jurisdiction could constitutionally exist; or, perhaps, (4) to recover when no other American forum is available.

Preclusion. In quasi in rem actions of the second subtype, where the court acts by virtue of its jurisdiction over property only, without jurisdiction over the defendant's person, the judgment will effectively determine the plaintiff's right to the property. That matter cannot be relitigated, even if the judgment was obtained by default. But the judgment decides no more.

The plaintiff's underlying claim is not precluded by the judgment in such an action. Even if the property is sufficient to satisfy the claim completely, the plaintiff is theoretically free to sue again for higher damages on the claim in a later action in personam or another action quasi in rem based on jurisdiction over other property.[25] It is sometimes urged that if the defendant is subject to personal jurisdiction at the situs of the property, but the plaintiff elects to proceed on a quasi in rem basis instead, the resulting judgment should preclude any later action on the claim.[26] However, case authority endorsing this reform is hard to find.

Whether issue preclusion could apply at all depends, of course, upon whether issues were actually litigated and determined. If the judgment was entered by default, no issues were actually litigated, and so it would not be

24. 433 U.S. 186 (1977).

25. See Restatement of Judgments § 34 cmt. i, illus. 4 (1942); see also Developments in the Law—Res Judicata, 65 Harv. L. Rev. 818, 834 (1952) (discussing the rationale for this curious proposition).

26. See Restatement (Second) of Judgments § 30 cmt. b (1982).

accorded issue preclusion effect. If the defendant chose to make a general appearance, the resulting personal judgment would have full res judicata effects, including issue preclusion.

But what issue preclusion effects should ensue if the defendant did appear and litigate, but did so pursuant to a limited appearance, whereby a defendant can limit the appearance to defending a nonpersonal proceeding on the merits without submitting to personal jurisdiction? This is an especially troubling question, which deserves extended treatment, because of the oddity that in quasi in rem actions of the second subtype the issues that must be decided in order to render judgment are the same ones that would be involved in a purely personal action. If, say, the underlying claim was in tort for a traffic accident, the quasi in rem action and the personal action would both involve trial on issues of negligence, causation, and injury. So what is the preclusion law on this point?

Limited Appearance. First some background is in order. Recall that the defendant in a proper nonpersonal action who is denied the option of a limited appearance would have to choose between (1) losing the property by default and (2) making a general appearance. When does the law provide the third option of a limited appearance?

Confusion shrouds the availability of a limited appearance. The answer lies in scattered case law. The best view is that a limited appearance should be available if it is constitutionally unreasonable for the forum to exercise personal jurisdiction with respect to the additional claim concurrently with hearing the nonpersonal action.[27] To understand that view, contrast two cases. First, in order to recover for personal injuries from a traffic accident in Japan, a New York plaintiff sues in New York for $60,000 by attaching the French defendant's property in New York worth $30,000. The defendant wishes to defend her property by contesting negligence, but without submitting to personal jurisdiction. Fairness counsels that the defendant should be able to make a limited appearance in this case resting on attachment jurisdiction, because exercising personal jurisdiction in New York would be unreasonable. Second, in order to foreclose a mortgage on a French defendant's land in New York, a New York plaintiff sues in New York by attaching the land. The defendant wishes to defend on the merits without submitting to personal jurisdiction for any excess amount owing on the underlying debt. Efficiency counsels that the defendant should not be able

27. See Restatement (Second) of Judgments § 9 (1982); I. Daniel Stewart, Jr., Note, Limited Appearances, 7 Utah L. Rev. 369 (1961).

to make a limited appearance, because a New York court hearing the foreclosure suit has power by virtue of the defendant's appearance and concurrently may reasonably exercise personal jurisdiction with respect to the associated claim for debt.

Given this approach to the availability of a limited appearance, and since *Shaffer v. Heitner* prohibited unreasonable nonpersonal jurisdiction, there will be *few occasions that permit a limited appearance.*[28] If the nonpersonal jurisdiction is reasonable, then likely the desired personal jurisdiction will be reasonable too, making a limited appearance unavailable.[29] But there may be rare situations where liability limited to the property is reasonable but unlimited personal liability would not be, as in certain instances of attachment jurisdiction when no other American forum is available, so that the court should allow a limited appearance.[30]

The defendant then must make clear at the very outset the intention to limit the appearance. If the court permits the limited appearance, the defendant can participate in the action fully. If the defense on the merits succeeds, the defendant gets to keep the property. If the defense on the merits fails, the property is gone, but the defendant will not be personally liable on the resulting judgment. That is, the property will go to satisfy the plaintiff's claim, but the defendant is not liable for any deficiency.

Even after a limited appearance, the plaintiff can sue the defendant again in a separate action—either in personam or quasi in rem. Even though the parties have vigorously and thoroughly contested the claim, the first judgment still does not have merger or bar effect on the claim. It purports only to determine the plaintiff's interest in the property.

Now, finally, we reach the tough question. Will a judgment in a quasi in rem action of the second subtype, defended on the merits via a limited appearance, have issue preclusion effect? The question is a "close" one according to the authorities.[31] Different courts have expressed different views on the point.[32] The First Restatement took seemingly contradictory posi-

---

28. See Restatement (Second) of Judgments § 8 cmt. g (1982).

29. See, e.g., Campbell v. Murdock, 90 F. Supp. 297 (N.D. Ohio 1950).

30. See, e.g., Salmon Falls Mfg. Co. v. Midland Tire & Rubber Co., 285 F. 214 (6th Cir. 1922); Cheshire Nat'l Bank v. Jaynes, 112 N.E. 500 (Mass. 1916).

31. Restatement (Second) of Judgments § 32(3) cmt. d (1982); 18 Charles Alan Wright, Arthur R. Miller & Edward H. Cooper, Federal Practice and Procedure § 4431, at 298 (1981).

32. Compare Cheshire Nat'l Bank v. Jaynes, 112 N.E. 500, 502 (Mass. 1916), with United States v. Balanovski, 236 F.2d 298, 302 (2d Cir. 1956).

tions.[33] The question, basically, is whether issue preclusion is seen as inconsistent with the modern notion of a limited appearance or whether issue preclusion requires only that issues essential to the judgment were fully and fairly litigated.

If the latter is the proper view, judgments rendered after a limited appearance should be accorded issue preclusion effect even if claim preclusion effect is to be denied. The Second Restatement endorses, without citing any case support, this view that quasi in rem judgments should have issue preclusion effect as to the issues litigated through the defendant's limited appearance.[34] Instead, any unfairness to the defendant in being held to a judgment of a court that could not exercise personal jurisdiction would factor into deciding whether there was a full and fair opportunity to litigate, which, of course, is a general exception to issue preclusion under the Second Restatement. Litigation over that exception's application would be costly. That exception might, indeed, eat up the rule here, because a limited appearance should be allowed only in a court constitutionally unreasonable for personal jurisdiction. So, ultimately, the Second Restatement's position is not very clear.

Giving issue preclusion effect would significantly reduce the value of the limited appearance as a means of preventing abuses of the quasi in rem procedure. Indeed, giving issue preclusion effect is basically inconsistent with the essence of a limited appearance. The limited appearance's purpose is to allow litigation without deciding the underlying personal claim, that is, to limit the risk of protecting the property to the value of the property. Because the issues are the same in the attachment claim and the underlying personal claim, the purpose of a limited appearance in this peculiar setting clashes with allowing issue preclusion. On the one hand, the losing defendant would receive little benefit from a limited appearance with issue preclusion effect, as the plaintiff could just sue again and win almost automatically by issue preclusion—the defendant's appearance would, after all, turn out to be not limited to the nonpersonal proceeding, as was expected. On the other hand, a limited appearance with issue preclusion effect would give the winning defendant the small windfall of foreclosing the whole claim while having directly risked only the property.[35]

---

33. Compare Restatement of Judgments §40 cmt. a (1942) (no collateral estoppel where defendant contests the claim without submitting to personal jurisdiction), with id. §76(2) cmt. c (collateral estoppel applies to questions actually litigated).

34. See Restatement (Second) of Judgments §32(3) (1982).

35. See Developments in the Law—Res Judicata, 65 Harv. L. Rev. 818, 835 (1952).

Moreover, a limited appearance should be available only when it is constitutionally unreasonable for the forum to exercise personal jurisdiction. This means that this whole debate swirls about a pretty rare occurrence, as attested by the total absence of recent cases dealing with the issue preclusion effect of a limited appearance. It also means that applying issue preclusion would most often involve giving personal effect to a judgment of a court that constitutionally could not have entertained the underlying personal claim. Only here, in all of litigation, does a finding that jurisdiction for a claim is unreasonable fail to block litigation of that claim's issues, because the issues on the merits are the same in the proper attachment claim and the improper personal claim. Thus, only for a limited appearance in attachment jurisdiction (and not for limited appearances in other nonpersonal jurisdiction), does a special blanket exception to issue preclusion need to apply.[36]

Picture now a case in a state that uses attachment jurisdiction when personal jurisdiction could constitutionally exist and that liberally grants limited appearances. Is relitigation desirable after a limited appearance when personal jurisdiction is reasonable? Of course not. But how should the state head off relitigation? The choice is *either* offering a limited appearance and then in the second action surprising the defendant with issue preclusion that makes the appearance rather unlimited after all *or* denying a limited appearance in the first place in order frankly to indicate what is at stake for the defendant and to avoid the need for duplicative actions. The better choice is obvious. The cure for the waste of litigating the merits without attaining preclusion is to deny a limited appearance whenever fairness does not demand one—not to apply preclusion illogically and unfairly to a limited appearance. Indeed, most recent cases do take the desirable route of denying a limited appearance.

In summary, although there is disagreement, the preferred view is that adjudication under subtype two of quasi in rem jurisdiction pursuant to a limited appearance should have no res judicata effects other than determining interests in the thing and, hence, no issue preclusion effect.[37]

---

36. See Minichiello v. Rosenberg, 410 F.2d 106, 112 (2d Cir. 1968), aff'd on reh'g en banc, 410 F.2d 117 (2d Cir. 1969).

37. See Arthur T. von Mehren & Donald T. Trautman, Jurisdiction to Adjudicate: A Suggested Analysis, 79 Harv. L. Rev. 1121, 1139 n.38 (1966); Ernest L. Schmider, Note, Limited Appearances and Issue Preclusion: Resetting the Trap?, 66 Cornell L. Rev. 595 (1981).

C. Noncivil Judgments

The question here is what effects of preclusion a criminal judgment has in a subsequent civil action, assuming that it was a valid and final decision.

Criminal judgments are now widely viewed as giving rise to normal issue preclusion in a subsequent civil action. Thus, a convicted defendant will generally be bound on essential issues actually litigated and determined, unless some exception applies as where the criminal offense was of such piddling importance as to deny the accused an adequate incentive to litigate. However, the government will almost never be bound by an acquittal, because an exception to issue preclusion (e.g., more favorable burden of persuasion) almost always applies.[38]

The contrasts and similarities between res judicata and the doctrine of double jeopardy applicable in criminal cases have been discussed in Chapter 2-I above. Matters adjudicated in a criminal case may also become relevant in later civil actions. In such a civil case, there is no role for claim preclusion. But a question of the issue preclusion effect of the criminal judgment may arise in the civil action.

Take as an example that the government by trial convicts *D* of arson involving a government building. The government later sues *D* civilly for damage to the building. Should *D* be subject to preclusion on the common issues? Yes.

Beyond this simple example, two factors have served to limit the issue preclusion effect of a criminal judgment in a later civil action, even where the issues involved are identical. One is the doctrine of mutuality, because the second action most often involves some new party in lieu of the government. The other is the different standard of proof required in criminal as opposed to civil proceedings. The significance of mutuality has, of course, waned since the *Bernhard* decision, but the standard of proof remains a serious limiting factor.

With the decline of the mutuality doctrine, it followed that issue preclusion based on a criminal conviction could be asserted by nonparties to the prior action. Most courts have accepted this proposition.[39] Others have continued to apply the rule of mutuality, thus denying issue preclusion in favor of a nonparty to the prior proceeding. A few in the middle have been willing to permit issue preclusion in favor of a nonparty only when the previ-

---

38. See generally Restatement (Second) of Judgments § 85 (1982).

39. See, e.g., Teitelbaum Furs, Inc. v. Dominion Ins. Co., 375 P.2d 439 (Cal. 1962).

ously convicted party is seeking in the civil action to benefit from his crime, as in trying to collect insurance after committing arson.[40]

Because of the different standards of proof, a judgment of acquittal will rarely if ever receive issue preclusion effect in a later civil suit. O.J. Simpson could not use his acquittal in the later civil action by a victim's family against him. Even when the parties remain the same (i.e, the government and the former defendant), so that no stranger or mutuality problem exists, the judgment of acquittal normally means that the government failed to establish beyond a reasonable doubt the existence of one or more of the facts essential to conviction. It does not necessarily follow that the government would be unable to meet the lesser standard of proof on that same issue in a civil action. Thus, a widow, who had been acquitted of the murder of her husband, could not use preclusion, on the issue of whether she had killed her husband, in her later claim for the proceeds of his governmental life insurance policy.[41] Moreover, the judgment of acquittal normally means that the government had no right to appeal, providing a separate argument against issue preclusion.

A judgment of conviction, contrariwise, rests upon proof beyond a reasonable doubt of all of the elements of the crime. If that high standard of proof has been satisfied, it would seem a fortiori that the usual civil standard of preponderance of the evidence is satisfied. Even as to determinations of peripheral issues on lower standards of proof, such as rejection of a pretrial motion to suppress evidence, issue preclusion can apply. If the same issues arise in the civil action, and they were actually litigated and determined and were essential to conviction, issue preclusion is appropriate. The only obstacles to giving collateral estoppel effect to the conviction in the later civil action are those exceptions applying to issue preclusion generally. It is through these exceptions that the courts take into account the tactical and procedural disadvantages of being a criminal defendant—including possibly lackadaisical assigned counsel, limited discovery, prejudicial setting, and reluctance to take the stand—which might amount to a lack of a full and fair opportunity to litigate the common issues.[42]

---

40. See Allan D. Vestal, Res Judicata/Preclusion 378-82 (1969).

41. Burns v. United States, 200 F.2d 106 (4th Cir. 1952); see One Lot Emerald Cut Stones v. United States, 409 U.S. 232, 235 (1972).

42. See generally 18 Charles Alan Wright, Arthur R. Miller & Edward H. Cooper, Federal Practice and Procedure § 4474 (1981 & Supp. 1999); Jonathan C. Thau, Collateral Estoppel and the Reliability of Criminal Determinations: Theoretical, Practical, and Strategic Implications for Criminal and Civil Litigation, 70 Geo. L.J. 1079 (1982).

An area where these questions frequently arise involves a convicted defendant's later seeking relief against the government. When the subsequent action is a habeas corpus proceeding collaterally attacking a conviction, some special considerations are relevant. The doctrine of res judicata has historically been regarded as inapplicable to habeas corpus proceedings, which have the unique purpose of release from unlawful confinement.[43] The Supreme Court of the United States has specifically declared res judicata inapplicable to habeas corpus in federal courts.[44] So, even if the issues asserted in a federal habeas corpus proceeding were litigated in the course of the original state prosecution, they may be relitigated under some circumstances. The circumstances under which relitigation is permitted are determined not by general principles of res judicata, but by a separate and complex body of statutory and decisional habeas corpus law,[45] which has incidentally become progressively more hostile to relitigation in recent years.[46]

Habeas corpus is not the only federal remedy for unconstitutional state convictions, however. The Federal Civil Rights Act in 42 U.S.C. § 1983 provides injunctive, declaratory, and damage remedies for the deprivation under color of state law of rights, privileges, and immunities secured by the Federal Constitution. Constitutional rights, privileges, and immunities may be infringed in the course of state criminal investigations and prosecutions. A criminal defendant may therefore have a claim for damages or other relief under § 1983 based upon the conduct of state officers. The same conduct, however, may sometimes have been asserted as a defense or as grounds for the exclusion of evidence in the state prosecution. For instance, an unlawful search and seizure in the defendant's home would have provided a basis for excluding from the state trial any evidence obtained through the search, but it could also provide the basis for an action for damages under § 1983.

If the issue was raised and decided in the state prosecution, would the issue be precluded when later raised in a federal action under § 1983? In contrast to the position expressed in habeas corpus cases, the Supreme Court has held that res judicata is fully applicable to federal civil rights ac-

43. See Ronald P. Sokol, Federal Habeas Corpus 157 (2d ed. 1969).

44. Fay v. Noia, 372 U.S. 391, 423 (1963).

45. See Developments in the Law—Federal Habeas Corpus, 83 Harv. L. Rev. 1038 (1970).

46. See 17A Charles Alan Wright, Arthur R. Miller & Edward H. Cooper, Federal Practice and Procedure §§ 4265-4267 (2d ed. 1988 & Supp. 1999).

tions brought under § 1983.[47] Many arguments exist against this result, but the Supreme Court brushed them all aside to embrace res judicata with true ardor. Unless a defendant could not fully and fairly litigate his constitutional right during the state prosecution, he will be collaterally estopped from relitigating the issue in a later federal civil rights action. Habeas corpus may be available in some circumstances, and appellate review in the Supreme Court of the state determination of federal constitutional law is theoretically possible, but these avenues are not always open. Thus, the defendant may simply be unable to get a federal-court determination of the federal constitutional issue.[48]

1. Plea of Guilty

On the one hand, because a guilty plea means the issues were not actually litigated and determined, the general and increasingly accepted view is that a conviction based thereon does not give rise to issue preclusion.[49] It is true, however, that a good number of courts persist in yielding to the temptation to preclude issues admitted by guilty pleas.[50]

On the other hand, the plea itself will normally be admissible in evidence, as an admission, in a subsequent civil action. It may also later equitably estop defendant from taking an inconsistent position in a subsequent civil action.

2. Conviction as Evidence

The question of issue preclusion has sometimes been confused with the question of admissibility of prior judgments as evidence of issues necessarily adjudicated. Recall that normally a judgment is inadmissible under the hearsay rule.[51] However, it should be noted that some jurisdictions have adopted a special exception to their hearsay rule.[52] This exception makes a conviction for a serious offense, by trial or guilty plea, admissible evidence

47. Allen v. McCurry, 449 U.S. 90 (1980).

48. See generally 18 Charles Alan Wright, Arthur R. Miller & Edward H. Cooper, Federal Practice and Procedure § 4471 (Supp. 1999).

49. See Haring v. Prosise, 462 U.S. 306 (1983); David L. Shapiro, Should a Guilty Plea Have Preclusive Effect?, 70 Iowa L. Rev. 27 (1984).

50. See 18 Charles Alan Wright, Arthur R. Miller & Edward H. Cooper, Federal Practice and Procedure § 4474, at 759-61 (1981).

51. See supra Chapter 2-C.

52. See, e.g., Fed. R. Evid. 803(22).

on any issue of fact that had been essential to the conviction. This half-way approach represents a recognition that the heavy burden of persuasion and other protections in criminal cases justify giving a conviction at least some effect in a subsequent civil case, even if not a preclusive effect.

3. Plea of Nolo Contendere

Such a plea and the resultant conviction have none of these preclusive or evidentiary effects in a subsequent civil action. It is simply a way of saying "no contest."

D. Nonjudicial Proceedings

The question here is what effects of claim and issue preclusion a nonjudicial decision has in a subsequent civil action, assuming that it was a valid and final decision.

1. Administrative Adjudications

Res judicata is a product of the judicial process. It does not apply to legislative or executive determinations. The question here concerns the extent to which res judicata applies to the determinations of those hybrid bodies known as administrative agencies or tribunals.

An adjudication by an administrative tribunal is treated like a court judgment, unless the essential elements of judicial adjudication were not employed or unless legislative policies support relitigation.[53]

There have been numerous cases that seem baldly to declare that res judicata does not apply to administrative agency decisions.[54] It seems generally to be recognized today, however, that *some* decisions of *some* administrative agencies will be accorded preclusive effects, not only by other administrative tribunals but by the courts as well. The Supreme Court has said: "When an administrative agency is acting in a judicial capacity and resolves disputed issues of fact properly before it which the parties have had an adequate opportunity to litigate, the courts have not hesitated to apply res judicata to enforce repose."[55]

---

53. See generally Restatement (Second) of Judgments § 83 (1982).

54. See, e.g., Pearson v. Williams, 202 U.S. 281 (1906); Warburton v. Warkentin, 345 P.2d 992 (Kan. 1959).

55. United States v. Utah Constr. & Mining Co., 384 U.S. 394, 422 (1966).

To determine when preclusion will be applied to decisions of administrative agencies, it is necessary to look at the particular decision and at the circumstances—particularly the procedural setting—in which it was rendered. Facts found by the agency in the process of exercising its rulemaking function will not be accorded preclusive effects. But when the administrative function consists of finding historical facts and determining their legal significance in accordance with previously established procedures through the medium of an adversary proceeding, the agency is essentially acting judicially. The decisions it reaches should be binding on the parties in the same ways as decisions of a court would bind them.

Basically, then, preclusion depends on whether the party to be bound had a full and fair opportunity to present its case in a manner of its own choosing, as well as on whether there is any substantive reason aside from procedural fairness to justify relitigation. Of course, if the procedures by which the agency acts are dissimilar to judicial procedures, preclusion may be inappropriate; different rules relating to the admission of evidence, access to compulsory process to compel production of evidence and witnesses, and mode of trial are relevant in this regard. Commonly parties have a right to judicial review of administrative rulings, which preclusion would normally demand; discretionary denial of such direct judicial review of the administrative ruling is a factor to be considered in deciding whether the matter should be precluded in a later action.[56]

2. Arbitration Awards

An award by arbitration is generally treated like a court judgment, usually having claim preclusion effect, and also having issue preclusion effect unless the essential elements of judicial adjudication were not employed or unless legislative policies or contractual provisions support relitigation.[57]

Although res judicata is, technically, an attribute only of a judgment of a court or a decision of an administrative tribunal, many cases have held that an award of an arbitration tribunal, for or against the claimant, has res judicata effects in the same ways.[58]

---

56. See generally 18 Charles Alan Wright, Arthur R. Miller & Edward H. Cooper, Federal Practice and Procedure § 4475, at 762-70 (1981).

57. See generally Restatement (Second) of Judgments § 84 (1982).

58. See 2 A.C. Freeman, A Treatise of the Law of Judgments 1339-41 (5th ed. 1925).

In some, but not all, of these cases, the award had been judicially confirmed. Because an unconfirmed arbitration award derives its authority from the agreement of the parties, not by act of the sovereign, presumably its res judicata effects are dependent upon the parties' intent.[59] Most recent cases do not seem to treat the question primarily as a matter of the parties' intent, however.[60] Indeed, in some jurisdictions or in some industries, there may be a sort of presumption in favor of res judicata that will apply in the absence of any contrary indication of the parties' intent.

In one way or another, by one theory or another, an arbitration award often enjoys res judicata effects. Which effects? Claim preclusion is on relatively solid ground, because often an arbitration should work to end the dispute once and for all. The parties likely agreed to arbitration with the idea that it would produce a binding result. Contrariwise, issue preclusion on the basis of a freewheeling arbitrator's decision often would be inappropriate, so courts are more wary. The parties likely were not even thinking about issue preclusion when they agreed to arbitration.[61]

59. See Allan D. Vestal, Res Judicata/Preclusion 233 (1969).

60. See, e.g., Overseas Motors, Inc. v. Import Motors Ltd., 375 F. Supp. 499 (E.D. Mich. 1974), aff'd, 519 F.2d 119 (6th Cir. 1975).

61. See generally 18 Charles Alan Wright, Arthur R. Miller & Edward H. Cooper, Federal Practice and Procedure § 4475, at 770-72 (1981).

CHAPTER 10

NONDOMESTIC JUDGMENTS

A. General Considerations

The problem here is what treatment a judgment should receive in a subsequent civil action in a different judicial system. Judgments rendered in the courts of one state or nation frequently bear on litigation conducted in the courts of another. For example, a plaintiff who has obtained a judgment in one jurisdiction may wish to enforce it against the defendant or the defendant's assets in another jurisdiction. In such a situation, the plaintiff may ask a forum in the second jurisdiction (F-2) to enforce the judgment of the first jurisdiction (F-1). Historically, this relief required the plaintiff to bring an action upon the judgment in the F-2 court for the purpose of enforcement,[1] unless some statute provided a more summary enforcement procedure.

Enforcement is not the only effect that the courts of F-2 may be asked to give to a judgment of F-1. If the parties have previously litigated in F-1 the claim involved in the F-2 action, the F-2 court may be asked to recognize the F-1 judgment's merger or bar effect. If the parties have previously litigated in F-1 some of the issues involved in the F-2 action, the F-2 court may be asked to recognize the F-1 judgment's issue preclusion effect. Recognition of nondomestic judgments, then, involves giving effects to such judgments under the law of res judicata that has been the subject of this book up to this point. Recognition, indeed, is a prerequisite to enforcement.

The subject of this chapter is court judgments. Judicially unreviewed administrative determinations and judicially unconfirmed arbitration awards

1. See supra Chapter 6-A-2-a.

often get respect in the courts of a different jurisdiction. But this respect normally flows from F-2's conflict of laws doctrine: F-2 can choose, as a matter of comity, to give effects to them. There is, however, no general obligation to give full faith and credit to these nonjudgments.[2]

In sum, this chapter will cover the extent of recognition and enforcement of nondomestic judgments in American courts. It will treat truly foreign judgments separately from nondomestic American judgments—and for these American judgments, it will treat sequentially all four combinations of state and federal judgments raised in state or federal court. But to begin, here is a summary statement of the general rules of recognition and enforcement of judgments, which this chapter will eventually explain and justify as applicable to all those different settings:

1. Recognition

A court will recognize, or give effects under the doctrine of res judicata to, a nondomestic judgment that is valid and final.

When the second court faces the question of whether the prior judgment is *valid and final*, it applies the law of the judgment-rendering sovereign—which, of course, is subject to any applicable external restraints, such as due process and other federal provisions imposed on and becoming part of state law. When the second court faces a question of the extent of *res judicata* based on the prior judgment, it similarly applies the law that the rendering court would apply, including any applicable external restraints. The basic approach to judgments thus is "retroverse," in the sense of turning backward to look at the rendering court's view of its own judgment. The second court lets the first court's law decide what it conclusively adjudicated.

2. Enforcement

The second court will enforce a judgment entitled to recognition.

With respect to the method of enforcement, the second court applies its own law. Its law is, however, subject to the federal requirement that the

2. See generally University of Tenn. v. Elliott, 478 U.S. 788 (1986) (suggesting that some state administrative findings might fall within the Full Faith and Credit Clause applicable in state courts, although not within 28 U.S.C. § 1738 applicable in federal courts); 18 Susan Bandes & Lawrence B. Solum, Moore's Federal Practice §§ 130.60-.66 (3d ed. 1999) (discussing, inter alia, the 1958 U.N. Convention on the Recognition and Enforcement of Foreign Arbitral Awards).

method not be so complex or expensive as to burden unduly the enforcement of nondomestic American judgments.

B. Judgments of American Courts

The above rules for handling a nondomestic judgment are in large part obligatory on American courts when that judgment comes from another American court. These rules help us to realize the benefits of a unified nation. "The animating purpose of the full faith and credit command...'was to alter the status of the several states as independent foreign sovereignties, each free to ignore obligations created under the laws or by the judicial proceedings of the others, and to make them integral parts of a single nation throughout which a remedy upon a just obligation might be demanded as of right, irrespective of the state of its origin.'"[3]

1. State Judgments

a. State—State

When the prior judgment was rendered by a state court and the second action is brought in a court of another state, the *Full Faith and Credit Clause* of the Federal Constitution requires the second court to give the same effects to a valid and final judgment as the judgment would have in the courts of the rendering state.[4]

Recognition. The prevalent view is that full faith and credit requires the second court to give neither more effect nor less effect than the rendering state would, but rather the same effect, even if the judgment is erroneous or against local public policy.

Rule of Full Faith and Credit. The Full Faith and Credit Clause of Article IV, Section 1 of the United States Constitution provides simply that "Full Faith and Credit shall be given in each State to the public Acts, Records, and judicial Proceedings of every other State." Certainly, this clause requires F-2 to accord to a valid and final F-1 judgment "at least the res judicata effect" that it has in F-1.[5] No one contends that F-2 can give less effect to an F-1 judgment than it has in F-1. But whether F-2 can, if its policy permits,

3. Baker v. General Motors Corp., 522 U.S. 222, 232 (1998) (quoting Milwaukee County v. M.E. White Co., 296 U.S. 268, 277 (1935)).

4. See generally Restatement (Second) of Conflict of Laws §§ 93, 100 (1971).

5. Durfee v. Duke, 375 U.S. 106, 109 (1963).

give *more* effect to an F-1 judgment than it has in F-1 is a question that has not yet received a definitive answer. Justice Jackson, in a famous article, suggested that F-2 could do so: "States under their voluntary policy may extend recognition when they could not constitutionally be required to do so ...."[6] Yet most authorities have asserted, to the contrary, that recognition of a judgment for full faith and credit purposes means giving the judgment "the same effect that it has in the state where it was rendered."[7]

On the one hand, the argument in favor of giving more effect runs like this. Assume that the F-1 judgment is valid and final, that the F-1 res judicata rule in the situation under discussion would permit relitigation of the claim or issue, that the F-2 rule would not permit relitigation, and that the F-2 res judicata rule does not exceed due process or other such constitutional limitations when applied to F-2 judgments. If F-2 has a significant connection to the parties or to the events involved in the F-1 litigation, and if the relitigation is to take place in F-2's court, F-2 is presumably free to conduct the litigation in accordance with its applicable substantive as well as procedural law. If F-2 has sufficient connection with the litigation to permit the application of its substantive law to the claims or issues without violating the Due Process Clause or the Full Faith and Credit Clause,[8] it would seem to have sufficient connection to apply its res judicata law to claims or issues relevant in the F-2 action that were previously litigated in F-1. Thus, application of F-2's broader preclusion rules is arguably permissible. And, of course, F-2 has interests in avoiding the burden of relitigation.

On the other hand, if F-2 accords claim preclusion or issue preclusion effects to the F-1 judgment, the result will be a new judgment that will then be entitled to res judicata effects and full faith and credit in every other state—even in F-1. The effect of F-2's application of its own broader res judicata standards could significantly change the effects of the F-1 adjudi-

---

6. Robert H. Jackson, Full Faith and Credit—The Lawyer's Clause of the Constitution, 45 Colum. L. Rev. 1, 30 (1945); see Robert C. Casad, Intersystem Issue Preclusion and the Restatement (Second) of Judgments, 66 Cornell L. Rev. 510, 521-23 (1981).

7. Restatement (Second) of Conflict of Laws introductory note to ch. 5, topic 2, at 277 (1971); see id. § 93 cmt. b; Farmland Dairies v. Barber, 478 N.E.2d 1314 (N.Y. 1985); Barbara Ann Atwood, State Court Judgments in Federal Litigation: Mapping the Contours of Full Faith and Credit, 58 Ind. L.J. 59, 69 n.54 (1982).

8. See Allstate Ins. Co. v. Hague, 449 U.S. 302 (1981); Home Ins. Co. v. Dick, 281 U.S. 397 (1930).

cation.[9] For instance, if F-2 held that the F-1 judgment was a bar to a later suit on the claim, the F-2 judgment would then prevent relitigation of the claim even in F-1, under whose rules the first judgment was not a bar. Similar permanent effects can result if F-2 precludes relitigation of issues that were not regarded as conclusively determined under the rules of F-1. Note that F-1 does not have the symmetrical power to give F-2's judgment less effect than it has in F-2. So, F-2's application of its own res judicata law has a significant impact on F-1. Surely, F-1 has significant substantive and procedural interests in specifying the effects of its own judgments. F-2's interest in avoiding relitigation is arguably insufficient to justify such an impingement on F-1's interests.

More is at stake, however, than the balancing of the two states' interests. The way to resolve this problem is to return to the purpose of the Full Faith and Credit Clause. It meant to give us the benefits of a judicially unified nation. A judgment of F-1 should mean the same thing everywhere within the nation, whether a person manages to sue subsequently in a broad or narrow res judicata state. Additionally, fairness argues that the parties litigating in F-1 know *then* what is at stake and what any judgment will mean anywhere in the nation.[10]

Even more basically, res judicata is the law that specifies what a judgment decides and what it does not decide. What it does not decide is just as important as what it decides. Res judicata defines the boundaries of the judgment. The boundaries are an intrinsic part of the judgment. To respect a judgment requires respecting its boundaries. For F-2 to give more credit to the content of F-1's judgment than F-1 would give—more rather than the same credit—necessarily implies that F-2 is giving less credit to the judgment's boundaries. Consequently, the Full Faith and Credit Clause must require giving the same effect to the judgment's content and its boundaries as would the rendering state.

It should finally be noted that 28 U.S.C. § 1738, substantially similar to the statute passed in 1790 to implement the Full Faith and Credit Clause, provides for the credit to be the same: "The records and judicial proceedings of any court of any such State, Territory or Possession... shall have the same full faith and credit in every court within the United States and its Territories and Possessions as they have by law or usage in the courts of

9. See Roche v. McDonald, 275 U.S. 449 (1928).

10. See Nelson v. Adams USA, Inc., 120 S. Ct. 1579 (2000) (due process concerns).

such State, Territory or Possession from which they are taken." This statute so sheds light on how to read the clause itself.

Validity. A state could not give effect to a judgment that is invalid. It would constitute a denial of due process to do so. So, only valid F-1 judgments are entitled to recognition in F-2. Validity in this context generally means that the F-1 court must have had subject-matter and territorial jurisdiction and given adequate notice under its own standards, and under federal due process standards as well.[11] Thus, recognition of the F-1 judgment in F-2 can be resisted by showing on collateral attack that the F-1 court lacked jurisdiction or slighted notice.

The F-2 court on such a collateral attack can make an independent determination of the facts regarding jurisdiction and notice, unless those issues were decided in the F-1 action under conditions that would entitle those F-1 court's findings to res judicata effect.[12] If F-1 and F-2 prescribe different criteria to determine when a party may be precluded from relitigating issues of validity, F-1's criteria should be applied in F-2.

Finality. Likewise, only final F-1 judgments are entitled to recognition in F-2. The governing criteria as to finality are those of F-1's law.[13]

Claim Preclusion. A valid and final judgment of a court of F-1 is entitled to recognition for its claim preclusion effect in F-2. This is true without regard to whether the F-1 judgment was for the plaintiff (merger) or for the defendant (bar). In the event that F-1 and F-2 apply different criteria to determine the claim preclusion effect, the local law of F-1 governs.[14]

Issue Preclusion. Full faith and credit also requires F-2 to accord issue preclusion effect to matters adjudicated in the F-1 judgment. If the F-1 judgment was a valid and final judgment, issues precluded from relitigation under F-1's doctrine may not be relitigated in F-2. If there are differences between the laws of F-1 and F-2 with respect to the issue preclusion effect, the local law of F-1 controls all questions, including the questions of who is bound and benefited by issue preclusion.[15]

Others have suggested that this particular rule is not constitutionally based, and so that F-2 is in some circumstances free to apply its own

---

11. See infra Chapter 12.

12. See infra Chapter 13.

13. See Parsons Steel, Inc. v. First Ala. Bank, 474 U.S. 518 (1986), on remand, 825 F.2d 1475 (11th Cir. 1987); Restatement (Second) of Conflict of Laws § 107 (1971).

14. See Restatement (Second) of Conflict of Laws § 95 (1971) (amended 1988).

15. See Restatement (Second) of Conflict of Laws § 95 cmt. g (1971) (amended 1988).

broader standards relating to the issues or parties affected by issue preclusion stemming from the F-1 judgment.[16] *Hart v. American Airlines*[17] faced the question whether New York could validly apply its rule of nonmutual offensive collateral estoppel in an air-crash action, which would permit the assertion of issue preclusion against the airline in favor of a nonparty to the prior judgment from Texas. In Texas the mutuality rule then prevailed, so that such a prior judgment would have no such issue preclusion effect there. Nevertheless, because the plaintiffs before it were from New York, this New York trial-level court found New York to have sufficient interest in the subject of the action to warrant application of its broader preclusion rule. As already argued, however, this book takes the position that the *Hart* view is suspect. And some courts have directly so held.[18]

Exceptions to Full Faith and Credit. There is no general exception based on the second state's public policy.[19] Thus, the fact that the underlying claim is contrary to F-2's public policy—for example, a claim on a gambling transaction—is not a valid ground for denying recognition and enforcement to an F-1 judgment on that claim.[20]

Tax judgments of sister states are accordingly entitled to recognition and enforcement in other states.[21] The status of penal judgments is a little less clear. Although the Supreme Court of the United States once declared that F-1 penal judgments need not be enforced in F-2, the Court's definition of penal for this purpose was quite narrow.[22] A judgment awarding punitive damages to a private party would clearly not be penal in this sense.[23] Prob-

---

16. E.g., Paul D. Carrington, Collateral Estoppel and Foreign Judgments, 24 Ohio St. L.J. 381 (1963); Jeffrey E. Lewis, Mutuality in Conflict— Flexibility and Full Faith and Credit, 23 Drake L. Rev. 364 (1974); Note, Collateral Estoppel in Multistate Litigation, 68 Colum. L. Rev. 1590 (1968); Gregory S. Getschow, Comment, If at First You Do Succeed: Recognition of State Preclusive Laws in Subsequent Multistate Actions, 35 Vill. L. Rev. 253, 266 (1990) (acknowledging that majority rule favors giving same effect).

17. 304 N.Y.S.2d 810 (Sup. Ct. 1969) (federal-state setting, although the New York court ignored the bearing of the fact that the prior judgment was from a federal court in Texas); cf. Williams v. Ocean Transp. Lines, 425 F.2d 1183 (3d Cir 1970) (state-federal setting).

18. E.g., Columbia Cas. Co. v. Playtex FP, Inc., 584 A.2d 1214, 1218 (Del. 1991) ("This result is clearly at variance with the purpose and spirit of the full faith and credit clause.").

19. See Baker v. General Motors Corp., 522 U.S. 222 (1998).

20. See Fauntleroy v. Lum, 210 U.S. 230 (1908).

21. See Milwaukee County v. M.E. White Co., 296 U.S. 268 (1935).

22. Huntington v. Attrill, 146 U.S. 657 (1892) (dictum).

23. See James-Dickinson Farm Mortgage Co. v. Harry, 273 U.S. 119 (1927).

ably F-2 can deny only enforcement and only when the F-1 judgment is truly penal, that is, a judgment actually imposing a punitive fine or other penalty by the state for a public offense.[24]

Thus, there can only be extremely narrow exceptions where some or all of the dictates of full faith and credit do not apply, namely, where recognition or enforcement in F-2 would so grossly and improperly interfere with F-2's important interests as to create a national interest against such recognition or enforcement. Distinguish that national interest against recognition or enforcement from F-2's local distaste for the nature of the underlying claim. Specific examples of proper exceptions are rare: the rendering state has purported directly to transfer title to land in the second state[25] or has enjoined litigation in the second state's courts.[26] A congressionally created exception lies in the 1996 statute[27] that placed same-sex marriages outside the Full Faith and Credit Clause (which clause, by the way, expressly authorizes congressional exceptions[28]). But even where full faith and credit does not compel recognition or enforcement, the second court can still choose, as a matter of comity, to give effect.

One illustrative but very thorny problem relating to the interstate respect for judgments arises in connection with judgments or decrees affecting land in states other than the forum state (F-1).[29] At a very early time, the Supreme Court held that a court exercising equitable powers and having personal jurisdiction over the parties could issue a decree requiring one of the parties to convey land in another state.[30] The decree is not enforceable in rem, because the rendering court did not have jurisdiction over the res. The decree can be enforced by the court's contempt power against the person of the defendant upon refusal to execute the conveyance as ordered. If

---

24. See Restatement (Second) of Conflict of Laws § 120 (1971).

25. See Fall v. Eastin, 215 U.S. 1 (1909); Restatement (Second) of Conflict of Laws § 102 cmt. d (1971).

26. See James v. Grand Trunk W.R.R., 152 N.E.2d 858 (Ill. 1958); Restatement (Second) of Conflict of Laws § 103 (1971) (amended 1988).

27. 28 U.S.C. § 1738C.

28. See Brainerd Currie, Full Faith and Credit, Chiefly to Judgments: A Role for Congress, 1964 Sup. Ct. Rev. 89.

29. See generally Russell J. Weintraub, Commentary on the Conflict of Laws 412-60 (3d ed. 1986); Moffatt Hancock, Full Faith and Credit to Foreign Laws and Judgments in Real Property Litigation: The Supreme Court and the Land Taboo, 18 Stan. L. Rev. 1299 (1966).

30. Massie v. Watts, 10 U.S. (6 Cranch) 148 (1810).

the defendant does execute the conveyance, the defendant cannot later avoid it in the state of the situs of the property on the ground that the conveyance was under duress rather than a free act and deed. The "duress" of the court's order does not support rescission or cancellation.

However, if the defendant does not convey, can anything be accomplished in the state of the situs of the land (F-2)? The Supreme Court in *Fall v. Eastin*[31] held that F-2 is not bound to recognize as owner the party who was successful in the F-1 action. The case was a curious one, its authority has been seriously questioned, and its exact meaning is unclear.[32] The majority opinion of Justice McKenna seemed to say not only that full faith and credit does not require F-2 to accord in rem effect to the F-1 judgment, but also that F-2 is not required to recognize any issue preclusion effect either. "[T]he decree in Washington gave no such equities as could be recognized in Nebraska as justifying an action to quiet title . . . ."[33] The Court did, however, note without disapproval an Ohio case that had attributed issue preclusion effect in Ohio to a Kentucky decree ordering specific performance regarding Ohio land. Thus, the Court seemed to say that F-2 may give issue preclusion effect to an F-1 judgment relating to F-2 land or it may refuse to do so, as F-2 sees fit.

Although *Fall v. Eastin* has not been overruled, the basic rationale of issue preclusion seems as appropriate in application to foreign land decrees as to any other valid personal judgment. The trend of modern decisions is to accord issue preclusion effect to decrees relating to land in other states when the issues are otherwise appropriate for issue preclusion. Some courts have even based such decisions on the proposition that full faith and credit requires that result. At present, it may not be possible to say with complete assurance that such decrees are constitutionally entitled to recognition for their issue preclusion effect. But it is becoming increasingly safe to speak in such a way.[34] In fact, the Supreme Court itself recently summarized *Fall v. Eastin* in this way: "Thus, a sister State's decree concerning land ownership in another State has been held ineffective *to transfer title* [citing *Fall v. Eastin*], although such a decree may indeed preclusively adjudicate the

31. 215 U.S. 1 (1909).

32. See Brainerd Currie, Full Faith and Credit to Foreign Land Decrees, 21 U. Chi. L. Rev. 620 (1954).

33. 215 U.S. at 14.

34. See, e.g., Restatement (Second) of Judgments § 28 cmt. e (1982); Restatement (Second) of Conflict of Laws § 102 cmt. d (1971).

rights and obligations running between the *parties* to the foreign litigation . . . ."[35]

Enforcement. Although valid and final judgments of the courts of one state of the United States are constitutionally entitled to recognition and enforcement in the courts of another, it is not a denial of full faith and credit for F-2 to require the party seeking enforcement of the F-1 judgment in F-2 to bring an F-2 action for that purpose.[36]

Indeed, historically the common method of enforcement was for the plaintiff to bring in F-2 a new action upon the prior judgment and thus obtain a regularly enforceable domestic judgment. Today, federal law provides for registration in any district court of another district court's judgment for recovery of money or property, thus automatically converting the registered judgment into a regularly enforceable local judgment and avoiding the jurisdiction, service, and venue requirements of an independent action upon the judgment.[37] Almost all states have built on this idea, as by the Uniform Enforcement of Foreign Judgments Act,[38] to permit registration of sister-state or federal judgments and so obviate the need for an independent action upon the judgment.

Equity decrees are entitled to full faith and credit, although acceptance of this proposition has come only recently.[39] F-2's law controls the method of enforcing. In fact, F-2 has some freedom to enforce the decree in a manner of its own choosing, as long as the manner is evenhanded.

Full faith and credit, however, does not require F-2 to enforce an F-1 judgment that would be barred from enforcement by lapse of time under F-2's limitations statute applicable to enforcement of a domestic judgment.[40] This seemingly anomalous result is explained on the ground that full faith and credit does not require F-2 to provide special procedures for enforcing sister-state judgments. Nevertheless, if the judgment-holder gets F-1 to revive its dormant judgment into a new judgment, then F-2 must enforce it.[41]

---

35. Baker v. General Motors Corp., 522 U.S. 222, 235 (1998) (dictum).

36. See McElmoyle v. Cohen, 38 U.S. (13 Pet.) 312 (1839).

37. 28 U.S.C. § 1963.

38. 13 U.L.A. 149 (1986).

39. See Baker v. General Motors Corp., 522 U.S. 222, 234-35 (1998).

40. See McElmoyle v. Cohen, 38 U.S. (13 Pet.) 312 (1839); Restatement (Second) of Conflict of Laws § 118(2) (1971).

41. See Union Nat'l Bank v. Lamb, 337 U.S. 38 (1949); Restatement (Second) of Conflict of Laws § 118(2) cmt. c (1971).

The same argument has been used to justify F-2's denial of enforcement of an F-1 judgment when F-2 had no existing judicial machinery appropriate for granting the relief that F-1 had awarded. An explanation lies in the much-quoted statement of Justice Holmes: "If the plaintiff can find a court into which it has a right to come, then the effect of the [F-1] judgment is fixed by the Constitution.... But the Constitution does not require the [F-2] State to provide such a court."[42] In that case, the Court allowed F-2, consistent with its ordinary practice, to refuse to entertain an action upon a judgment between two out-of-state corporations. Note, nevertheless, that it is irrelevant to full faith and credit whether F-2 has courts competent to entertain the underlying claim.[43]

Under these very narrow and uncertain statute-of-limitations and judicial-machinery exceptions, F-2 can deny enforcement to F-1 judgments of a particular type on the ground that they are not appropriate for enforcement in F-2 courts. These two exceptions thus give further indication that the policy of uniformity reflected in the Full Faith and Credit Clause does not require sacrifice of all local concerns for effective judicial administration.

b. State—Federal

When the second court is instead a federal court, then *28 U.S.C. § 1738* likewise compels the second court to give the same effects to a valid and final judgment as the judgment would have in the courts of the rendering state.[44]

Governing Law. Picture a plaintiff, who has lost a state action for employment discrimination, now bringing a Title VII discrimination case in federal court. Although the Full Faith and Credit Clause of the Constitution does not refer to federal courts, the implementing statute, § 1738, requires every court "within the United States" to accord full faith and credit to the judgments of courts of states, territories, and possessions. Here the Supreme Court has been entirely explicit. The federal court must apply the res judicata law of the rendering state.[45]

42. Anglo-American Provision Co. v. Davis Provision Co., 191 U.S. 373, 374 (1903); see Restatement (Second) of Conflict of Laws § 117 cmt. d (1971).

43. See Kenney v. Supreme Lodge, 252 U.S. 411 (1920).

44. See generally Restatement (Second) of Judgments § 86 (1982).

45. See Kremer v. Chemical Constr. Corp., 456 U.S. 461, 466 (1982).

The same is true even when the claim in federal court is within exclusive federal jurisdiction.[46] Thus, in considering the preclusive effects of an earlier state judgment rendered on a state claim, the federal court must apply the state res judicata law even though a state court could not hear the federal claim. The federal court cannot give the state judgment less credit than the rendering state court would. The Supreme Court has also repeatedly held that the federal court is not free to give the state judgment more preclusive effects than would the rendering state court.[47]

Nevertheless, that body of state res judicata law does not absolutely always govern in federal court. After all, it governs in federal court by virtue of a federal statute, § 1738, so federal law can make exceptions to that statute. In narrow circumstances grounded on strong federal substantive or procedural policies, federal law may provide against (or by statute conceivably for) recognition or enforcement. A few infrequent examples lie where federal courts construe occasional federal statutes bestowing exclusive federal jurisdiction so as to permit relitigation of certain issues in federal court.[48] Normally, however, such an exception to the general retroverse approach would arise only upon a clearly expressed congressional purpose to override § 1738 in a particular area of law.[49]

Nature of Governing Law. Of course, the normally governing state res judicata law is not free of federal command. Most importantly, due process requires that the state not preclude on the basis of a judgment if the proceedings did not afford a full and fair opportunity to litigate.[50] That is, the state must have a basically fair res judicata law, which will apply in that state's own courts as well as in federal court to specify the effects of that state's judgments.[51] It is accurate to call this res judicata law

46. See Matsushita Elec. Indus. Co. v. Epstein, 516 U.S. 367 (1996) (securities case).

47. See, e.g., Marrese v. American Academy of Orthopedic Surgeons, 470 U.S. 373, 384-86 (1985).

48. See, e.g., Brown v. Felsen, 442 U.S. 127 (1979) (bankruptcy case).

49. See Kremer v. Chemical Constr. Corp., 456 U.S. 461, 468 (1982); cf. 18 Charles Alan Wright, Arthur R. Miller & Edward H. Cooper, Federal Practice and Procedure § 4469.1 (Supp 2000) (treating the troublesome *Rooker-Feldman* doctrine, which uses preclusion-like concepts to deny subject-matter jurisdiction to federal district courts for actions in the nature of appeal from a state judgment).

50. See Kremer v. Chemical Constr. Corp., 456 U.S. 461, 480-83 (1982).

51. See William V. Luneburg, The Opportunity to Be Heard and the Doctrines of Preclusion: Federal Limits on State Law, 31 Vill. L. Rev. 81 (1986).

a body of state law, even though the state formulates its law within federally imposed limits.

2. Federal Judgments

a. Federal—State

When the prior judgment was rendered by a federal court and the second action is brought in a state court, the second court must similarly give the same effects to a valid and final judgment as the judgment would have in the rendering court, with federal res judicata law controlling in the state court by virtue of the *Supremacy Clause.*[52]

Governing Law. It is understood that state courts must accord similar respect to judgments of federal courts, although the exact source of this requirement is unclear.[53] Neither the Full Faith and Credit Clause nor its implementing statute applies to a federal judgment in state court. So whence the same rule of retroversion?

The best view is that like any court system, the federal courts operating under Article III of the United States Constitution have necessarily produced a body of res judicata law. This federal law comprises occasional statutes and court rules but also the federal common law of res judicata, which follows the modern rules described in this book. Moreover, the federal system has developed a retroverse approach to the conflicts question regarding judgments, in that a subsequent court applies the res judicata law that the rendering court would. These federal principles are applicable to a federal judgment and thus become binding in a state court by virtue of the Supremacy Clause of Article VI.[54]

Nature of Governing Law. Under the simpler but hotly disputed view, a uniform federal law applies regardless of the basis of federal subject-matter jurisdiction in the first court.[55] Thus, even when the federal judg-

---

52. See generally Restatement (Second) of Judgments § 87 (1982).

53. See Hancock Nat'l Bank v. Farnum, 176 U.S. 640 (1900).

54. See 18 Susan Bandes & Lawrence B. Solum, Moore's Federal Practice § 133.12 (3d ed. 1999).

55. See Semtek Int'l Inc. v. Lockheed Martin Corp., 736 A.2d 1104 (Md. Ct. Spec. App. 1999) (federal res judicata law governs federal judgment rendered in removed diversity case), rev'd, 2001 WL 182650 (U.S.); Ronan E. Degnan, Federalized Res Judicata, 85 Yale L.J. 741 (1976).

ment issued in a diversity action, the effects of that judgment are governed by a uniform federal law of res judicata. Such a result is, however, exceedingly difficult to accept in certain circumstances of high state interests.[56]

Imagine a case of toxic tort (such as exposure to asbestos), where the plaintiff in a federal diversity action has sued successfully for injury (from asbestosis) but chosen not to sue for considerably increased risk of injury (from cancer). Can the plaintiff sue again when the risk of cancer later becomes the actuality of cancer? Imagine further that the federal law takes a strict claim preclusion view against claim-splitting, while the state law has carefully decided to give such plaintiffs a choice to split.[57] Could it really be that the plaintiff has lost that substantively based right to choose, merely by having sued in federal court?

Or imagine a mass accident case. Should a federal diversity judgment for the plaintiff open the door to nonmutual offensive collateral estoppel, even if the local state adheres to mutuality of estoppel and even if the local state is where the accident occurred? Should the defendant lose rights to relitigate, merely by being sued in federal court? Alternatively, how broad would be the effect of a judgment for the defendant, if the state privity law aggressively binds nonparties?

A strong argument exists in these special cases of heavy substantive import that the federal law of judgments should at least adopt the pertinent state law as federal common law.[58] The argument is weaker, however, in the mass accident case than in the toxic tort case. In more usual cases, the argument for state law weakens considerably further.

So what is the proper approach? *Semtek* (U.S. 2001) opted for federal common law normally adopting state law to govern diversity judgements. With some hesitancy, we suggest that the better position is that the federal

---

56. See Heiser v. Woodruff, 327 U.S. 726, 733 (1946) (limiting its opinion to nondiversity cases). Compare Lane v. Sullivan, 900 F.2d 1247, 1249-50 (8th Cir. 1990) (state law governs), with Hauser v. Krupp Steel Producers, Inc., 761 F.2d 204, 207 (5th Cir. 1985) (federal law governs).

57. See Note, Claim Preclusion in Modern Latent Disease Cases: A Proposal for Allowing Second Suits, 103 Harv. L. Rev. 1989 (1990); supra Chapter 6-A-1-b.

58. See 18 Charles Alan Wright, Arthur R. Miller & Edward H. Cooper, Federal Practice and Procedure §4472 (1981 & Supp. 1999); cf. Stephen B. Burbank, Interjurisdictional Preclusion, Full Faith and Credit and Federal Common Law: A General Approach, 71 Cornell L. Rev. 733 (1986) (considerable rendition-state law should apply by virtue of direct application of the *Erie* doctrine).

law of res judicata should apply to all federal judgments, but with rare adoption of state law as federal common law.[59]

A uniform federal law of judgments should usually govern, for three reasons. *First*, although state interests are admittedly sometimes at stake, the federal interests are stronger. The federal judgment is the product of an organ of the federal government, which should be able to define the limits of its own output. "One of the strongest policies a court can have is that of determining the scope of its own judgments."[60] Also, applying state res judicata law to a federal judgment would overly complicate an already complicated process of recognition and enforcement, would destroy the uniformity of federal judgments law, and could undercut the federal interest in its judgments' disposing of the whole litigation to a just extent. Much of res judicata law is indeed tied to the way a case was or should be litigated in the initial action, so that linking res judicata law to state law while providing that federal procedure otherwise governs the case's litigation could lead to illogical or undesirable results. *Second*, using federal res judicata law under these circumstances accords with the general practice under the Full Faith and Credit Clause and § 1738 of the second court's looking to the rendering court's law to determine the effect of its judgments, thus giving the benefits of a judicially unified nation. Also, this retroverse practice parallels the practice followed in analogous situations, such as state courts' looking to federal law to determine the effect of federal judgments in cases turning on Federal Rules of Civil Procedure 13(a) and 41. *Third*, the concerns of *Erie* are not fully implicated by applying federal law in this particular context. It is unlikely that the plaintiff in the first action chose federal court because of the res judicata effects of its judgments. Also, the *Erie* concerns are even more attenuated in this context because the judge in the second court is asking whether there was impermissible forum-shopping in the choice of the first forum, rather than the usual question of whether there was impermissible forum-shopping in the instant case.

Exceptions are necessary, nevertheless. Sometimes, albeit rarely, the force of state substantive policies may spike too high to ignore, despite all the background interests in a uniform and federal law of judgments. The proposed approach, using the usual balancing methodology for federal com-

---

59. See generally Howard M. Erichson, Interjurisdictional Preclusion, 96 Mich. L. Rev. 945 (1998).

60. Kern v. Hettinger, 303 F.2d 333, 340 (2d Cir. 1962).

mon law in the federal courts,[61] would lead to the adoption of the pertinent state law as federal common law in those special cases. That is, although the governing law is still federal, it will not be uniform in these instances. Instead, the federal court will choose to adopt the appropriate state's res judicata law. This deference serves to accommodate the high state interests involved. But such rare and flexible adoption of state law as federal law is distinguishable from the broad and binding application of state law in federal court under *Erie*'s command.

b. Federal—Federal

When the second court is instead another federal court, still the same precept of looking to the rendering court's law prevails, because the two courts are *arms of the same sovereign*.[62]

Federal courts should treat federal judgments just as state courts treat federal judgments. The federal retroverse approach to the conflicts question regarding judgments binds federal courts throughout the nation. Indeed, even in case of difference in law between circuits, the subsequent federal court should apply the rendering federal court's view of the federal law of res judicata.[63]

C. Judgments of Foreign Nations

American courts treat judgments of foreign nations pretty much like American judgments, although their approach to such foreign judgments can be more flexible because their respect generally flows from *comity* rather than from legal obligation.[64]

1. Rules for Recognition and Enforcement

a. General Practices

The acts of foreign governments have no effect within another government's territory, unless the latter government chooses to give them effect. As to foreign judgments, there is no internationally binding law compara-

---

61. See Kevin M. Clermont, Civil Procedure 234-35 (5th ed. 1999).

62. See generally Restatement (Second) of Judgments § 87 (1982).

63. See generally 18 Charles Alan Wright, Arthur R. Miller & Edward H. Cooper, Federal Practice and Procedure § 4466 (1981).

64. See generally Restatement (Second) of Conflict of Laws § 98 (1971) (amended 1988).

ble to the Full Faith and Credit Clause. Thus, when a prior judgment bears on American litigation, a fundamental difference exists between foreign country judgments and American judgments.

Yet the general policies underlying res judicata are no less applicable when the prior judgment was rendered in a foreign country than when it was rendered in an American court. Indeed, American courts tend to give respect to foreign judgments not only because finality is a fair and efficient policy, but also because American courts hope to encourage abroad similar respect for their own judgments. Therefore, freed from constitutional obligations but motivated by similar policies, American courts generally respect foreign judgments if valid and final under the foreign law. If the court that granted the judgment had subject-matter and territorial jurisdiction and if the circumstances of the adjudication were such that the parties can be said to have had a fair day in court, F-1's res judicata law should be applicable and F-1's judgment should be enforceable in F-2.

Nevertheless, a closer look at the actual holdings suggests that slightly different standards are applied to judgments of foreign nations, as compared to those applied to domestic, sister-state, or federal judgments. The principal reason for difference is that an American court has no guarantee that a foreign judgment, although comporting with the basic requirements of the foreign law, is minimally acceptable to Americans. The foreign laws concerning validity vary widely. Moreover, the Due Process Clause does not control foreign sovereigns, of course, and so the workings of the foreign legal system could be quite, well, foreign. An American court will give no respect to a foreign judgment that it views as repugnant. An American court will not recognize or enforce a foreign judgment resulting from proceedings that failed to meet the basic notions of American due process. An American court can ask whether territorial jurisdiction existed under the foreign law, but more importantly, the American court may examine whether the foreign assertion of jurisdiction satisfied the American tests of due process. For example, an American court would disregard a French judgment for which personal jurisdiction was based solely on the plaintiff's French nationality. Furthermore, an American court might apply other limitations on comity, such as allowing collateral attack on the stronger equitable grounds, and such as refusing recognition or enforcement if the original claim is directly contrary to strong local public policy as explained below.

Still, America in fact behaves pretty generously in respecting foreign judgments, compared to most other countries. Most countries have demonstrated a more heightened notion of sovereignty than America endorses in this regard. In other countries, even if an American judgment passes the foreign court's jurisdictional reexamination, which very well might involve meeting all the standards of the foreign jurisdictional law, the foreign court tends to reexamine the merits vigorously to ensure that the applied law conformed to local policy.

b. Preclusion Specifics

Claim Preclusion. A foreign country judgment against the claimant offered as a defense of *bar* to the claimant's reassertion of the claim in American courts will usually be accorded full claim preclusion effect. The judgment can be challenged on somewhat broader grounds than a domestic, sister-state, or federal judgment could be, however. In addition to jurisdictional and equitable attacks, the bar effect of a foreign judgment may be avoided in some American courts on such grounds as recognition being contrary to strong local public policy.

Although a foreign country judgment against the claimant could be asserted as a bar in American courts, the traditional view had been that a judgment in favor of the claimant would not be given *merger* effect. Thus, in American courts following this view, a plaintiff who had won an unsatisfied judgment in a foreign country had an election to sue upon the judgment or to sue on the original claim.[65] The view apparently was rooted in the old limitations on the common-law action for enforcement of judgment, but its persistence in modern practice is hard to justify.[66] Many courts have refused to follow this view.[67] Today, it can be said that the traditional view has largely disappeared, and courts accord merger as well as bar effect to foreign judgments.

Issue Preclusion. It is generally understood that parties who have litigated particular issues in a foreign country court will be precluded from relitigating the same questions in American courts.[68] Again, the foreign

---

65. See Hessel E. Yntema, The Enforcement of Foreign Judgments in Anglo-American Law, 33 Mich. L. Rev. 1129, 1139 (1935).

66. See Albert A. Ehrenzweig, A Treatise on the Conflict of Laws 217-18 (1962).

67. See, e.g., Alaska Commercial Co. v. Debney, 2 Alaska 303 (1904).

68. See Overseas Motors, Inc. v. Import Motors Ltd., 375 F. Supp. 499 (E.D. Mich. 1974), aff'd, 519 F.2d 119 (6th Cir. 1975); Eugene F. Scoles & Peter Hay, Conflict of Laws 996-1018 (2d ed. 1992); Courtland H. Peterson, Res Judicata and Foreign Country Judgments, 24 Ohio St. L.J. 291 (1963); Willis L.M. Reese, The Status in This Country of Judgments Rendered Abroad, 50 Colum. L. Rev. 783, 789 (1950).

judgment is somewhat more subject to challenge than is an American judgment.

Given a lack of constitutional constraint, American courts could, and some do, give the foreign judgment more effects than the foreign court would give its own judgment. For example, an American court could, although it should not, give a foreign mass-tort judgment a nonmutual collateral estoppel effect, even though the foreign court would not.[69]

c. *Governing Law*

Insofar as recognition and enforcement of judgments of foreign nations go, the matter is regulated by general principles of comity. The principles of comity that govern such questions are the principles recognized by F-2 law.

Thus, state statutory[70] and common law on comity governs in state court, and federal common law on comity governs on federal claims in federal court. However, in a diversity action, the federal court under *Erie* looks to state law on how to treat a foreign judgment.[71] An argument could be made that in all federal cases, and even in all state cases as well, federal law should control because of strong federal interests including the interest in foreign relations, but that is not how things have worked out. At any rate, state and federal law on comity are basically similar.

Ideally, both state and federal law on comity should refer to the foreign rendering court's law for specifying the extent of recognition and enforcement.[72]

Oddly enough, international law itself currently plays no real role in American treatment of foreign judgments, except to the extent that the American approach is already a manifestation of the generally recognized principles that constitute part of international law. The United States has not a single treaty on the subject, although obviously this subject could be regulated by treaty.

---

69. See Restatement (Third) of Foreign Relations Law of the United States § 481 cmt. c (1987).

70. See, e.g., Uniform Foreign Money-Judgments Recognition Act, 13 U.L.A. 263 (1986), discussed in 18 Susan Bandes & Lawrence B. Solum, Moore's Federal Practice § 130.52 (3d ed. 1999).

71. See Restatement (Second) of Conflict of Laws § 98 cmt. c (1971) (amended 1988).

72. See generally Robert C. Casad, Issue Preclusion and Foreign Country Judgments: Whose Law?, 70 Iowa L. Rev. 53 (1984).

2. Special Exceptions to Recognition and Enforcement

For the most part, as already explained, foreign country judgments are treated in American courts similarly to American judgments. There are a few notable differences, however.

a. Reciprocity

In the much-criticized decision of *Hilton v. Guyot*[73]—involving French plaintiffs trying to enforce in federal court a French money judgment against U.S. citizens—a sharply divided Supreme Court of the United States ruled that a federal court should not accord enforcement without relitigation of the merits to a judgment of a foreign country if the courts of that country would not enforce judgments of American courts rendered under similar circumstances. This reciprocity exception was said to apply only where the foreign judgment was rendered in favor of a plaintiff who was a national of that country and against a defendant who was a foreigner to that country. It thus did not apply to cases where the judgment was against the plaintiff, where the plaintiff was a foreigner to that country, or where both parties were nationals of that country. In all these other cases, the reciprocity exception did not apply, the Court said, so that the foreign judgment could be enforced in federal court without reconsideration of the merits, regardless of the treatment accorded American judgments in that foreign country.

It has been generally understood that the holding of *Hilton v. Guyot* is not an exception binding on the states, but merely an exception governing enforcement of judgments in federal courts.[74] And even in federal courts, in view of the later-announced *Erie* doctrine, the exception does not apply in diversity cases unless the state in which the federal court sits has adopted it—which not many states have done.[75]

---

73. 159 U.S. 113 (1895); see Restatement (Second) of Conflict of Laws § 98 cmt. f (1971) (amended 1988); Restatement (Third) of Foreign Relations Law of the United States § 481 cmt. d (1987).

74. See Johnston v. Compagnie Générale Transatlantique, 152 N.E. 121 (N.Y. 1926). But see John Norton Moore, Federalism and Foreign Relations, 1965 Duke L.J. 248, 265.

75. See Bank of Montreal v. Kough, 612 F.2d 467 (9th Cir.1980); Svenska Handelsbanken v. Carlson, 258 F. Supp. 448 (D. Mass. 1966). But see John D. Brummett, Jr., Note, The Preclusive Effect of Foreign-Country Judgments in the United States and Federal Choice of Law: The Role of the Erie Doctrine Reassessed, 33 N.Y.L. Sch. L. Rev. 83 (1988).

One can persuasively argue against *Hilton v. Guyot* that courts should not be pursuing a role in foreign relations that belongs to the other branches of government, especially when American courts have failed to present a united front on the reciprocity matter; that the Court's unclear albeit narrow exception of reciprocity undermines the fairness and efficiency of res judicata law; and that it is unfair to punish a foreign litigant for its government's policy.[76] Still, a feeling lingers that, in the absence of supranational authority, a federal reciprocity statute is about all that America could threaten in order to give foreign courts an incentive to abandon their stinginess in respecting its judgments.[77]

b. Public Policy

American courts sometimes refuse to recognize or enforce foreign country judgments on the ground that the underlying claim is contrary to some strong public policy of the forum.[78] An example might be an English judgment for defamation that impinges on American principles of free speech. In such cases, unlike the case where recognition or enforcement is refused on reciprocity grounds, there can be no recovery on the underlying claim either. This power to deny respect on public policy grounds is sparingly used, however.[79]

In this connection, it should be noted that judgments of foreign countries imposing tax obligations or penal sanctions generally are not regarded as entitled to recognition or enforcement in American courts, although cases actually so holding are hard to find. Moreover, the underlying claims usually cannot be sued on in American courts.[80]

---

76. See Richard H.M. Maloy & Desamparados M. Nisi, A Message to the Supreme Court: The Next Time You Get a Chance, Please Look at Hilton v. Guyot; We Think It Needs Fixing, 5 J. Int'l Legal Stud. 1 (1999).

77. See Michael Whincop, The Recognition Scene: Game Theoretic Issues in the Recognition of Foreign Judgments, 23 Melb. U. L. Rev. 416 (1999) (analyzing recognition as an iterative prisoner's dilemma game).

78. See, e.g., De Brimont v. Penniman, 7 F. Cas. 309 (C.C.S.D.N.Y. 1873) (No. 3715); Restatement (Third) of Foreign Relations Law of the United States § 482(2)(d) (1987).

79. See Restatement (Second) of Conflict of Laws § 117 cmt. c (1971).

80. See Restatement (Third) of Foreign Relations Law of the United States § 483 (1987); Thomas B. Stoel, Jr., Enforcement of Foreign Non-Criminal Penal and Revenue Judgments in England and the United States, 16 Int'l & Comp. L.Q. 663 (1967).

3. Hague Treaty

The principal European countries appear ahead of America on the treatment of foreign judgments. The European Union has an enlightened, albeit far from perfect, treaty called the Brussels Convention on Jurisdiction and the Recognition and Enforcement of Judgments in Civil and Commercial Matters. By it, the member states agree to provide virtually automatic recognition and enforcement of the judgments of the other member states. This provision is like the Full Faith and Credit Clause of the U.S. Constitution. In order to make this agreement acceptable, the Convention is a "double convention" that also defines the bases of territorial jurisdiction. This latter agreement works as the Due Process Clause does in the United States. The European member states can give respect to the others' judgments because they know that the Convention restricts the others to appropriate jurisdictional reach. The current time is exciting in Europe as the supranational European Court of Justice, overseeing the national courts, actively works out the details, much as the Marshall Court united the American judicial systems two centuries ago.

Of course, the Brussels Convention's jurisdictional bases follow the civil-law approach. The defendant's domicile is the usual place for suit, although there is additionally long-arm-like jurisdiction for tort and contract actions. There is authorization for forum selection clauses. There is exclusive local jurisdiction in actions concerning real property and the like. Certain disadvantaged plaintiffs, such as consumers, can sue at home. On the prohibited side, each member state gave up its exorbitant jurisdiction, so that for example France gave up its personal jurisdiction based on the plaintiff's French nationality.

The Brussels Convention applies only to defendants domiciled in a member state, however. Indeed, it openly discriminates against outsiders. Accordingly, although France cannot use its exorbitant jurisdiction in a suit by a French person against an English person, it can still use it when the defendant is an American instead. Moreover, the resulting French judgment gets automatic recognition and enforcement in England, Germany, and elsewhere in the European Union against the American or the American's assets there.

Similarly, the virtually automatic recognition and enforcement under the Brussels Convention does not extend to judgments rendered by countries that are not member states. The European countries, in fact, have traditionally been and continue to be rather stingy in extending respect to foreign judgments not covered by treaty.

So Americans are being whipsawed. Not only are they still subject to the far-reaching jurisdiction of European courts and the wide recognition and enforceability of the resulting European judgments, but also American judgments tend to be given short shrift in European courts. In the long run, this situation is untenable for the United States.

Therefore, the United States has initiated a push to conclude a worldwide treaty on jurisdiction and judgments. It is working through the Hague Conference on Private International Law. A treaty would resolve the whipsawing predicament in which Americans today find themselves regarding recognition and enforcement of judgments.

An obvious concern with a multilateral treaty is that the United States might be forced to give respect to distasteful foreign judgments. Americans are confident about sister-state and federal judgments, but there the Due Process Clause applies, with the U.S. Supreme Court in place to review its application. Perhaps Americans could muster confidence in the judgments of a small number of like-minded legal systems, even in the absence of a supranational oversight authority. But a worldwide treaty is altogether another matter. Americans could not be sure of the fundamental fairness of all foreign judgments. Accordingly, any treaty would have to contain a provision giving each signatory country broad control over which countries can sign on vis-à-vis that country, as well as a narrowly drawn public-policy exception for procedural due process violations and other repugnancies.

Will such a treaty come into existence? The United States has little bargaining power. It needs a treaty, while the Europeans have little to gain over their presently favorable situation. The expectation therefore is that any eventual treaty will be similar to the Brussels Convention. That is, the treaty will agree on certain bases of territorial jurisdiction, but chiefly those palatable to the Europeans—and judgments based thereon will receive virtually automatic recognition and enforcement in other signatory countries, except perhaps those judgments that the Europeans consider too generous or punitive. Such a prospect is not to the United States' liking. Reaching agreement on a treaty is therefore far from a certainty. Certainly, the path to international agreement will not be smooth.

Yet reaching agreement on a multilateral treaty could yield great returns for the United States on both jurisdictional and judgments law. The negotiations are definitely worth the effort.[81] In particular regard to the treatment of foreign judgments, a Hague treaty appears quite desirable. It would

81. See Kevin M. Clermont, Jurisdictional Salvation and the Hague Treaty, 85 Cornell L. Rev. 89 (1999).

mean that the United States could get returns for the respect it is already according other nations' judgments.

PART III

Practice

Res judicata pro veritate accipitur.

A thing adjudged is taken for truth.

(Roman maxim)

CHAPTER 11

Invoking Res Judicata

Taking something as the truth is serious business. The law wants to proceed carefully in conducting any business that is like application of res judicata. It therefore should lay out a detailed procedure, but it has not succeeded in doing this clearly. To the study of how the law handles the res judicata doctrine in practice, this book now turns.

A. Raising

Res judicata is not self-executing. The person wishing to rely on it must raise it. Failure to do so means waiver. This result flows from the premises of our adversary system, coupled with the fact that the policies underlying res judicata are not so essential as to require judicial invocation.

The norm, then, is that the interested party must raise res judicata.[1] But almost every generalization is subject to exception. Here, one must note that a court has the power to raise res judicata on its own, although it seldom will. The court usually will use its sua sponte power only when it sees its own interests in avoiding repetitive litigation as especially and unnecessarily endangered.[2]

1. See, e.g., Carbonell v. Louisiana Dept. of Health & Human Resources, 772 F.2d 185 (5th Cir. 1985).

2. See, e.g., Arizona v. California, 120 S. Ct. 2304, 2318 (2000); Plaut v. Spendthrift Farm, Inc., 514 U.S. 211, 231-32 (1995); Disimone v. Browner, 121 F.3d 1262 (9th Cir. 1997).

1. Timing

As already explained, in Chapter 1-C above and subsequently with regularity, res judicata applies only after judgment, outside the context of the initial adjudicatory process and any direct review such as appeal. Thus, the plaintiff in Action #2 might invoke res judicata to preclude the defendant from defending on the underlying merits in an action upon the judgment rendered in Action #1 or might invoke res judicata to foreclose relitigation of certain issues decided in Action #1. Similarly, the defendant in a subsequent action might invoke claim or issue preclusion as a defense. Accordingly, it is the court handling the subsequent litigation that decides the applicability of res judicata.

In unusual circumstances, the invoker of res judicata after judgment may secure an injunction from the initial court against the invokee's later attempt to relitigate.[3] The circumstances must be unusual because such equitable relief lies only where the legal remedy of asserting res judicata in the subsequent action is an inadequate remedy. A misbehaving invokee, a very complex initial proceeding, very foreseeable subsequent proceedings, a danger that the second court would not respect res judicata—all these factors increase the chances for an injunction. But still such injunctions are rare indeed.[4]

2. Method

The defendant in a subsequent action usually should plead res judicata as an affirmative defense. The plaintiff in a subsequent action usually should raise res judicata by a pretrial motion. To get an idea of what this means in practice, consider separately claim and issue preclusion.

a. Claim Preclusion

Res judicata in its claim preclusion aspect is usually a defense, to be asserted by a defending party in the answer or an amendment thereto.[5] Normally, it must be specially pleaded as an affirmative defense, and so it can-

---

3. See, e.g., Harrelson v. United States, 613 F.2d 114 (5th Cir. 1980) (egregiously abusive plaintiff).

4. See, e.g., Bluefield Community Hosp. v. Anziulewicz, 737 F.2d 405 (4th Cir. 1984); supra Chapter 2-H.

5. See, e.g., Fed. R. Civ. P. 15(a).

not be raised by a mere denial.[6] Undue delay in pleading the affirmative defense will result in waiver.[7] If the defending party properly raises the defense of res judicata in a responsive pleading, a party can submit the question for pretrial decision by the judge through a motion for judgment on the pleadings.[8] The judge will treat such a motion as a motion for summary judgment when materials outside the pleadings are offered in support of it.[9]

Courts permit the defendant also to raise the defense, in some circumstances, by a pre-answer motion or demurrer.[10] That is, if the fact of the prior judgment on the same claim appears on the face of the complaint, many courts allow the defense of res judicata to be raised by such a motion asserting the failure of the pleading to state a claim upon which relief can be granted. Some courts tolerate this practice even if the prior judgment does not appear on the face of the complaint, as long as there is no apparent harm from this irregular motion practice; the motion will charge that the complaint fails to state a claim upon which relief can be granted and might offer the prior judgment in support of that challenge; when such outside materials are offered, the court will treat the motion as though it were a motion for summary judgment.

Although courts often do tolerate this motion practice, it is arguably impermissible not only by a technical reading of the court rules, but also under a view toward the proper purpose of motion practice.[11] A good defense lawyer will therefore avoid the risks of procedural dispute and raise the defense correctly in the answer.

As for plaintiffs' occasional reliance on claim preclusion, the basic rule remains that they must provide the opponent and the court with fair notice of its assertion. If the plaintiff is asserting claim preclusion against a counterclaim, the plaintiff's reply should include that affirmative defense. If the plaintiff is asserting claim preclusion against a defense, the plaintiff may proceed by motion. If the plaintiff unduly delays, waiver will result by

---

6. See, e.g., Fed. R. Civ. P. 8(c).
7. See Arizona v. California, 120 S. Ct. 2304, 2316-17 (2000).
8. See, e.g., Fed. R. Civ. P. 12(c).
9. See, e.g., Fed. R. Civ. P. 56.
10. See 5 Charles Alan Wright & Arthur R. Miller, Federal Practice and Procedure § 1277 (2d ed. 1990); 18 Charles Alan Wright, Arthur R. Miller & Edward H. Cooper, Federal Practice and Procedure § 4405 (1981).
11. See, e.g., Concordia v. Bendekovic, 693 F.2d 1073 (11th Cir. 1982).

the operation of the ordinary discovery, pretrial conference, or evidence rules.

b. Issue Preclusion

The invocation of issue preclusion is by no means limited to defending parties. In a proper case either party may seek to establish elements of its claim or defense or parts thereof, or disprove those of its adversary's case, by showing that the matters were decided previously. The party *may* assert issue preclusion by specific reference in a pleading to the fact that a particular issue has been decided in a prior action. Whether the party *must* raise issue preclusion by pleading, however, is a question that has received varying answers in the cases.

Issue preclusion is an aspect of res judicata in the broad sense of that term, and many cases have declared that issue preclusion must be pleaded as an affirmative defense because res judicata is an affirmative defense. Indeed, Federal Rule of Civil Procedure 8(c) refers to both res judicata and estoppel as affirmative defenses. The Supreme Court of the United States lent support to this view in declaring, "Res judicata and collateral estoppel are affirmative defenses that must be pleaded.... The purpose of such pleading is to give the opposing party notice of the plea of estoppel and a chance to argue, if he can, why the imposition of an estoppel would be inappropriate."[12]

Some authorities therefore have expressed the view that failure to plead issue preclusion constitutes a waiver of the right to avoid relitigation of the issue. Statements such as these, however, cannot be interpreted as imposing a strict requirement that issue preclusion must be pleaded in every case in which it is to be invoked. In the first place, references to Rule 8(c) and to like provisions are inapposite when issue preclusion would work to establish a plaintiff's claim, rather than the defendant's defense. Rule 8(c) thus cannot be read as requiring the pleading of issue preclusion in every case. But if plaintiffs do not have to plead it, why should defendants have to do so? A reason is not apparent. In the second place, as noted above, a defendant may in some situations raise even claim preclusion by motion. It should therefore be possible to invoke issue preclusion, too, by motion to

---

12. Blonder-Tongue Lab. v. University of Illinois Found., 402 U.S. 313, 350 (1971). But see Southern Pac. R.R. v. United States, 168 U.S. 1 (1897) (plaintiff, United States, which had pleaded a "general replication" in its quiet title action, could prove an element of its case by collateral estoppel, even though it had not specifically pleaded the prior judgment).

dismiss or for summary judgment, especially when the matter on which preclusion is sought would destroy the claim with an effect similar to claim preclusion's. In the third place, the issue preclusion defense may not be available until late in the game because the other action has not yet gone to judgment. Surely, the party need not plead an as yet unavailable ground. Instead, the party can later raise res judicata by supplemental pleading[13] or by motion.

Beyond those three irrefutable points, one could argue that issue preclusion is functionally different from claim preclusion. Usually issue preclusion works to prove or disprove only parts of a case. Its function in the lawsuit then is essentially evidentiary, in the sense that it takes the place of evidence. Is there any more reason to require a party to plead how the party is going to establish the elements of claim or defense when the proof will be in the form of the record of a former judgment rather than in the usual form of testimonial, real, or demonstrative evidence of the fact—or when a legal issue will be concluded by issue preclusion rather than remain open to argument? That is, what is the special need to notify the opposing party or the court in the pleadings when a point will be established through resort to issue preclusion? Should the party instead be able simply to introduce the prior judgment at trial?

On the one hand, certain authorities hold that a former judgment may, in appropriate circumstances, be used for issue preclusion purposes without any special pleading or even a motion.[14] They allow foreclosure of a legal issue when the former judgment is first raised at trial. On factual matters, they allow assertion of the former judgment just as they would allow introduction of evidence at trial. If the judgment proves or disproves a fact material to the case, it comes in by the manner mere evidence would. If the opposing party objects to the assertion of the judgment because of the absence of specific reference to it in the pleadings, the party seeking to invoke issue preclusion might be allowed to amend the party's pleading, in the absence of real harm; if the former judgment comes in without objection by the opposing party, the matter will be said to have been tried with the implied consent of the parties.[15] Accordingly, when issue preclusion is asserted at trial, even if not raised earlier, some courts have been willing to give it

---

13. See, e.g., Fed. R. Civ. P. 15(d).

14. See Overseas Motors, Inc. v. Import Motors Ltd., 375 F. Supp. 499, 512-15 (E.D. Mich. 1974), aff'd, 519 F.2d 119 (6th Cir. 1975); 18 Susan Bandes & Lawrence B. Solum, Moore's Federal Practice § 132.05[8] (3d ed. 1999).

15. See, e.g., Fed. R. Civ. P. 15(b).

full effect. However, even this permissive approach has limits. If the party does not invoke issue preclusion in timely manner, the party will have waived it. Most courts therefore will hold that the party seeking to assert it cannot do so after trial.[16]

On the other hand, requiring a pleading, or at least a motion, would ensure better notice. Moreover, issue preclusion is different from factual evidence or legal argument, because issue preclusion results in the point being conclusively established. The prior judgment is not merely probative of the matters it decided, it is conclusive on those matters. It is like a new rule of law dispensing with an element of claim or defense. Also, the opponent may have to do some work to prepare to defeat the prior judgment's issue preclusion effect. So allowing the party to wait until trial to assert the prior judgment seems to be pushing laxity a bit too far.

In sum, fair notice is probably all that courts require before assertion of the former judgment for issue preclusion purposes. That is, courts tend to be pretty lax as to waiver. Nevertheless, the cases indicating that it is necessary to plead issue preclusion are sufficiently numerous, and the policy calling for early notice is sufficiently cogent, that the safest course for the parties is to avoid procedural dispute and raise issue preclusion as soon as possible. A defendant should include in the answer, when possible, some reference to the former judgment's issue preclusion effect. Analogously, a plaintiff normally should raise issue preclusion by pretrial motion.

B. Proving

1. Burden

The burden of persuasion that res judicata applies—that the situation satisfies the requirements of a rule—is on the party raising res judicata. But then the burden of proof that an exception to res judicata applies is on the other side. That opponent must raise the exception by appropriate response to however the proponent raised res judicata, and then must persuade the court that the exception applies.

One situation does not fit this simple scheme. Upon an attempt at relief from judgment by attacking its validity, the attacker bears the burden, at least when the attacker had knowledge of the prior action. In this late post-

16. See, e.g., Harvey v. United Transp. Union, 878 F.2d 1235 (10th Cir. 1989) (waiver by plaintiffs).

judgment setting, the presumption should shift in favor of validity. Consequently, the burden of production and persuasion would be on the attacker to establish invalidity, rather than on the proponent of the judgment to show its validity.[17]

2. Evidence

A party invoking res judicata normally needs to submit evidence of the prior judgment, such as the formal record of judgment.[18] However, sometimes the court will be willing to take judicial notice of the prior judgment.[19]

Often it is necessary for the party invoking res judicata, especially in its issue preclusion aspect, to prove additional matters, such as *what was actually litigated* in the prior action. These questions may require extrinsic evidence beyond the record itself, including a transcript showing that issues outside the pleadings were tried by consent, or evidence of stipulations or agreements of the parties removing some issues from contention. Such extrinsic evidence is broadly admissible today under the rules of evidence in most jurisdictions, and the extrinsic evidence can even contradict the formal record in order to show the true prior situation.[20] In some states, however, extrinsic evidence may be inadmissible; or it may not be used to show that an issue reflected in the record was not actually litigated, although extrinsic evidence may be used to show that an issue not reflected in the record actually was litigated.[21] Of course, to minimize later difficulties, the party expecting to rely on res judicata should make every effort in the initial action, such as by amending the pleadings, to make the record both accurate and expressive.

Proving precisely *what was actually determined* in the prior action is especially tricky. Testimony of the jurors who tried the facts in the prior action is sometimes offered for this purpose. But the Supreme Court of the United States long ago declared "that the secret deliberations of the jury, or grounds of their proceedings while engaged in making up their verdict, are not competent or admissible evidence of the issues or finding. The jurors

17. See Theresa L. Kruk, Annotation, Who Has Burden of Proof in Proceeding Under Rule 60(b)(4) of Federal Rules of Civil Procedure to Have Default Judgment Set Aside on Ground That It Is Void for Lack of Jurisdiction, 102 A.L.R. Fed. 811 (1991).

18. See, e.g., 28 U.S.C. § 1738; Fed. R. Civ. P. 44; Fed. R. Evid. 902.

19. See, e.g., St. Louis Baptist Temple v. FDIC, 605 F.2d 1169 (10th Cir. 1979).

20. See Restatement (Second) of Judgments § 19 cmt. h, § 27 cmt. f, § 77 (1982).

21. See, e.g., Slater v. Skirving, 70 N.W. 493 (Neb. 1897).

oftentimes, though they may concur in the result, differ as to the grounds or reasons upon which they arrive at it."[22] And most of today's laws of evidence agree in excluding such juror evidence.[23] Similarly, judges cannot testify as to their mental workings, although they are competent witnesses on open, objective events in the course of a prior action.[24] Allowing judges to testify as to the grounds of their prior decisions would be too susceptible to after-the-fact rationalization and modification, as well as being an undue burden on the judiciary. So what to do? Careful examination of the record may reveal the grounds of decision, as often a judgment necessarily implies resolution of certain issues. Arranging for a special verdict by the jury can overcome the remaining obscurity, as can ensuring that the judge makes detailed findings of fact and conclusions of law in a nonjury trial. Extrinsic evidence can occasionally help. But ultimately in the absence of adequate proof on what was determined, res judicata will not apply.

3. Decision

In most cases, the judge before trial will determine from the evidence submitted whether res judicata applies, including what was actually litigated and determined in the former action and so whether any issues in the later action are precluded.

If, however, there is a genuine dispute as to the truth of the evidence offered as extrinsic proof, and if a party demands a jury trial of that factual dispute, some courts submit the question to the jury along with the evidence on the other questions in the case, including the ones on which preclusion is sought. If the jury in such a case decides that res judicata should apply, the jury will not proceed to the precluded part of the merits in order to decide on the basis of the evidence adduced in the later case.[25] This procedure seems not only suspect as to reliability, but also anomalous in the light of preclusion's purpose to avoid relitigation.

---

22. Packet Co. v. Sickles, 72 U.S. (5 Wall.) 580, 593 (1867).

23. See, e.g., Fed. R. Evid. 606.

24. See, e.g., Grip-Pak, Inc. v. Illinois Tool Works, 694 F.2d 466 (7th Cir. 1982); Fleming James, Jr., Civil Procedure 579-80 (1965); 18 Charles Alan Wright, Arthur R. Miller & Edward H. Cooper, Federal Practice and Procedure § 4420, at 189-91 (1981). But cf. Timothy E. Travers, Annotation, Judge as Witness in Cause Not on Trial Before Him, 86 A.L.R.3d 633, 665-68 (1978) (citing authorities permitting judge's testimony to explain unclear record).

25. See, e.g., Packet Co. v. Sickles, 72 U.S. (5 Wall.) 580 (1867).

Therefore, it would be a better practice to regard the question of res judicata as one to be decided by the judge, even when it turns on disputed factual evidence, and furthermore a question to be decided before trial. Moreover, this shift to pretrial judicial disposition would foster the articulation of the reasons behind res judicata decisions, and hence the sound development of the doctrine.

But if a court wants to pursue this policy that favors judicial decision-making on res judicata, how can it overcome the plausible argument that a jury right exists on any genuine factual disputes in a common-law action? This argument should give the judge pause, because whether a jury right exists with respect to res judicata disputes remains unsettled. So the prevailing judicial response is to sidestep the argument by defining "fact" very narrowly in this context of res judicata disputes.[26] Not only does this narrowness put res judicata into the hands of the judge, but also it facilitates pretrial disposition by summary judgment. Most of res judicata is therefore treated as presenting questions of "law."

Labels aside, minimizing the real role of fact in the doctrine is desirable. To the extent that res judicata law does turn on facts, it tends to be undesirable doctrine. It thereby departs from the virtues of clear, simple, and rigid doctrine. Accordingly, the lawmaker should try, all else being equal, to mold res judicata law so as to minimize the role of disputable facts and thus avoid this jury problem altogether.

4. Review

Appellate review likewise raises the distinction between fact and law.[27] Again by broadly defining the realm of "law," the appellate courts can and do lean heavily toward de novo review.[28] It is true that more deferential review would tend to limit litigation over whether to relitigate, because decisions on res judicata would become more fixed upon the trial court's resolution. Relegating res judicata to the trial court would also facilitate developing a doctrine that turns on an intuitive weighing of a lot of factors in the pursuit of individualized precision. However, the appellate courts nevertheless lean against deference because they want instead to tighten up the res judicata doctrine and to supervise closely its application. For ad-

---

26. See, e.g., Wahl v. Vibranetics, Inc., 474 F.2d 971 (6th Cir. 1973); cf. Markman v. Westview Instruments, Inc., 517 U.S. 370 (1996) (fact/law distinction for jury right).

27. See 1 Steven A. Childress & Martha S. Davis, Standards of Review § 3.9 (1986).

28. See, e.g., Blasi v. Williams, 775 F.2d 1017 (9th Cir. 1985).

ministrative reasons, they also want to favor the characterization of the doctrine as being more purely legal in nature and hence more subject to pretrial judicial disposition by summary judgment.

If, however, the trial judge or jury has decided a blatantly factual subquestion after hearing extrinsic evidence, the appellate court will give the judge's or jury's decision on that subquestion moderately deferential (clearly erroneous standard) or highly deferential review (irrational jury standard), respectively.[29] To avoid giving that deference, the appellate courts will view "facts" to include only findings "based ultimately on the application of the fact-finding tribunal's experience with the mainsprings of human conduct."[30]

Also, if the trial judge in handling res judicata has made a decision that was of an expressly discretionary nature, as is the case of nonmutual issue preclusion, the appellate court will apply an abuse-of-discretion standard of review.[31] But the appellate courts will do so begrudgingly, with minimal deference.[32]

---

29. See, e.g., Bayless v. Industrial Comm'n, 880 P.2d 654 (Ariz. Ct. App. 1993).

30. Commissioner v. Duberstein, 363 U.S. 278, 289 (1960).

31. See, e.g., Parklane Hosiery Co. v. Shore, 439 U.S. 322 (1979).

32. See 18 Charles Alan Wright, Arthur R. Miller & Edward H. Cooper, Federal Practice and Procedure § 4465, at 590-91 (1981).

CHAPTER 12

Defeating Res Judicata

The previous chapters have discussed various exceptions to the operation of res judicata, both in its claim preclusion and issue preclusion aspects. Imagine one party invoking some aspect of res judicata against the opponent, or invokee. To defeat the rule of res judicata, the invokee can raise and prove that one of those exceptions apply. Alternatively, the invokee can defeat the invoker's attempt to establish that the rule of res judicata applies in the first place by overcoming the invoker's support for any of the doctrinal requirements of the rule. For example, the invokee could defeat issue preclusion by overcoming the invoker's showing that the current case involves the same issue as the prior case, that the issue was actually litigated and determined, or that its determination was essential to the prior judgment.

All that is rather obvious. What is less intuitive is that the invokee can avoid res judicata by raising the absence of res judicata's prerequisites of the prior judgment's being valid and final. That is, a party who seeks to avoid the binding effects of a judgment can make an attack against the judgment itself. Of course, the party may do so on many grounds by immediate post-judgment motion or by appeal. But even outside the ordinary course of review in the trial and appellate courts, the party can attack the judgment at least for the lack of finality or validity.

Finality was treated in Chapter 5 above. Attacks on validity are especially complicated. This chapter will explore how to avoid res judicata by establishing the invalidity of the prior judgment.

A. Methods of Attack

For a judgment to have res judicata effects, it must be "valid." To be treated as valid, the judgment must be of sufficient quality to withstand an attack in the form of a request for "relief from judgment." The focus of study should first fall on those late post-judgment processes that afford relief from judgment. Requests for relief from judgment, in the technical sense, refer to certain procedural techniques, other than in the ordinary course of review in the trial and appellate courts, for avoiding the effects of the judgment. Relief from judgment encompasses three techniques:

1. Motion for Relief

A party or privy may attack the judgment in the rendering court by a motion for relief from judgment.[1] Such a motion is technically a continuation of the initial action, and so is a form of attack called direct attack. Nevertheless, it lies only in fairly extraordinary situations, designedly not serving as a cure for carelessness. In appropriate cases, however, it is the preferred means of giving relief from judgment, being the most direct and orderly technique.[2]

2. Independent Suit

If adequate relief from judgment is unavailable by motion because of any applicable procedural limitations on use of such motion, a person may properly bring an independent suit against the judgment-holder to nullify the judgment, to enjoin the enforcement of the judgment, or otherwise to get relief from the judgment.[3] The essence here is a separate claim, but one aimed directly at the prior judgment. This independent action in equity to obtain relief from judgment is preferably, but not necessarily, brought in

---

1. See, e.g., Fed. R. Civ. P. 60(b); Bank of Montreal v. Olafsson, 648 F.2d 1078 (6th Cir. 1981) (applying Rule 60(b)).

2. See generally 11 Charles Alan Wright, Arthur R. Miller & Mary Kay Kane, Federal Practice and Procedure §§ 2857-2866 (2d ed. 1995).

3. See, e.g., Britton v. Gannon, 285 P.2d 407 (Okla. 1955) (equitable claim asserted as counterclaim or defense).

the rendering court, which can exercise continuing jurisdiction over such an action.[4]

3. Defensive Attack

If a party in a subsequent action relies on a prior judgment as a basis for claim or defense (as where the plaintiff sues upon the judgment to enforce it or where the defendant pleads res judicata), and if adequate relief from judgment is not available and more convenient by the two other procedural techniques, then the opposing party may properly launch an attack in the subsequent action on the prior judgment to prevent its use.[5] This is often called a collateral attack, as opposed to a direct attack. Because invocation of res judicata tends to provoke collateral attack, the study of res judicata frequently involves problems of collateral attack.

The term "direct attack," then, merely refers to a challenge to a judgment made in a proceeding brought specially for that purpose, such as by appeal or by motion or independent suit for relief from judgment. If a judgment was infected with serious error, the court can reverse it or set it aside through such a direct attack, and thus destroy its res judicata effects. Any serious error can provide the basis of a direct attack on the judgment, including but not limited to the fundamental or jurisdictional errors that may be the basis also of collateral attack.

"Collateral attack," then, means any attempt to avoid, defeat, or evade the effects of a judgment by attacking its validity otherwise than through a direct attack. Attacks on the validity of a judgment launched when defending against either an attempt to enforce the judgment or an assertion of the judgment as res judicata in a later action are the prime instances of collateral attacks.

B. Grounds for Attack

As suggested, a judgment must be deemed valid in order to have any res judicata effects. To be so deemed, the judgment must be able to withstand

---

4. See generally 11 Charles Alan Wright, Arthur R. Miller & Mary Kay Kane, Federal Practice and Procedure § 2868 (2d ed. 1995).

5. See, e.g., Marshall v. Lockhead, 245 S.W.2d 307 (Tex. Civ. App. 1952).

an attack by any of the three methods of requesting relief from judgment. So what grounds will support an attack by these methods?

1. Jurisdiction and Notice

a. Jurisdiction

Among the major defects that will normally render a judgment invalid are defects of jurisdiction. The judgment of a court that lacked jurisdiction of the subject matter, of the person (in an action in personam), or of the res (in an action in rem or quasi in rem) can be challenged in any later litigation to which that judgment is relevant. Jurisdictional challenges can be made on direct attack or even on collateral attack, according to conventional doctrine.

That is, conventional law allows even collateral attack for lack of jurisdiction, whether the exercise of jurisdiction violated constitutional or subconstitutional requirements, provided that the attacker did not induce another person's substantial reliance on the judgment. Conventional law does not allow collateral attack on the ground of a defect of venue or a violation of forum non conveniens or other such doctrines of judicial self-restraint, but only for defects of jurisdictional stature.[6]

By subject-matter jurisdiction, or competence, we mean the requirement that the court have, under applicable constitutional and statutory provisions, authority to adjudicate the type of controversy before it. Constitutions and statutes, speaking in essentially nongeographic terms, specify the scope of the court's subject-matter jurisdiction in order to divide functions among the organs of government, thus accommodating federal and state authority, separating courts from the other branches, and differentiating one court from another.

By territorial jurisdiction, or judicial jurisdiction, we mean the important restrictions on the court's authority to entertain cases with nonlocal elements in their parties and events. The relevant doctrine, speaking in terms of the geographic relationship among the parties, the forum, and the litigation, specifies the scope of the court's territorial jurisdiction in order to confine the place of litigation to appropriately located courts.[7]

---

6. See generally 18 Charles Alan Wright, Arthur R. Miller & Edward H. Cooper, Federal Practice and Procedure §§4428-4431 (1981).

7. See generally Robert C. Casad & William B. Richman, Jurisdiction in Civil Actions (3d ed. 1998); Kevin M. Clermont, Civil Procedure: Territorial Jurisdiction and Venue (1999).

The concept of territorial jurisdiction embraces both jurisdiction in personam and also nonpersonal jurisdiction, be it in rem or quasi in rem. The difference between personal and nonpersonal jurisdiction turns on whether the target of the action is a person or a thing.

Under the usual law, for a court to perfect territorial jurisdiction, it must not only have a sufficient nexus or basis for jurisdiction—such as the defendant's presence, domicile, consent, or forum-directed acts—but also have formally asserted its power over the target of the action. The court's assertion comes through the plaintiff's service of process. On collateral attack on the ground of territorial jurisdiction, the attacker could either raise a lack of nexus to the person or thing targeted by the prior action or raise a failure of service of process.

b. Notice

Similarly, the invokee of res judicata can directly or collaterally attack the prior judgment for a failure to afford adequate notice to the invokee or the invokee's representative in that prior action.[8] The Due Process Clause requires fair notice of the pendency of the action to the affected person or the representative—fair notice must be suitably formal in tenor and informative in content; fair notice must be either actual notice or notice that is reasonably calculated to result in actual notice; and fair notice must afford a reasonable opportunity to be heard.[9] Beyond this constitutional requirement, the local law on service of process further specifies the manner of giving adequate notice.

Conventional law allows collateral attack for inadequate notice, whether in violation of constitutional requirements or the more important subconstitutional requirements, provided that the attacker did not induce another person's substantial reliance on the judgment. It does not allow collateral attack for technical violations of the subconstitutional requirements for giving notice, but only on grounds that go to basic fairness. The judicial trend goes toward ignoring minor irregularities either where the party actually received suitably formal and informative notice or where the form of the notice and the manner of transmitting it substantially complied with the prescribed procedure.[10]

---

8. See generally Restatement (Second) of Judgments §§ 65-66, 81 (1982).
9. See Mullane v. Central Hanover Bank & Trust Co., 339 U.S. 306 (1950).
10. See generally Restatement (Second) of Judgments §§ 2-3 (1982).

The term "adequate notice," which we take directly from the Second Restatement of Judgments,[11] could be misleading. Obviously, it does not set up an ironclad requirement of actual notice. A valid judgment can result from notice reasonably calculated to result in actual notice, even if the defendant never received the notice.

Less obvious is that, under the case law, adequate notice here is a shorthand expression that stands for a broader concern with the most basic commands of procedural due process. On direct or collateral attack, the court will entertain any ground that truly goes to the heart of fairness. Thus, in the case of class actions, due process requires that absent members of the class be adequately represented by named parties whose interests in the litigation are such as to assure effective presentation of the claims or defenses of the class members—more precisely, the absentees must truly agree with the general objectives on the merits of some party, who vigorously and competently pursues those objectives, and the absentees must have some ties to that party, whether through their substantive interests or their procedural conduct.[12] When a judgment rendered in a class action is sought to be asserted against an absent class member, the latter can directly or collaterally attack the judgment on the ground that the representation was inadequate to comport with due process, in addition to the other usual grounds for attack. If successful, such an attack will enable the absentee to avoid the effects of the class-action judgment.

c. *Summary*

The requirements of subject-matter jurisdiction, territorial jurisdiction, and adequate notice are normally grounds for later attack, either direct or collateral. The reason is that these requirements are so basic to the authority of the initial forum that they should remain open to testing. Generally, even in a wholly different subsequent action, the court can inquire into the prior satisfaction of these three forum-authority defenses.

Questions of law or fact relating to jurisdiction and due process may be litigated on the direct or collateral attack, including such matters as the existence of a particular basis for jurisdiction and the adequacy of notice in the circumstances. If these issues were already decided in the first action,

---

11. See Restatement (Second) of Judgments § 1 (1982) (using the terms "jurisdiction of the subject matter," "territorial jurisdiction," and "adequate notice" for the three critical requirements).

12. See Richards v. Jefferson County, Ala., 517 U.S. 793 (1996); Hansberry v. Lee, 311 U.S. 32 (1940).

however, the party seeking to avoid the res judicata effects of that judgment may be precluded from attacking the judgment on that ground, as will be explained in the next chapter.

2. Equitable Grounds

a. General

The effects of a judgment may sometimes be avoided on equitable grounds, such as the fact that it was procured by fraud, duress, or mistake.[13] At common law, such procurement of a judgment did not render it vulnerable to collateral attack, but courts of equity would, in some cases, enjoin the enforcement of the judgment or grant other appropriate equitable relief when the enforcement of the judgment would be grossly unfair or unconscionable. It was said that such judgments were merely "voidable" rather than "void."[14] Still today, such an equitable attack on a judgment for extraordinary injustice has to come by direct attack, such as by motion or independent suit for relief from judgment, rather than by collateral attack.

The aggrieved can seek *relief by motion*. Consider the wording of Federal Rule of Civil Procedure 60(b):

> On motion and upon such terms as are just, the court may relieve a party or a party's legal representative from a final judgment, order, or proceeding for the following reasons: (1) mistake, inadvertence, surprise, or excusable neglect; (2) newly discovered evidence which by due diligence could not have been discovered in time to move for a new trial under Rule 59(b); (3) fraud (whether heretofore denominated intrinsic or extrinsic), misrepresentation, or other misconduct of an adverse party; (4) the judgment is void; (5) the judgment has been satisfied, released, or discharged, or a prior judgment upon which it is based has been reversed or otherwise vacated, or it is no longer equitable that the judgment should have prospective application; or (6) any other reason justifying relief from the operation of the judgment. The motion shall be made within a reasonable time, and for reasons (1), (2), and (3) not more than one year after the judgment, order, or proceeding was entered or taken. A motion under this subdivision (b) does

13. See generally Restatement (Second) of Judgments §§ 67-68, 70-74 (1982).

14. See 18 Susan Bandes & Lawrence B. Solum, Moore's Federal Practice § 130.04[3] (3d ed. 1999).

> not affect the finality of a judgment or suspend its operation. This rule does not limit the power of a court to entertain an independent action to relieve a party from a judgment ....

As with equitable remedies generally, an *independent action for relief* from judgment is subject to a large element of judicial discretion, and the cases are often difficult to reconcile. Consider the formulation of one federal court:

> The indispensable elements of such a cause of action are (1) a judgment which ought not, in equity and good conscience, to be enforced; (2) a good defense to the alleged cause of action on which the judgment is founded; (3) fraud, accident, or mistake which prevented the defendant in the judgment from obtaining the benefit of his defense; (4) the absence of fault or negligence on the part of the defendant; and (5) the absence of any adequate remedy at law.[15]

Many, but not all, kinds of misconduct or misfortune, then, are sufficient for relief from judgment by direct attack. One kind of case in which relief is almost always granted, however, is the case wherein the defending party was prevented from a fair opportunity to be heard by fraud on the part of the adversary. It merits a closer look.

b. Fraud

Will any kind of fraud suffice? Federal Rule of Civil Procedure 60(b)(3) expressly extends relief by motion to fraud generally, but is subject to a one-year limitation. The independent-action cases, although not subject to a strict time limitation, traditionally drew a distinction between "intrinsic" and "extrinsic" fraud. Fraud that was intrinsic to the first action would not be grounds for relief against the judgment by independent action, but fraud that was extrinsic would. Thus, the grounds for relief by motion appear broader than the grounds for independent action.

Although these terms of intrinsic and extrinsic were widely used in this context, and still are to a lesser extent, no very clear distinction between the two classes of fraud has emerged. The terms themselves are certainly not very descriptive of the difference between the cases that do not, or should

15. National Sur. Co. v. State Bank, 120 F. 593, 599 (8th Cir. 1903).

not, permit and those that do, or should, permit equitable attack.[16] To get a sense of the difference, one must dive into the case law.

Generally speaking, intrinsic fraud has been held to include evidential misrepresentations made in the course of the proceeding leading to the prior judgment. False statements in pleadings, false testimony of witnesses, and the like have usually been classified as instances of intrinsic fraud. They are misrepresentations that normally can be avoided or corrected in the proceeding itself—by countervailing evidence, cross-examination, impeachment of witnesses, and so on—or through appeal.

Extrinsic fraud has been held to include misconduct unrelated, or extrinsic, to the underlying merits. "Extrinsic fraud has been defined as any fraudulent conduct of the successful party which was practiced outside of an actual adversary trial directly and affirmatively on the defeated party whereby he was prevented from presenting fully and fairly his side of the cause. Included in such definition are false representations that the defeated party is merely a nominal party against whom no relief is sought, false promises of compromise, concealment of the suit, kidnapping of witnesses, and the like."[17] When the fraud has had the effect of denying to the defrauded party a fair day in court, the normal trial and appellate processes cannot be relied on to correct misstatements or false testimony. In such a case, equitable relief by independent action may be necessary to avoid injustice.

Some courts go further, however, in expanding the scope of extrinsic fraud. Although the use of perjured testimony does not, under the usual view, constitute extrinsic fraud, the active concealment of material evidence that the party has a duty to disclose may amount to extrinsic fraud.[18] Thus the distinction between extrinsic and intrinsic fraud blurs.

Additionally, extrinsic fraud intrudes on the realm of due process notice. Sometimes the same fraudulent misbehavior could support a collateral attack on notice grounds. But fraud, by its own name, will support only a direct attack. The traditional schema, then, is that a collateral attack lies for notice defects, an independent action lies for extrinsic frauds as well,

---

16. Compare 18 Susan Bandes & Lawrence B. Solum, Moore's Federal Practice § 130.04[3] (3d ed. 1999) (using the distinction), with 11 Charles Alan Wright, Arthur R. Miller & Mary Kay Kane, Federal Practice and Procedure §§ 2861, 2868 (2d ed. 1995) (criticizing the distinction).

17. Britton v. Gannon, 285 P.2d 407, 409-10 (Okla. 1955).

18. See, e.g., Weyant v. Utah Sav. & Trust Co., 182 P.189 (Utah 1919).

and a motion lies additionally for all frauds. But, as usual, the reality is much fuzzier, because the relevant definitions are imprecise.

C. Approaches to Attack's Methods and Grounds

Now we must put all this information together in order to understand validity. The initial step is to realize that the legal history of validity is one of failed compartmentalization, with the law trying unsuccessfully to allocate certain grounds for attack among the conceptual boxes of certain methods of attack. The distinction between extrinsic and intrinsic fraud did not work, as we have just seen by way of example.

Moreover, the basic distinction between collateral and direct attack, or equivalently between void and voidable judgment, turns out to be a mirage. Consider the traditional view of extrinsic fraud, which made the judgment voidable and subject to direct attack in the form of an independent action. Even before the merger of law and equity, however, it became possible to assert some equitable claims as counterclaims, and some equitable defenses as defenses, against legal claims in the same action asserting the legal claims themselves. If an action were brought to enforce a judgment that was procured through extrinsic fraud, the equitable challenge to its enforcement could be made by way of counterclaim in the enforcement action. Because the relief sought in the counterclaim would be the invalidation of the other party's claim, the assertion of extrinsic fraud could indeed be called a defense rather than a counterclaim.[19] If the defense were upheld, the judgment would be denied enforcement, just as it would be if the defendant had established a lack of jurisdiction for the prior judgment. In this situation—assertion of the fraud as a defense in a legal action to enforce the judgment—all semblance to an independent action in equity that could logically be called a direct attack is gone, and the fraud defense is a collateral attack in all but name.[20] Thus, the utility of the traditional and common distinction between collateral and direct attack is more than questionable.

19. See Massari v. Einsiedler, 78 A.2d 572, 575-76 (N.J. 1951).

20. See Britton v. Gannon, 285 P.2d 407 (Okla. 1955). But see Gannon v. American Airlines, 251 F.2d 476, 482 (10th Cir. 1957) (2–1 decision) (in a different enforcement action based on the same Illinois judgment as in the Britton case, the court disagreed with the still nonfinal Britton ruling and held the Illinois judgment "not open to collateral attack in this proceeding upon the ground of fraud not going to the jurisdiction of the court"), vacated per stipulation, 251 F.2d 486 (10th Cir. 1958).

(After all is said and done, where does an independent action fall? An independent action was and is referred to as a direct attack in most cases.[21] However, other cases have called it a collateral attack,[22] and some cases, to distinguish it from both direct and collateral attack, have referred to it as an indirect attack.[23])

Compartmentalization has failed, because the precision of the compartments' definitions has broken down. The courts must therefore return to the basic point behind the validity concept. It is, simply, that certain fundamental flaws are of such seriousness that they can be raised any time and any place, even in the subsequent and distant setting of a defensive attack; other lesser kinds of flaws must be presented for correction through the processes of more direct attack that the law specifically provides for that purpose—or not at all. Distinguishing between flaws in this context seems to call for at least some discretionary balancing by the subsequent court. The outcome of that balancing will define validity.

So, what is the current law by which the subsequent court defines validity? Well, it varies from court to court. The urge to compartmentalize persists, and therefore in each court the law lies somewhere between rigid compartmentalization and fluid decisionmaking. In other words, the law lies somewhere between the following two approaches embodied respectively in the First and Second Restatement of Judgments.

1. Traditional, Rigid Approach

Generally, an attack on validity, when it comes by various procedures in subsequent litigation outside the ordinary course of review in the trial and appellate courts, lies on grounds set by the judgment-rendering sovereign. Of course, that sovereign's law is subject to any applicable external restraints, an example being where due process and other federal provisions are imposed on and become part of state law.

So in, say, an action upon a default judgment of a state court, that state's law governs the grounds for collateral attack. The grounds have been very limited. The traditional rule there has been that a collateral attack will succeed on the ground that the rendering court failed to satisfy the require-

21. See Comment, The Value of the Distinction Between Direct and Collateral Attacks on Judgments, 66 Yale L.J. 526, 531 (1957).

22. See, e.g., Griffith v. Bank of N.Y., 147 F.2d 899, 901 (2d Cir. 1945).

23. See, e.g., Eichhoff v. Eichhoff, 40 P. 24, 25 (Cal. 1895).

ment of subject-matter jurisdiction, territorial jurisdiction, or adequate notice; indeed, such an attack will succeed only on one of those three grounds and not on the ground of any other error, which should have been corrected on appeal or other direct attack. In other words, the common formulation provided that the judgment was subject to collateral attack *if and only if* the rendering court had failed to satisfy the requirement of (1) subject-matter jurisdiction, (2) territorial jurisdiction, or (3) adequate notice.[24]

If the defaulting party had instead proceeded promptly to the rendering court to move for relief from judgment, the list of grounds would have been slightly longer. Relief then would have lain in a situation of extraordinary injustice, such as in the case of fraud. In case of certain kinds of extraordinarily severe misbehavior or misfortune, such as classic extrinsic fraud, the defaulting party could have alternatively proceeded by independent action for relief.

In sum, motions and independent actions for relief from judgment have traditionally been limited to cases of extraordinary injustice, although not as limited as collateral attack with its focus on jurisdiction and notice.[25]

2. Ultramodern, Fluid Approach

There have been some inroads on the traditional doctrine, and hence on its relative certainty. The ultramodern, or postmodern, view is that courts should, and to some extent apparently do, approach relief from judgment as a discretionary balancing. According to some theorists and in some cases, relief from judgment should turn more expressly on a discretionary balancing of equities. Under the judgment-rendering sovereign's law, various factors would determine the availability of relief:

- the nature and importance of the judgment's alleged infirmity;
- the procedural technique of relief from judgment employed, this factor being based on the view that such techniques form a spectrum and that the list of available grounds for relief should contract as the mode, place, and time of attack become more distant from the initial action;
- the impact of the relief requested; and

24. See Restatement of Judgments §4 (1942).
25. See Restatement of Judgments ch. 5 (1942).

- the position of the parties, including diligence in seeking relief and reliance on the judgment.

Under this fluid approach, it can still be said that judgments usually are treated as valid for res judicata purposes if and only if they meet the requirements of subject-matter jurisdiction, territorial jurisdiction, and adequate notice. That is, this fluid approach approximates the traditional doctrine. But there are exceptions. Sometimes and for some purposes, judgments not meeting the three requirements of competence and nexus and notice nevertheless would have effect (even on motion in the rendering court),[26] and other judgments meeting those requirements would have no effect (even in a later action upon the judgment)[27]—when all the above fluid factors are taken into account. For example, even if the attacker could show a lack of jurisdiction or notice in the first action and even if the attacker used a direct attack under Federal Rule of Civil Procedure 60(b)(4), the judgment would stand if the attacker had shown an intent to treat the judgment as valid and someone else had substantially relied on it. Contrariwise, even when jurisdiction and notice were fine and even on a collateral attack, a judgment will fall, at least for some purposes, if serious fraud were involved in the first action and the attacker were seeking relief with due diligence. Ultimately, it comes down to a discretionary balancing of the equities.

3. Resolution

At least to some extent, the Second Restatement's fluid approach prevails everywhere. This chapter implicitly recognized this fact in its opening definition of validity: "To be treated as valid, the judgment must be of sufficient quality to withstand an attack in the form of a request for 'relief from judgment.'" A key idea here is that validity should be defined in terms of relief from judgment. A valid judgment is not one that necessarily results

---

26. See, e.g., Gschwind v. Cessna Aircraft Co., 189 F.R.D. 643 (D. Kan. 1999) (subject-matter jurisdiction lacking); Marshall v. Lockhead, 245 S.W.2d 307 (Tex. Civ. App. 1952) (personal jurisdiction lacking); Restatement (Second) of Judgments §§ 65-66 (1982).

27. See, e.g., Lee v. Carroll, 146 So. 2d 242 (La. Ct. App. 1962) (collateral attack on fraud ground); Restatement (Second) of Judgments §§ 67-68, 70-74, 82 (1982).

from certain processes. Instead, a valid judgment is one that can withstand certain processes aimed at upsetting the judgment.[28]

This seemingly indeterminate, retrospective approach to validity requires some justification. Does it put the cart before the horse?

It is true that litigants and courts need a working, prospective sense of validity. As we have suggested, a working sense exists: A valid judgment will normally result when the rendering court had jurisdiction over the subject matter and over the target of the action and it afforded adequate notice to the interested parties. In other words, a valid judgment is one free from the most basic defects, even if it is otherwise erroneous. Using this rough definition, litigants and courts routinely respect valid judgments, while disregarding the rare invalid judgment.

This rough approach works well for almost every judgment. But in the unusual case that involves a subsequent attack on validity, the situation becomes fuzzier.

In the first place, a confluence of errors has already occurred, and so the case under attack has arrived in a bit of a mess. The plaintiff arguably erred in satisfying one of litigation's most basic requirements. The defendant failed to straighten out the matter promptly. The rendering court may have bobbled the matter of validity, as well as the merits.

In the second place, the mess comes before a subsequent court, which confronts a unique array of post-judgment developments. People may have relied on the judgment. The attack comes by a certain method, before a certain court, and at a certain time. All those factors bear on the propriety of relief. The attack might rest on a defect of jurisdiction or notice only in a technical sense, so that those basic requirements do not look so sacrosanct in context. Or the attack might rest on some defect other than jurisdiction or notice, yet appear so terrible in context that it should be fatal. On attack, the requested relief is a declaration of invalidity for a certain purpose. But that implies that a judgment can be valid for some purposes, while invalid for other purposes. True, the prior judgment coming before the subsequent court is presumed valid, and the court will so treat it unless the attacker can upset it. But in deciding the success of the attack, the subsequent court must take account of this broad range of considerations, and can do so only by a discretionary balancing.

Therefore, to say a judgment is valid—as opposed to roughly or presumptively valid—is to make a predictive general statement about the out-

28. See generally Restatement (Second) of Judgments introductory note to ch. 2, at 19-22 (1982).

come of a contextual balancing. Only a retrospective definition of validity—the judgment must be of sufficient quality to withstand an attack in the form of a request for relief from judgment—can be truly accurate. It is framed in terms of the procedural setting where the question of validity actually arises, namely, a retrospective setting. It properly uses the label of validity to describe a result, rather than invoking validity to pose as a reason for the result.

This retrospective definition, while more accurate, is undeniably more complex than the conventionally rough definition. But retrospectivity here has a low level of the usual costs associated with such indeterminacy. The vast run of judgments remain wholly unaffected by the slight indeterminacy of the rare irregular case. Most judgments are well within the core of obvious validity. Moreover, the irregular cases are so messy and unique that they are inevitably subject to being finessed by the subsequent court. No conceivable definition of validity could avoid that uncertainty. Thus, a frankly retrospective definition does not seriously undermine the virtues of finality.

In summary, it is fine to use validity in its conventionally rough sense of requiring subject-matter jurisdiction, territorial jurisdiction, and adequate notice. It is a useful shorthand expression for describing judgments that will normally have res judicata effects. But one should use it carefully, with a sense of its roughness. One should remain aware that a full understanding of validity and invalidity necessitates a retrospective definition, as elaborated in this chapter.

CHAPTER 13

Jurisdiction to Determine Jurisdiction

After this book's coverage of res judicata and then of attacks on validity to defeat res judicata, the appropriate final topic would be the effect of res judicata in repulsing attacks on validity. So, that interaction is the concern of this chapter.

The court in the initial action may pass on jurisdiction and notice. If one of the basic forum-authority defenses—subject-matter jurisdiction, territorial jurisdiction, or adequate notice—is raised in the ordinary course of the initial action, the judge without jury either may hear and determine the defense in a pretrial proceeding, on the application of any party, or may choose to defer the issue until trial.[1] Moreover, in the post-trial period of that initial action, a defense of lack of subject-matter jurisdiction will be determined whenever raised.[2]

After determination of a forum-authority defense in the initial action, there may arise the question of its res judicata effects. The normal rules and exceptions of res judicata apply. For example, if the question of a party's domicile is actually litigated and determined to uphold jurisdiction, and if that question of domicile arises as part of the merits of another claim, the prior finding could have issue preclusion effect. For a quite different example, if an attacker later loses a collateral attack made on the ground of inadequate notice, that loss will preclude further attacks on that ground, under the normal doctrine of issue preclusion.[3]

---

1. See, e.g., Fed. R. Civ. P. 12(d).
2. See, e.g., Fed. R. Civ. P. 12(h).
3. See, e.g., Arecibo Radio Corp. v. Puerto Rico, 825 F.2d 589 (1st Cir. 1987).

But there is the important additional question of the effect that a determination rejecting a forum-authority defense in the initial action has on an attack on the resultant judgment, when the attack comes not in the ordinary course of review in the trial and appellate courts but in subsequent litigation. This is a different kind of question: it does not involve preclusive use of determinations embedded in a valid judgment, but instead involves preclusive use of prior determinations in order to establish validity. Here the desire for finality generally outweighs the concern for validity, giving the determination preclusive effect and thus generating a special variety of res judicata labeled "jurisdiction to determine jurisdiction." That is to say, affirmative rulings on jurisdiction or notice can preclude the parties from attacking the resultant judgment on that ground in subsequent litigation.

The impact of the jurisdiction to determine jurisdiction doctrine is a bit shocking upon first impression. After all, seemingly implicit in the concept of due process embodied in the Fifth and Fourteenth Amendments of the U.S. Constitution is the principle that one cannot be bound by a judgment of a court that lacked jurisdiction or failed to give notice. This principle would seem to imply not only that such a judgment cannot be entered against the person or the person's property, but also that the judgment will not be enforced or recognized as valid judgments would be. The fact is, however, that this validity principle does not exist.

It is true that if a defendant is sued in a court that lacks jurisdiction or fails to give notice, ordinarily the defendant is not obliged to respond in any way. If the defendant takes no action of any kind in response to the suit, the court may enter a default judgment, but such a judgment is said to be invalid. If the plaintiff should attempt to assert rights based on that judgment in a later suit against the same defendant, the defendant will ordinarily be permitted to avoid the effects of the judgment by showing that it was entered without jurisdiction or notice. The defendant is entitled to a day in court on the question of the authority of the court that rendered that earlier judgment.

The defendant may, instead, choose to raise the jurisdiction or notice issue in the initial action before the challenged court itself. A court that otherwise lacks authority could conceivably have jurisdiction to determine whether it has jurisdiction and whether its notice was good, and its rulings on such questions could be binding on the parties and preclude relitigation of the same questions. The defendant's appearance in the challenged court would then be the defendant's only day in court.

Our law in fact accepts this so-called bootstrap principle, which allows a court lacking fundamental authority to issue a judgment that will nevertheless be immune from late attack. Because the issue of jurisdiction or notice was actually litigated and determined, even if erroneously, the parties are precluded from relitigating the same issue in subsequent litigation. The erroneous ruling can be reviewed on appeal from the judgment, of course, but it cannot be challenged in seeking relief from judgment.

Indeed, our law accepts the bootstrap principle's value of finality with enthusiasm, despite its conflict with the intuitive value of validity. Our law applies the principle even more broadly than the foregoing illustration of actually litigated and determined forum-authority defenses. But before getting into the doctrinal details of jurisdiction to determine jurisdiction, the reader should first get clearly in mind the nature of this doctrine.

A. Status of This Subdoctrine

The doctrine of jurisdiction to determine jurisdiction is a separate body of res judicata law. It is obviously similar to issue preclusion, but it differs in several respects. First, issue preclusion requires a valid prior judgment. Jurisdiction to determine jurisdiction does not require validity, but instead works to make invulnerable an otherwise invalid judgment. Second, issue preclusion applies only in a subsequent action, and so does not apply on a motion for relief from judgment, which is technically a continuation of the initial action.[4] Jurisdiction to determine jurisdiction, however, does apply to preclude a validity attack by such a motion, as well as by the other methods for relief from judgment.[5] Third, issue preclusion usually does not work to bind the party prevailing on the issue. Jurisdiction to determine jurisdiction will preclude the successful plaintiff if the unsuccessful defendant would be precluded on the forum-authority issue.[6] Fourth, issue preclusion applies only to issues actually litigated and determined. Jurisdiction to determine jurisdiction sometimes applies to issues of subject-matter jurisdiction that were not litigated at all, and even against a defaulting party, as we shall soon see. Fifth, and most importantly, special policies and concerns

4. See, e.g., Harduvel v. General Dynamics Corp., 801 F. Supp. 597, 601 (M.D. Fla. 1992) (Rule 60(b)).

5. See, e.g., Nemaizer v. Baker, 793 F.2d 58, 64-66 (2d Cir. 1992) (Rule 60(b)).

6. Cf. McDonald v. Mabee, 243 U.S. 90 (1917) (plaintiff can collaterally attack default judgment, as could defendant).

are at work with respect to the forum-authority defenses, so the law needs to develop special rules and exceptions for jurisdiction to determine jurisdiction.

Therefore, it is desirable to view res judicata as comprising three subdoctrines: claim preclusion, issue preclusion, and jurisdiction to determine jurisdiction. The law can then develop separate and appropriate rules and exceptions for the jurisdiction to determine jurisdiction subdoctrine.

B. Content of This Subdoctrine

On any late attack on a judgment, res judicata may apply. In particular, the res judicata subdoctrine of jurisdiction to determine jurisdiction may foreclose relitigation of a prior determination of the existence of subject-matter jurisdiction, territorial jurisdiction, or adequate notice. The application of preclusion rests on different theoretical bases when the reference is to territorial jurisdiction or adequate notice, rather than to subject-matter jurisdiction.

1. Territorial Jurisdiction and Adequate Notice

A defendant can always submit to territorial jurisdiction or accept service of process. Indeed, if a defendant participates in the action in any substantial way without first raising the issue of territorial jurisdiction or adequate notice, the defendant is usually deemed to have waived the objection by consent, whether knowingly intended or not.

In every state and federal court, however, a defendant is permitted to participate in the proceedings for the purpose of challenging the court's territorial jurisdiction or adequate notice without thereby submitting generally. This sort of participation is commonly called a special appearance. By such an appearance, the defendant submits to the court's authority only for purpose of the challenge. Submission for that sole purpose, however, does result in being bound by the court's ruling on the challenge.

Under such a special appearance the defendant can raise issues of fact, law, or application of law to fact. He can challenge the existence of a basis for the exercise of jurisdiction over him. He can challenge the form of process or the manner of service. In challenging either the basis or the service, he can raise not only questions predicated upon the relevant statutes and court rules, but also constitutional due process issues, including whether his contacts with the forum were sufficient and the circumstances satisfied the fair-play-and-substantial-justice standard and whether the method of invoking jurisdiction provided adequate notice and opportunity to be heard.

If the court rules that the requisites of territorial jurisdiction and adequate notice are present, the defendant will be bound by that ruling and hence by the judgment ultimately rendered in the action, whether the defendant participates further or not. If the judgment is not set aside on appeal, it will be binding, and the territorial jurisdiction and adequate notice issues cannot again be litigated. Indeed, upon a challenge to the existence of *either* territorial jurisdiction *or* adequate notice, an affirmative ruling precludes the defendant from attacking the resultant judgment on either ground in subsequent litigation.[7]

The basic lesson, then, is that once a defendant starts litigating in Action #1, the defendant must stay there and correct any errors by appeal, because the threshold forum-authority issues will be foreclosed in Action #2. In *Baldwin v. Iowa State Traveling Men's Association*,[8] an erroneous determination by a Missouri federal court, after a special appearance, of the existence of territorial jurisdiction over the person was held to preclude a later attack by the defendant. In *Durfee v. Duke*,[9] a determination by a Nebraska state court, after active litigation of the quiet-title action, of the issue of territorial jurisdiction over the land, a determination that rested on an erroneous finding that the land on the banks of the shifting river was in Nebraska rather than Missouri, was held to preclude later attack by the defendant. Although the Supreme Court referred to the issue in *Durfee v. Duke* as one of "jurisdiction over the subject matter," its characterization was sloppy. The issue there was conceptually one of quasi in rem jurisdiction over particular land, not one of general competence to hear suits to quiet title. Moreover, the policies at stake were those of territorial jurisdiction, not those of subject-matter jurisdiction.[10]

In summary, if the defendant appears and does not litigate the threshold defense of territorial jurisdiction or adequate notice, the defendant waives it. If the defendant litigates one of these threshold defenses but the court finds authority, the ruling precludes the defendant on both. Either way, the appearing defendant cannot attack the resulting judgment on these

---

7. See generally Restatement (Second) of Judgments § 10 cmt. d (1982).

8. 283 U.S. 522 (1931).

9. 375 U.S. 106 (1963); cf. Johnson v. Muelberger, 340 U.S. 581 (1951) (jurisdiction over status).

10. See Restatement (Second) of Judgments § 11 cmt. b (1982).

grounds in subsequent litigation. Thus, relief from judgment on the ground of territorial jurisdiction or adequate notice can lie only from a judgment entered after the attacker had completely defaulted.

2. Subject-Matter Jurisdiction

The issue of subject-matter jurisdiction is regarded as being of fundamental importance. It is generally said that the issue can be raised at any time by anyone—even on appeal by the court itself, or even by a party who participated actively in the action without challenging the jurisdiction or invoked the jurisdiction in the first place. Subject-matter jurisdiction, unlike territorial jurisdiction, cannot be conferred by the defendant's consent, collusion, waiver, or estoppel.[11]

Accordingly, if a defendant appears in the action and fails to raise the question of the court's subject-matter jurisdiction, it cannot be said, as it could of territorial jurisdiction, that the court has jurisdiction because of the defendant's waiver. Or if a defendant appears in the action to litigate the question of the court's subject-matter jurisdiction, it cannot be said, as it could of territorial jurisdiction, that the court has jurisdiction simply because of the defendant's submission of the question of its jurisdiction.

The bootstrap principle, nevertheless, operates in connection with rulings by a court on the question of its own subject-matter jurisdiction, in spite of the seeming conflict between that result and the traditional lore about subject-matter jurisdiction. The bald theory underlying the application of the principle to questions of subject-matter jurisdiction is simply the point that—apart from any waiver or consent on the part of the defendant—a court inherently has jurisdiction to decide whether it has subject-matter jurisdiction over a case presented to it. Its ruling on that question, even if erroneous, will be binding unless set aside on appeal and will have preclusive effect on a later attack.

Thus, despite any lingering sense of incongruity, it is clear today that preclusion can apply to affirmative rulings on subject-matter jurisdiction that have been actively litigated and expressly determined, except when very important jurisdictional limits are involved such as some of those carving out areas of exclusive federal jurisdiction. Moreover, preclusion can extend to affirmative rulings on subject-matter jurisdiction even when they were not actively litigated—a declaration by the court of its own motion that

11. See, e.g., Thompson v. Whitman, 85 U.S. (18 Wall.) 457 (1874).

jurisdiction exists is enough to preclude late attack on its subject-matter jurisdiction. Furthermore, preclusion can extend to affirmative rulings on subject-matter jurisdiction even when they were not expressly determined—an implicit conclusion by the court that it has jurisdiction suffices— and supposedly the court so implicitly concludes before rendering judgment in any litigated action.[12]

In *Chicot County Drainage District v. Baxter State Bank*,[13] the Supreme Court precluded even a defaulting party from attacking an earlier illegal exercise of subject-matter jurisdiction, because other defendants had contested the initial action, although they had not questioned the court's subject-matter jurisdiction. In this and other less extreme cases, the Court has recognized the propriety of giving preclusive effect to a court's determination of its own subject-matter jurisdiction. But on the same day, in *Kalb v. Feuerstein*,[14] the Supreme Court held that a foreclosure judgment by a state court after contested proceedings, rendered illegally during the pendency of federal bankruptcy proceedings, was subject to collateral attack. The Court so acknowledged that sometimes the illegal exercise of subject-matter jurisdiction really can undermine the authority of other courts, and so the ruling must remain open to collateral attack.

This bootstrap principle is embodied in the Second Restatement of Judgments in the following terms:

> **When a court has rendered a judgment in a contested action, the judgment precludes the parties from litigating the question of the court's subject matter jurisdiction in subsequent litigation except if:**
> **(1) The subject matter of the action was so plainly beyond the court's jurisdiction that its entertaining the action was a manifest abuse of authority; or**
> **(2) Allowing the judgment to stand would substantially infringe the authority of another tribunal or agency of government; or**
> **(3) The judgment was rendered by a court lacking capability to make an adequately informed determination of a question concerning its own jurisdiction and as a matter of procedural fairness**

12. See Dan B. Dobbs, Beyond Bootstrap: Foreclosing the Issue of Subject-Matter Jurisdiction Before Final Judgment, 51 Minn. L. Rev. 491 (1967).

13. 308 U.S. 371 (1940).

14. 308 U.S. 433 (1940).

> **the party seeking to avoid the judgment should have opportunity belatedly to attack the court's subject matter jurisdiction.**[15]

It is to be noted that preclusion of the issue under this section does not necessarily require in all cases that the question be actively litigated, and it may be enough that the court implicitly determined its own jurisdiction. At the same time, by virtue of the section's exceptions, there may be no preclusion in some cases where the issue was actually litigated and determined. Generalization is difficult, and so the Second Restatement's black-letter rule does little more than identify certain factors to be considered in weighing the competing policies in each case.

Putting the cases and the Second Restatement together, then, we can say that a holding of the existence of subject-matter jurisdiction precludes the parties from attacking the resultant judgment on that ground in subsequent litigation, except in special circumstances such as where the court plainly lacked subject-matter jurisdiction or the judgment substantially infringes on the authority of another court or agency. Because unraised subject-matter jurisdiction is supposedly always implicitly determined to exist in any action litigated to judgment, such determination has the res judicata consequences of an actually litigated determination of the existence of subject-matter jurisdiction insofar as foreclosing attack on the judgment, although the court in subsequent litigation may be more likely to find applicable an exception to res judicata. The bottom line is that relief from judgment on the ground of subject-matter jurisdiction is readily available only in cases where all defendants defaulted.

Note that the subdoctrine of jurisdiction to determine jurisdiction for subject-matter jurisdiction is both narrower and broader than jurisdiction to determine jurisdiction for territorial jurisdiction and adequate notice. On the one hand, because subject-matter jurisdiction entails systemically important interests, jurisdiction to determine jurisdiction has more exceptions with respect to subject-matter jurisdiction, such as where the initial court stepped on some toes in invading the subsequent court's realm of authority. On the other hand, because any court in rendering judgment in a litigated action implicitly determines its own subject-matter jurisdiction—but does not necessarily determine the strictly personal defenses of territorial jurisdiction and adequate notice—jurisdiction to determine jurisdiction may apply to subject-matter jurisdiction even when the issue was not

15. Restatement (Second) of Judgments § 12 (1982).

actually litigated and determined, and even when the judgment's attacker defaulted in the initial action.

C. Jurisdiction to Determine *No* Jurisdiction

So far this chapter has discussed the res judicata effects of affirmative rulings on forum-authority. But what if the initial court decides that it lacks jurisdiction or failed to give notice? That is, can a court, which is admittedly without authority to enter a valid judgment, make any rulings that have preclusive effect? Yes.

The initial court's ruling that it lacks authority will prevent a second try that presents exactly the same issue. It had authority to determine its lack of authority. Common sense supports preclusion on the threshold issue, in order to prevent the plaintiff from suing repetitively. This common-sense doctrine works as a sort of direct estoppel. For such purposes only, the prior judgment is a valid one.[16]

Of course, the dismissal of the initial action on a threshold defense does not generate a bar to a second action in an appropriate court. Moreover, the initial court's ruling probably should have no res judicata effects in such later action, whether to establish the jurisdiction of the other court or to preclude an issue on the merits of the same or any other claim. For such purposes, the prior judgment is an invalid one.

D. A Final View of Validity and Finality

When all is said and done, an understanding of jurisdiction to determine jurisdiction is clearly essential to an understanding of validity. This chapter has revealed that attacks on judgments for invalidity play a much smaller role than they could. The law certainly does not treat all invalid judgments as nullities, because this subdoctrine of jurisdiction to determine jurisdiction heads off many attacks. Jurisdiction to determine jurisdiction precludes those attacks by establishing that courts have authority to determine their own judgments' validity. As a consequence, most successful attacks on invalidity come against default judgments.

---

16. See Ruhrgas AG v. Marathon Oil Co., 526 U.S. 574, 585 (1999); 18 Charles Alan Wright, Arthur R. Miller & Edward H. Cooper, Federal Practice and Procedure §4436 (1981 & Supp. 1999).

Why does the law, despite its fervent slogans, in fact downplay validity in this way? The reason is that the law ultimately favors finality. The basic tension in this area is validity versus finality. Validity here represents the yearning to get things right, to pursue truth to the end. Finality represents the concession to the brevity of life, to the reality that justice demands an end to litigation.

To reiterate, the subdoctrine of jurisdiction to determine jurisdiction comes down on the side of finality. That is as it should be, because unthinking invocation of the slogans of validity masks the fact that the forum-authority defenses are not and should not be sacrosanct. No good reason exists, for instance, to allow a defendant to litigate personal jurisdiction in two forums. The law instead tells the defendant to choose one forum and litigate fully there. Indeed, constitutionally the law probably could say in these modern times that the defendant can no longer choose to stay home but instead must litigate personal jurisdiction in the initial forum—or not at all. The law does not impose that burden on the defendant. But it can and does say to the defendant that personal jurisdiction will receive only one treatment.

The basic tension between validity and finality has been the central focus of this entire book. In the broader context of general res judicata, the law recognizes that it must value truth. It values truth, but does so within limits. Outside those limits, it values more an end to litigation. Fixing those limits—which depends on the profound but practical undertaking of discovering the tipping point between validity and finality—is the doctrine of res judicata. The law fixes those limits in response to the welter of fairness, efficiency, and substantive policies heretofore discussed at length.

We hope that this book has illuminated that law of res judicata for you.

Table of Cases

Index